Lecture Notes in Computer Science　　9848

Commenced Publication in 1973
Founding and Former Series Editors:
Gerhard Goos, Juris Hartmanis, and Jan van Leeuwen

More information about this series at http://www.springer.com/series/7409

Takaya Yuizono · Hiroaki Ogata
Ulrich Hoppe · Julita Vassileva (Eds.)

Collaboration and Technology

22nd International Conference, CRIWG 2016
Kanazawa, Japan, September 14–16, 2016
Proceedings

 Springer

Editors
Takaya Yuizono
Japan Advanced Institute of Science
  and Technology (JAIST)
Ishikawa
Japan

Hiroaki Ogata
Kyushu University
Fukuoka
Japan

Ulrich Hoppe
Universität Duisburg-Essen
Duisburg
Germany

Julita Vassileva
University of Saskatchewan
Saskatoon, SK
Canada

ISSN 0302-9743   ISSN 1611-3349   (electronic)
Lecture Notes in Computer Science
ISBN 978-3-319-44798-8   ISBN 978-3-319-44799-5   (eBook)
DOI 10.1007/978-3-319-44799-5

Library of Congress Control Number: 2016948249

LNCS Sublibrary: SL3 – Information Systems and Applications, incl. Internet/Web, and HCI

Printed on acid-free paper

This Springer imprint is published by Springer Nature
The registered company is Springer International Publishing AG Switzerland

Preface

This volume contains the papers presented at the 22nd International Conference on Collaboration Technologies, CRIWG 2016. The conference was held during September 14–16, 2016, in Kanazawa, Japan. The conference was supported and governed by the Collaborative Research International Working Group (CRIWG), an open community of collaboration technology researchers. Since 1995, conferences supported by CRIWG have focused on collaboration technology design, development, and evaluation.

This year, CRIWG was co-located and organized with CollabTech 2016 after the successful collaboration in CRIWG 2014 that was co-located and organized with CollabTech 2014 in Santiago, Chile. Both communities have similar research directions and topics, but have been geographically located in different regions. This joint endeavor will keep or promote a worldwide community on collaboration technology.

For CRIWG 2016, 27 papers were submitted and carefully reviewed through a double-blind review process involving at least three reviewers per full-paper submission or two reviewers per work-in-progress paper submission. Finally, ten submissions were selected as full papers and three were selected as work-in-progress papers. Thus, this volume presents the most relevant and insightful research papers carefully chosen among the contributions accepted for presentation and discussion at the conference.

The papers published in the proceedings of this year's and past CRIWG conferences reflect the current diversity of collaborative computing research and its evolution. The topics included group support, AR and 3D technology, wearable technology, intercultural collaboration, remote physical tasks, recommendation systems, collaborative learning, and health support.

This year had contributions from four regions: there were six papers from Europe — Germany (four papers), France, Portugal; four papers from Asian countries — Japan (three papers) and Thailand; two papers from North American countries — Canada and Mexico; and two papers from South American countries — Brazil and Chile.

As editors, we would like to thank everybody who contributed to the content and production of this book, namely, all the authors and presenters, whose contributions made CRIWG 2016 a success, as well as the Steering Committee, the members of the Program Committee, and the reviewers. Off course, we would like to acknowledge the local organizers of the conference. We are also deeply grateful for the financial support from Ishikawa Prefecture, Kanazawa City, SCAT foundation, and Hitachi, Ltd. Our thanks also go to Springer, the publisher of the CRIWG proceedings, for their continuous support.

July 2016

Takaya Yuizono
Hiroaki Ogata
Ulrich Hoppe
Julita Vassileva

Organization

Program Committee

Renata Araujo	UNIRIO, Brazil
Nelson Baloian	University of Chile, Chile
Lars Bollen	University of Twente, The Netherlands
Ivica Boticki	University of Zagreb, Croatia
Luis Carriço	University of Lisbon, Portugal
Cesar A. Collazos	University of Cauca, Colombia
Gj De Vreede	University of South Florida, USA
Dominique Decouchant	UAM Cuajimalpa, Mexico DF, Mexico, LIG de Grenoble, France
Alicia Diaz	La Plata University, Argentina
Yannis Dimitriadis	University of Valladolid, Spain
Orlando Erazo	University of Chile, Chile
Benjamim Fonseca	UTAD, INESC TEC, Portugal
Kimberly García	Université Pierre et Marie Curie, France
Marco Gerosa	University of São Paulo, Brazil
Valeria Herskovic	Pontificia Universidad Católica de Chile, Chile
Gwo-Jen Hwang	National Taiwan University of Science and Technology, Taiwan
Indratmo Indratmo	Grant MacEwan University, Canada
Tomoo Inoue	University of Tsukuba, Japan
Seiji Isotani	University of Sao Paulo, Brazil
Marc Jansen	University of Applied Sciences Ruhr West, Germany
Ralf Klamma	RWTH Aachen University, Germany
Michael Koch	Bundeswehr University of Munich, Germany
Thomas Largillier	GREYC, France
Stephan Lukosch	Delft University of Technology, The Netherlands
Wolfram Luther	University of Duisburg-Essen, Germany
Alejandra Martínez	University of Valladolid, Spain
Sonia Mendoza	CINVESTAV-IPN, Mexico
Roc Meseguer	Universitat Politècnica de Catalunya, Spain
Alberto L. Morán	UABC, Mexico
Cuong Nguyen	University of Nebraska at Omaha, USA
Sergio Ochoa	Universidad de Chile, Chile
Hugo Paredes	INESC TEC and UTAD, Portugal
Christoph Rensing	Technische Universität Darmstadt, Germany
Ana Respício	University of Lisbon, Portugal
Flavia Santoro	NP2Tec/UNIRIO, Brazil

Applying Learning Analytics to Collaborative Learning

(Keynote Speech)

Stephen J.H. Yang

Department of Computer Science and Information Engineering,
National Central University, Taoyuan City, Taiwan
jhyang@csie.ncu.edu.tw

Abstract. This study applies learning analytics to measure learners' interaction, collaboration, and engagement during the process of collaborative learning in a MOOCs enabled course. The learning analytics provide instructors with visualized analysis of learners' engagement for better understanding of learners' collaboration with co-learners and interaction with course context. In addition, the learning analytics enable instructors to identify at-risk learners who have difficulties in collaboration and then trigger early intervention strategy. Our study shows that the learning analytics can successfully identify 85 % of students who were at-risk in collaboration, and over 60 % of the identified at-risk learners can improve their collaboration with early interventions.

Contents

Private or Common Criteria in a Multi-criteria Group Decision Support System: An Experiment

Pascale Zaraté[1(✉)], D. Marc Kilgour[2], and Keith Hipel[3]

[1] IRIT, Toulouse University, Toulouse, France
pascale.zarate@irit.fr
[2] Wilfrid Laurier University, Waterloo, Canada
[3] University of Waterloo, Waterloo, Canada

Abstract. Because collective decision processes are central to the management function of most organizations, it is important to understand them better and to improve them if possible. One common view of group decision processes is that they should offer participants the opportunity to confront and resolve the differences in their points of view. New cognitive and technical tools may help to facilitate the sharing of individuals' reasoning and preferences, but only if they do not require participants to reveal information that they wish to keep private, perhaps for strategic or personal reasons. The aim of this study is to test experimentally one such approach, contained in the Group Decision Support System, GRUS, which allows decision makers to use a multi-criteria approach to problem structuring that can involve both public (shared) and private criteria.

Keywords: GDSS · Multi-criteria group decision making · Private criteria · Public criteria

1 Introduction

In most organizations, important decisions are made after intensive consultations involving numerous decision makers, rather than by individuals acting on their own [1]. Smoliar and Sprague [2] discuss how interactions involving several actors are input into decision processes in organizations. This interaction, which includes but is not limited to the communication of information, is generally aimed at achieving a joint understanding among the decision makers.

Many authors have analyzed the process of group decision making from a range of perspectives. Zaraté [3] demonstrated that the use of Information and Communication Technologies to support decisions within the increasing complexity of organizations implies a modification of decision processes, which become more complex and involve more actors. These modifications must be present both at the organizational level, with larger numbers of responsible actors, and at the individual level, as actors face the challenge of understanding and classifying information using new and more difficult cognitive processes. New kinds of decision processes, which could be called Collaborative Decision Making, are thus required.

© Springer International Publishing Switzerland 2016
T. Yuizono et al. (Eds.): CRIWG 2016, LNCS 9848, pp. 1–12, 2016.
DOI: 10.1007/978-3-319-44799-5_1

Simply put, within a collective framework decision makers may have difficulty balancing their own preferences with the development of common (group) preferences and a shared understanding. The purpose of this paper is to conduct an experiment to assess whether decision makers can feel comfortable with common preferences. This experiment is based on a multi-criteria approach using the Group Decision Support System GRoUp Support, or GRUS [4], and aims to assess the roles of private versus common (shared or collective) criteria. When do multi-criteria group decision processes work better? Under what circumstances are individuals more comfortable using private as opposed to common criteria and performance evaluations? Can we verify in practice that these advantages are significant and discover conditions that can strengthen them? More generally, we wish to observe how participants perceive the advantages of joint decision-making in a group multi-criteria approach.

This paper is structured as follows. In Sect. 2, the GRUS system is described. Then the experiment is set out, along with the hypotheses of our study, in Sect. 3. Next, in Sect. 4, the results of the experiment are analyzed, and then they are discussed in the Sect. 5, which compared our hypotheses to the experimental observations. Section 6 offers some concluding remarks and perspectives.

2   Related Work

Moulin [5] defined cooperative games as follows: "A cooperative game in society N consists of a feasible utility set for the grand coalition N as well as a utility set for each and every sub-coalition (non-empty subset) of N, including the coalitions containing one agent only." He then proposed a categorization of many Game Theory axioms. Inspired by his definitions, we define Collaborative Decision Processes as dynamic decision processes involving several actors, who may use Information and Communication Technologies, who interact not only by making moves but also by updating their information and beliefs as other participants move. For these Collaborative Decision Processes, the use of Group Decision Support Systems (GDSS) is called for, and the facilitation process takes a central place.

The facilitator role within group meetings has been studied for over 40 years. Facilitators contribute to the effectiveness of GDSS, making meetings more productive and efficient, by managing the content, the process, or the use of software, and sometimes all three. It is not surprising that facilitator know-how can made a great difference in the effectiveness of GDSS in practice. Bostrom et al. [6] try to answer to the question: "Is a facilitator necessary in GSS environments?" Even though researchers have promoted GSS as a substitute for a human facilitator, many answer "Yes" to the question; and Bostrom and co-authors conclude that a human facilitator is definitely required. They find that the important question is "How can different sources of facilitation (people, software) be combined to effectively design and support meetings?" Following this paradigm, Ackerman [7] proposed Strategic Options Development and Analysis (SODA) to group members (participants) who had used a GDSS for organizational decision making. SODA is indeed a methodology to guide participants during meetings.

Even though the facilitation process has been well studied for several decades, several questions remain difficult to answer. What kinds of skills are necessary to facilitate Collaborative Decision Making? Can Collaborative Decision Processes be conducted with no human facilitation at all?

3   The GRoUp Support System: GRUS

GRUS is a free web platform, available at http://www.irit.fr/GRUS; it is protected by a login and a password available upon request from the authors. GRUS supports several kinds of meetings: synchronous or asynchronous, distributed or face-to-face. In case of a distributed asynchronous meeting, the decision making process must be managed by a facilitator as if it were a classical project by imposing an agenda.

GRUS is designed as a toolbox and is implemented in the framework Grails, which is based on the programming language Groovy, a very high level language like Python or Ruby. Groovy can be compiled to Java Virtual Machine bytecode and can interoperate with other java codes or libraries (for more details about these tools, see [4]). GRUS can be used by different users, including designers of collaborative tools (application developers), designers of a collaborative process (collaboration engineers), session facilitators (users of GRUS), and decision makers (users of GRUS).

GRUS offers the basic services commonly available in Group Decision Support System (GDSS) such as definition/design of a static or dynamic group decision process, management (add, modify, delete, etc.) of collaborative tools, and management of automatic reporting as PDF files.

GRUS is conceived as a toolbox including several collaborative tools supporting collaborative decision processes such as Brainstorming, Clustering, multicriteria Analysis, Voting, Consensus determination, and Reporting. Users of the multicriteria tools can define several criteria and several alternatives, and then give their assessment of each alternative on each criterion, thus creating what is called a preference matrix. Each preference is reported on a scale from 0 to 20. The decision makers may also give their preferred weights for the criteria. To indicate these preferences, each decision maker must enter a suitability function, thereby defining his or her interpretation of each criterion. This is possible thanks to an indifference threshold. Finally, dependencies among criteria must also be taken into account. These dependencies are assessed by each decision maker on a scale from 0 to 20 for each pair of criteria.

Two aggregation techniques are implemented in the GRUS system. The first aggregation methodology is the weighted sum [8], under which dependencies among criteria are not taken into account. The second methodology is the Choquet Integral [9], which explicitly takes dependencies among criteria into account.

4   Hypotheses of the Experiment

One benefit of a group decision-making process is the sharing of information that supports the participants' preferences. If the participants announce their preferred alternative without providing arguments about why it is appropriate to the problem at hand, the process does not contribute to any deeper understanding of the problem, nor to better knowledge of the alternatives, nor the links between them. In other words, the decision does not benefit from being made by the group [10]. However, it may not be practicable for participants to share their reasoning, first because they may have personal information or considerations that they may not wish to divulge (due to strategic reasons or privacy concerns), and second because the reasons for their own preference may not be clear, even to themselves.

In the end, the result of a group decision-making process must be supported by a mix of objective and subjective reasons. To meet this requirement, Sibertin and Zaraté [11] proposed a methodology distinguishing collective criteria from individual criteria for the assessment of alternatives.

- According to Sibertin and Zaraté [11], a criterion is *collective* if the group participants agree on its relevance and on the score of each alternative on this criterion;
- A criterion is *individual* if it is considered relevant by one participant (or several, but not all), or if the participants do not agree on the scores of alternatives on this criterion.

Collective criteria contribute to the objective part of the group's assessment, while individual criteria contribute to its subjective part.

Hypothesis 1: *In a collaborative decision making process, there are benefits from allowing participants to use private criteria as well as common criteria.*

In order to achieve cohesion in the group and the consistency in the group decision, it is necessary to find a balance between the individual approach to the problem, i.e. the private criteria, and the collective approach, i.e. the common criteria.

Hypothesis 2: *In a collaborative decision making process, the number of private criteria should at least equal the number of common criteria.*

Collaborative decision making processes are generally supported by Group Decision Support Systems. The use of GDSS implies the need for group facilitation, defined as a process in which a person who is acceptable to all members of the group intervenes to help improve the way the group identifies and solves problems, and makes decisions [12]. Facilitation is a dynamic process that involves managing relationships between people, tasks, and technology, as well as structuring tasks and contributing to the effective accomplishment of the intended outcomes.

According to Ackermann and Eden [13], such facilitation helps groups to contribute freely to the discussion, to concentrate on the task, to sustain interest and motivation to solve the problem, to review progress and to address complicated issues rather than ignore them. A further task of facilitation is to engage the group in problem-formulation and creativity-enhancing techniques to bring structure to the issues they are facing [14]. Facilitators attend to the process of decision making, while the decision makers concentrate on the issues themselves.

Automated facilitation is the enrichment of a GDSS so as to guide decision makers toward successful structuring and execution of the decision-making process [15]. According to Nunamaker et al. [16], an electronic facilitator should execute four functions: (1) provide technical support by initiating and terminating specific software tools;

(2) chair the meeting, maintaining and updating the agenda; (3) assist in agenda planning; and finally (4) provide organizational continuity, setting rules and maintaining an organizational repository.

Because many of these tasks seem difficult to automate, it would seem that it would be difficult for decision makers to use GDSS without a human facilitator.

Hypothesis 3: *GDSS use remains difficult without a human facilitator.*

A questionnaire was given to all participants. This questionnaire was composed of seven questions, five about the common/private criteria and two about the facilitation.

5   The Experiment

The experiment was conducted while the first author visited Wilfrid Laurier University and the University of Waterloo in Waterloo, Canada. A group of 15 persons, mostly PhD students and visiting researchers, was selected to participate in the experiment.

The experiment is described as follows:

A case-study decision problem was proposed, as described below.

"You are a member of the Administrative Committee of the Play-On-Line Company, which develops Software Games. Its primary staff includes 150 collaborators, as follows:

- 80 % Computer Engineers
- 15 % Marketing and Sales Staff
- 5 % Administrative Staff.

During an earlier meeting, the Board decided to buy mobile phones for the entire staff (all the collaborators listed above) even though the usage of the phones will not be the same for the business staff, the engineers, and the administrative staff. The computer engineers need to test the software they develop on all kinds of operating systems, for example operating systems implemented on Androids or iPhones. The business staff will use their phones to demonstrate the software to potential clients (for example, they need large screens). Administrative needs are simpler, and include for example communication (email and text as well as phone calls).

The aim of the meeting today is to decide on the best solution for the Play-On-Line Company. The finances are strictly limited, so costs must be minimized. In order to satisfy the requirements of all stakeholders, your group must think up several solutions called scenarios. Nevertheless, the company's survival, from a financial point of view, is the highest priority. You can, for example, decide to buy the same smartphones for all users, or you could plan to buy different smartphones for different stakeholders, or use at least some smartphones exclusively for testing and assign others to the collaborators. The technical characteristics and prices of five preselected smartphones are given below.

First of all, you have to define the set of criteria (4 or 5) to solve this problem and several alternatives (4 or 5). One alternative is defined as a combination of several products, such as 80 % of Smartphone A plus 20 % of Smartphone B. You will be guided by the facilitator, and then you will enter in the GRUS system your own preferences that will be input to the group decision".

Using the GRUS system, the following process was applied:

- **Brainstorming** to generate criteria and alternatives (scenarios) electronically. Each decision maker's input is anonymous.
- **Clustering** to reduce the numbers of criteria and alternatives to 4 or 5. This step is conducted by the facilitator orally. Each decision maker expresses their own views about the categorization of ideas. The facilitator then assigns each criterion to a category of criteria and each alternative to a category of alternatives.
- **MultiCriteria Evaluation**, in which each decision maker gives their own assessment, on a scale of 0 to 20, of the performance of each alternative on each criterion, the weight of each criterion, and a suitability function reflecting the interpretation of each criterion (i.e. an indifference threshold as well as the pair-by-pair dependencies among criteria).
- **Direct Vote, in which** all preferences given by all users are combined using two techniques, weighted sum and Choquet Integral. During this step, the facilitator shows the results of the Multi-Criteria Evaluation. All alternatives are then ranked according to the two techniques, producing two total orders. A discussion is then initiated by the facilitator in order to classify all alternatives into three categories: Saved, Possible, Removed.
- **Conclusion** in which the facilitator proposes a conclusion for the meeting – the set of saved alternatives. If the group must decide on one specific alternative, it is still possible to go back to the Multi-Criteria Evaluation step in order to refine the solution.
- **Report.** The facilitator generates a report of the meeting as a PDF file.

Finally, after this 1-h meeting, the participants were asked to fill out a questionnaire assessing these methods for identifying criteria and evaluating alternatives.

Three groups of five participants each were created. Each worked within a meeting session of 60 min.

Figure 1 shows Experimental Group 2 carrying out the first step of the process, brainstorming on criteria and alternatives.

Fig. 1. Brainstorming step for Group 2

Group 1 agreed on the following criteria: Price, Operating System, Communication Autonomy, Battery Capacity, and RAM; and generated 4 alternatives. Group 2's criteria were as follows: Price, Battery, Communication, and Operating System; and used 3 alternatives. Group 3 proposed as criteria: Price, Autonomy, RAM, and Handling; and defined 4 alternatives. All of this information is summarized in Table 1.

Table 1. Groups and Criteria

Group number	Number of participants	Selected criteria	Number of identified alternatives
1	5	Price Operating System Communication Autonomy Battery Capacity RAM	4
2	5	Price Battery Communication Operating System	3
3	5	Price Autonomy RAM Handling	4

6 Results

The results for all groups are given in the following sections.

6.1 Common/Private Criteria Results

The questionnaire contained five questions about whether the decision makers felt comfortable using only common criteria. The participants answered on a 4-point scale, with one additional level for those who have no opinion: Completely agree, Rather agree, Rather disagree, Completely disagree, No opinion.

The first question was: Do you think it is difficult for the group to find a set of shared criteria? The results are shown in Fig. 2. No participant answered No opinion or Completely agree. A large majority (80 %, including those who chose Completely not agree or Rather not agree) thinks that it is not difficult to find shared criteria in a group.

The second question was: Do you think that group size makes it difficult for the group to find shared criteria? The results are shown in Fig. 3. No participant answered No opinion. A majority (60 %, including those who chose Completely agree or Rather agree) thought that the size of a group influences its ability to find shared criteria.

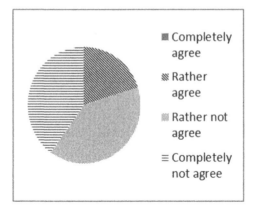

Fig. 2. Difficult to find shared criteria

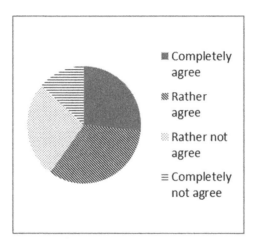

Fig. 3. Size of the group influences finding shared criteria

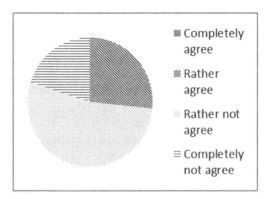

Fig. 4. Use private criteria

The third question was: Do you think it should be mandatory for all group members to use the same criteria?

No participant answered No opinion or Completely agree. A majority (74 %, including those who chose Rather not agree or Completely not agree) thought that it is not mandatory that the group work with the same criteria.

The fifth question was: Do you think that the number of private criteria for each decision maker should be at least as great as the number of shared criteria? The results are shown in Fig. 5.

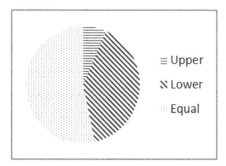

Fig. 5. Number of private criteria equal to number of shared criteria

No participant answered No opinion. A majority (53 %) thought that the number of private criteria should be the same as the number of shared criteria, but a large minority responded that the number of private criteria should be less than the number of public criteria (40 %).

6.2 Facilitation Results

Two questions about the facilitation process were asked to the stakeholders.

The participants answered on a 4-point scale, with one additional level for those who have no opinion: Completely agree, Rather agree, Rather disagree, Completely disagree, No opinion.

The first question was: Do you think that GRUS could be used without a facilitator? The results are shown in Fig. 6.

No participant answered No opinion. The result is balanced: 40 % rather agree and 40 % rather disagree with the idea that the system could be used without a human facilitator.

The second question was: Do you think that a decision process using the GRUS system is enough to support a group decision meeting? The results are shown in Fig. 7.

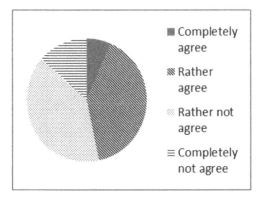

Fig. 6. Use of the system without a facilitator

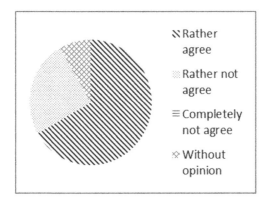

Fig. 7. Use of the system as a work process

One participant had no opinion. A large majority (74 %, including those who chose Completely agree or Rather agree) thought that the system could be used with a work process introduced in the GRUS system.

7   Discussion

The hypotheses were analyzed according to the results obtained in the experiment.

Hypothesis 1: *In a collaborative decision making process, there are benefits from allowing participants to use private criteria as well as common criteria.*

Most participants did not find it difficult to define shared criteria (see Fig. 1) and a small majority thought that the size of the group influences its ability to find common criteria (see Fig. 2). Referring to Fig. 3, a large majority believed that the group should not use only shared criteria and that the system worked better when participants could use private criteria. Based on these results, we conclude that Hypothesis 1 is confirmed.

Next, the question is to determine the number of criteria to be used and the proportions of private and common criteria.

Hypothesis 2: *In a collaborative decision making process, the number of private criteria should at least equal the number of common criteria.*

The results given in Fig. 4 show that the majority thought that the number of private criteria should at least equal the number of common criteria. Forty percent of participants also indicated that the number of private criteria should be less than the number of common criteria. We conclude that Hypothesis 2 is partially confirmed, and recommend that the number of private criteria be equal to or less than the number of common criteria.

GDSS use is generally conducted by a facilitator who, it has been suggested, may be replaced by a computer system. The next hypothesis aims to assess the participants' reactions to GDSS with and without a human facilitator.

Hypothesis 3: *GDSS use remains difficult without a human facilitator.*

For Fig. 5, the results are balanced. Forty percent of the participants thought that a human facilitator would help, but forty percent felt that a human facilitator is not mandatory. Turning to Fig. 6, we can see that a large majority (74 %) believed that an automated process implemented in the system could facilitate the decision making process. Therefore, we cannot interpret Hypothesis 3 as confirmed. We only can say that an automated process implemented to support the group could be helpful, but that a human facilitator may be at least equally effective.

8 Concluding Remarks and Perspectives

Group decisions can be complex and conflicting. Participants may feel dissatisfied and unmotivated, and they may not feel that their wishes and views have been properly considered. We have shown that using private and common criteria in Multi-Criteria Group Decision making can improve the participants' satisfaction with the process.

This study aimed to test the effects of using private and common criteria in group decisions. It addressed certain factors that should be considered carefully in designing a group decision process.

One such factor is the impact of the homogeneity of the group. Cohesive groups can agree more easily, especially if there are dominant leaders, and thereby limit creative solutions. Cultural effects could also have an influence on the results.

One limitation of this work is the low number of participants. In order to verify these first results, we will need to conduct more experiments.

Thus, our preliminary results should be checked using other experiments. We aim to conduct them in the near future, including in other countries. In addition to these new experiments, we plan to analyze all the experiments with respect to the demographic data of the participants (sex, age, occupation).

Another limitation of this first study is the analysis was conducted with students. These first results must therefore be verified with further experiments conducted in companies.

Acknowledgement. The authors would like to thank the CIMI Excellence Laboratory, Toulouse, France, for funding the visit of Pascale Zaraté as Visiting Professor at Wilfrid Laurier University, Waterloo, Canada, during the period of December 2015 to February 2016.

References

1. Gorry, G., Morton, M.S.: A framework for management information systems. Sloan Manage. Rev. **13**(1), 50–70 (1971)
2. Smoliar, S., Sprague, R.: Communication and understanding for decision support. In: Proceedings of the International Conference IFIP TC8/WG8.3, Cork, Ireland, pp. 107–119 (2002)
3. Zaraté, P.: Tools for Collaborative Decision-Making. John Wiley, Hoboken (2013)
4. Camilleri, G., Zaraté, P.: EasyMeeting: a group decision support system (Release 1). Rapport de recherche IRIT/RR–2014–10—FR (2014)
5. Moulin, H.: Axioms of Cooperative Decision Making (No. 15). Cambridge University Press, New York (1991)
6. Bostrom, R.P., Anson, R., Clawson, V.K.: Group facilitation and group support systems. Group Support Syst. New Perspect. **8**, 146–168 (1993)
7. Ackermann, F.: Participants' perceptions on the role of facilitators using group decision support systems. Group Decis. Negot. **5**(1), 93–112 (1996)
8. Yager, R.: On ordered weighted averaging aggregation operators in multicriteria decision making. IEEE Trans. Syst. Man Cybern. **18**, 183–190 (1988)
9. Choquet, G.: Theory of capacities. Ann. Inst. Fourier **5**, 131–295 (1953)
10. Schmidt, K., Bannon, L.: Taking CSCW seriously: supporting articulation work. Comput. Support. Coop. Work (CSCW) **1**(1), 7–40 (1992)
11. Sibertin-Blanc, C., Zaraté, P.: Cooperative decision making: a methodology based on collective preferences aggregation. In: Zaraté, P., Kersten, G.E., Hernández, J.E. (eds.) GDN 2014. LNBIP, vol. 180, pp. 1–10. Springer, Heidelberg (2014)
12. Schwarz, R.: The skilled facilitator. Jossey-Bass Publishers (1994)
13. Ackermann, F., Eden, C.: Issues in computer and non-computer supported GDSSs. Decis. Support Syst. **12**, 381–390 (1994)
14. French, S.: Web-enabled strategic GDSS, e-democracy and Arrow's theorem: a Bayesian perspective. Decis. Support Syst. **43**(4), 1476–1484 (2007)
15. Limayem, L., DeSanctis, G.: Providing decisional guidance for multicriteria decision making in groups. Inf. Syst. Res. **11**(4), 386–401 (2000)
16. Nunamaker, J., Briggs, R.O., Mittleman, D., Vogel, D., Balthazard, B.: Lessons from a dozen years of group support systems research: a discussion of lab and field findings. J. Manage. Inf. Syst. **13**(3), 163–207 (1997)

Communication Design for New Type of Showroom Dedicated to Value Co-creation

Kazunori Horikiri[✉]

Customer Co-creation Lab, Fuji Xerox Co., Ltd., Yokohama-shi, Japan
Kazunori.Horikiri@fujixerox.co.jp

Abstract. For enterprises today, in order to create new business, it is becoming more important to understand customers' business context, their potential problems, and their challenges rather than thinking of ideas to solve widely known problems. In these cases, many companies will provide a special type of facility similar to a showroom which we call a "Co-creation Showroom" in order to understand customers' business context and challenges.

This work analyzes the communication process of the "Co-creation Showroom" and identifies several key factors for successful dialogue between facilitators and customers. This work also introduces a new communication process using new communication tools as well as evaluations of this process.

Keywords: Design method · Co-creation · Critical design · Human centered design · Showroom · User evaluation · Communication tool

1 Introduction

Nowadays, a new type of showroom is becoming popular among enterprises aiming to develop innovative business based on the understanding of customers' business problems and challenges. The "Customer Technical Center (CTC)" of 3 M is one of the most historical examples of this type of showroom. The company has more than 40 CTCs worldwide [1]. In Japan in particular, they established a CTC in 1997. They define the mission of the CTC as "Creating value through collaborative dialogues with customers." Their special communication scheme is introduced as follows: "Engineers work in collaboration with our customers to develop ideas which address their technological problems," and "Customers can meet with engineers face-to-face to discuss problems and solutions and explore possible courses of action" [2].

Recently, similar types of co-creation showrooms are being established by other companies, for example as the "Customer Co-creation Lab" by Fuji Xerox Co., Ltd. in 2010 [3], the "Open Innovation Hub" by FUJIFILM Holdings Corporation in 2014 [4], the "IHI Innovation Centre" by IHI Corporation in 2014 [5] and the "Global Center for Social Innovation (CSI)" by Hitachi, Ltd. in 2015 [6].

These "Co-creation Showrooms" are characterized as follows by comparing them with conventional showrooms (Table 1).

However, an analytical view of the business process and communication taking place in a "Co-creation Showroom" is never clearly stated but rather seeps into and is held by the individual facilitators. Therefore, it is hard to improve performance and

© Springer International Publishing Switzerland 2016
T. Yuizono et al. (Eds.): CRIWG 2016, LNCS 9848, pp. 13–20, 2016.
DOI: 10.1007/978-3-319-44799-5_2

Table 1. Comparison between conventional showroom and co-creation showroom

	Conventional showroom	Co-creation showroom
Why	Sales promotion	Business development
What	Products	Technologies and prototypes
Who	Sales representatives	Engineers and planners
Whom	End users	Invited managers of a business unit
How	Explain and answer questions	Explain and ask questions, dialogue
Where	Sales rep sites	R & D sites or headquarters

quality of communications in the showroom as an organization. This work analyzes the communication processes of the "Co-creation Showroom" and extracts several key factors for successful dialogue between facilitators and customers. This work also introduces a new communication process using a new tool as well as evaluations of this process.

2   Background

Nowadays, it is becoming more important for many enterprises to create new values for customers. Furthermore, the focus of the market is drastically shifting from one that is "goods-centered" to one that is "service-centered" [7]. As the focus of the market shifts from "goods" to "service", the customer becomes a coproducer of service and an active participant in relational exchanges and coproduction. And "Value is perceived by the consumer on the basis of "value in use."

Koskinen identified three types of format for design, named "Lab," "Field" and "Gallery/Showroom," and defined the characteristics of each of them as follows: [8, 9]

- Lab: Studies are conducted in laboratory-like conditions by introducing explanatory variables.
- Field: Instead of bringing the context into a design experiment, it places design into a naturalistic setting.
- Gallery/Showroom: The exhibition presents concepts and design objects as well as ideas and visions by giving people the opportunity for first-hand experience.

A "Gallery" pushes knowledge to new domains by way of critical discourse through practices borrowed from the art world [8]. On the other hand, the space in which the artifacts are shown becomes a 'showroom' rather than a gallery, encouraging a form of conceptual consumerism via critical 'advertisements' and 'products' [10].

As for "Co-creation Showrooms" for enterprises, we observe that the format is very similar to the conventional showroom so the facilitators tend to behave like sales representatives and fail to extract customers' business context and problems to develop new businesses. The facilitation of communication in co-creation showrooms requires a wide range of knowledge regarding semi-structured interviews, experience design, business models and organization design as well as business communication manners. However, little attention has been paid to the communication design of the showrooms in which enterprise customers are invited to create value through collaborative dialogues [1, 10].

This work analyzes the communication process of these new types of Showrooms which we call "Co-creation Showrooms" and identifies several key factors for successful dialogue between facilitators and customers. This work also introduces a new communication process using new communication tools as well as evaluations of this process (Table 2).

Table 2. Key Goal Indicators of the co-creation showroom

ID	Key Goal Indicators
1-1	To create business through co-creation with customers
1-2	To increase the number of non-disclosure agreements with customers
1-3	To increase the number of sample evaluation requests from customers

3   Method

This section describes our steps of communication design, namely user study, identification of user requirements, prototype and evaluation in the field.

3.1   Understanding the Context of the Showroom Activities

To understand the context of the showroom activities, we started a project of an action research with a business partner who has communication process issues of their co-creation showroom. We observed to understand realistic context by participating as "customers" and interviewed two managers of the showroom to understand hidden context such as outputs and goals of the showroom activities and their reporting line. As a result, the activities are roughly categorized into three phases; pre-activities, customer visit and post-activities.

Pre-activities: showroom managers have a meeting with their sales representatives to understand customer's background of the visit.

Customer visit: it takes about 120 min and consists of mainly 4 parts, "Greetings (10 min)," "Introduction of the company history (20 min)," "Introduction of cutting-edge technologies and prototypes (60 min)," and "Discussion (30 min)."

Post-activities: notes of dialogues are gathered from facilitators, and a summary of the notes are distributed to customers and relevant divisions.

3.2   Hierarchical Goals of the Co-creation Showroom

We design a semi-structured interview based on the key activities extracted from the observation of the co-creation showroom. We take a 150-min semi-structured interview individually with each of two managers of the showroom to understand their activities and goals. Applying GTA [11], we segmented the output of each interview and merged it into 19 goals/sub-goals. Then we categorize these goals into three hierarchical layers

Table 3. Key Success Factors of the co-creation showroom

ID	Key Success Factors
–	To improve the quality and efficiency of face-to-face communication
2-1	To extract potential and promising customer problems
–	To get an opportunity for new business
2-2	To identify problems and their business context
–	To capture customers' needs at high quality level
2-3	To get all customers involved
2-4	To improve the quality and speed of action derived from the dialogue

based on their dependency, namely "Key Goal Indicators (KGIs)", "Key Success Factors (KSFs)" and "Key Performance Indicators (KPIs)". KSFs are intended to be sub-goals of KGIs, and KPIs are intended to be sub-goals of KSFs (Table 3).

Numbered KGIs, KSFs and KPIs are indicators/factors that are highly prioritized by the managers of the showroom.

3.3   Prototype

Using highly prioritized factors and indicators, we extract a typical current scenario of a showroom focusing on customer problems, as shown in Fig. 1.

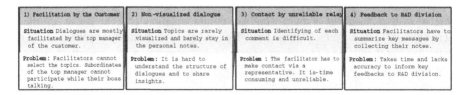

Fig. 1. A typical current scenario of the co-creation showroom

To solve problems in a typical current scenario, we have introduced a new communication scenario and communication tools with shared dual 80-in. digital boards as well as a tablet terminal for each customer, as shown in Figs. 2 and 3.

Fig. 2. Prototype of a typical future scenario of the co-creation showroom

Fig. 3. Facilitating dialogues using shared digital boards and tablet terminals

Using the new communication process and tools, customers and facilitators can communicate concurrently and visually via digital boards and tablet terminals handling digital sticky-notes (Table 4).

Table 4. Key Perfoemance Indicators of communication in the co-creation showroom

ID	Key Performance Indicators of Communication
–	To promote dialogue though visualization
–	To improve the quality and efficiency of structuring of topics during dialogue
3-1	To increase the number of visitors who discuss their business challenges
3-2	To narrow down topics during facilitation
3-3	To find out customers' hidden issues
3-4	To discuss topics in depth
–	To facilitate to extract the background and reason of the requirement
3-5	To improve the speed of feedback to relevant divisions
3-6	To improve the quality and efficiency of structuring of topics after discussion

3.4 Evaluation

In order to evaluate the performance improvement of the co-creation showroom from the perspective of KGIs, we trace the total number of (1-2) NDAs entered into and (1-3) sample requests over the course of 6 months. The average occurrence more than tripled, from 1.7 to 5.5 per month (Table 5).

For the perspective of KSFs and KPIs, we design a questionnaire for quantitative and qualitative evaluations. We use a 5-point scale in order to indicate the degree of improvement compared with the baseline, namely level 1: "much worsened", level 3: "same as before" and level 5: "much improved". We use a free description format for the qualitative evaluation. We pick up all the facilitators of the co-creation showroom including two managers and five assistant facilitators. Summary of the evaluation is as follows:

Table 5. Quantitative and qualitative evaluation of the new communication process

ID	KSF/KPI	Quantitative evaluation	Qualitative evaluation
2-1	To extract potential and promising customer problems	3.8	Numbers of comments can indicate the priority of problems.
2-2	To identify problems and their business context	4.0	Visualization of topics makes facilitation easy.
2-3	To get all customers involved	4.2	Topics are selected based on their contents rather than the job titles.
2-4	To improve quality and speed of action derived from dialogue	quality:4.2 speed:4.0	It is possible to make direct contact with the author of comments. Sharing digital board images as minutes leads to a quick response from the customer.
3-1	To increase number of visitors who discuss their business challenges with us	4.5	Many comments can be gathered concurrently, especially in a big group discussion.
3-2	To narrow down topics during facilitation	4.3	Facilitators can start dialogues on the topic of their own interests.
3-3	To find out customers' hidden issues	3.7	Customers' writings makes their opinions clear.
3-4	To discuss topics in depth	4.3	Understanding customers' interests and navigating related topics can lead the discussion in depth.
3-5	To improve speed of feedback to relevant divisions	quality:4.0 speed:4.2	Since the summary can be shared with attendees on-site, the efficiency is improves.
3-6	To improve quality and efficiency of structuring of topics after dialogue	quality:4.3 speed:4.7	Since the structuring process is shared among attendees, the outcome is convincible.

4   Discussion

We extracted three KGIs, four highly prioritized KSFs, and six KPIs of Communications for the co-creation showroom from the interviews. These KGIs/KSFs and KSFs/KPIs were identified to have cause-and-effect relations by the facilitators.

As we investigate the KSFs and KPIs carefully, strongly dependent factors/indicators are identified, such as (2-1) "extract potential and promising customer's problem" and (2-2) "find out problems and their business context." Factor (2-2) is a necessary condition of factor (2-1).

In order to make the relations between factors/indicators clear, we conducted an additional interview and derived a directed acyclic graph (DAG) of the relations, as shown in Fig. 4. Arrows indicate the dependencies; a left-to-right arrow denotes that the left item is dependent on the right.

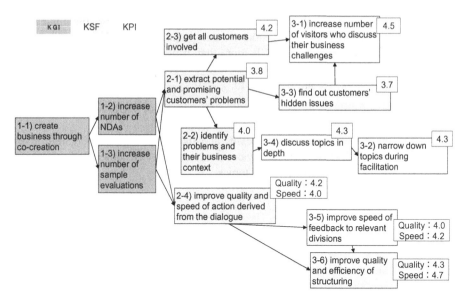

Fig. 4. DAG denoting dependencies of KGIs, KSFs and KPIs from user study

The DAG of the dependencies of indicators/factors tells that:

- Two main KSFs for the showroom are identified, namely, "(2-1) extract potential and promising customer's problems" and "(2-4) improve quality and speed of action derived from the dialogue"
- The subgraph starting from the node (2-1) is larger than the subgraph starting from the node (2-4). This implies that achieving condition (2-1) is more difficult than achieving (2-4). For example, condition (2-2) is to "identify problems and their business context" requiring discussion in depth (4-3). On the other hand, condition (2-3) requires "To get all customers involved" in widely. Therefore, satisfying both conditions (2-2) and (2-3) requires a special facilitation technique to avoid a contradiction.
- The performance gap between (3-1) "To increase number of visitors who discuss their business challenges" and (3-3) "To find out customers' hidden issues" is relatively big. This implies that the possibility of missing important KPIs related to the condition (3-3). The full set of KPIs involves the condition of "To facilitate to extract the background and reason of the requirement." This can be a good candidate to start further discussion.

5   Conclusion

This work analyzes the communication process of the co-creation showroom as an action research and extracts 19 key indicators/factors for successful dialogue between facilitators and customers. We introduce priorities and dependency relations into these indicators/factors to extract a typical current scenario of the co-creation showroom.

To solve problems in a typical current scenario, we introduce a new communication scenario between facilitators and customers using shared digital boards and tablet terminals. As a result, the average KGIs more than tripled from 1.7 to 5.5 per month and all the KSFs/KPIs are improved, whose average is greater than 4 in a 5-point scale.

For the future work, we are planning to;

- apply a statistical analysis to clarify the dependency of KGIs/KSFs/KPIs using evaluation data for each session with customers, and
- introduce other communication processes and mechanisms to support high level facilitation especially for achieving wide involvement of customers to seek topics and deep discussions on the selected topics.

References

1. Rahn, S.: 3M: beyond the 15 % rule. In: Gassmann, O., Schweitzer, F. (eds.) Management of the Fuzzy Front End of Innovation, pp. 195–199. Springer International Publishing, Heidelberg (2014)
2. The 3M Japan Group: Corporate Profile. http://www.mmm.co.jp/corporate/pdf/corporateprofile_e_201507.pdf
3. Horikiri, K.: A pattern language of process and environment to design value co-creation with customers. In: Collaborative Innovation Networks Conference (COINs) (2015)
4. Fujifilm opens the Open Innovation Hub - For "co-creation" of new values with business partners | FUJIFILM Holdings Corporation (2014). http://www.fujifilmholings.com/en/news/2014/0120_01_02.html
5. IHI Innovation Centre | IHI Corporation. http://www.ihi.co.jp/itl/en/index.html
6. News Releases : Hitachi Global, 27 February 2015. http://www.hitachi.com/New/cnews/month/2015/02/150227.html
7. Vargo, S.L., Lusch, R.F.: Evolving to a new dominant logic for marketing. J. Mark. **68**, 1–17 (2004)
8. Koskinen, I., Binder, T., Redström, J.: Lab, field, gallery, and beyond 1. Artifact **2**, 46–57 (2008)
9. Koskinen, I., Zimmerman, J., Binder, T., Redstrom, J., Wensveen, S.: Design Research Through Practice: From the Lab, Field, and Showroom. Elsevier, Burlington (2011)
10. Dunne, A.: Hertzian Tales: Electronic Products, Aesthetic Experience, and Critical Design. The MIT Press, Cambridge (2008)
11. Glaser, B.G., Strauss, A.L.: The Discovery of Grounded Theory: Strategies for Qualitative Research. Transaction Publishers, London (2009)

AR-based Modeling of 3D Objects in Multi-user Mobile Environments

Andrés Cortés-Dávalos$^{(\boxtimes)}$ and Sonia Mendoza

Computer Science Department,
Centro de Investigación y Estudios Avanzados del Intituto Politécnico Nacional,
Av. Instituto Politécnico Nacional No. 2508, Col. San Pedro Zacatenco,
Del. Gustavo A. Madero, 07360 México City, Mexico
`acortes@computacion.cs.cinvestav.mx`, `smendoza@cs.cinvestav.mx`
`https://www.cs.cinvestav.mx/`

Abstract. In animations and video games, Digital Elevation Maps (DEMs) are commonly used to model geometric assets, e.g., terrains on a landscape. When a DEM is edited by a group of collaborators, they are constrained to access the elevation data from their PC following a turn-taking policy, since most of the applications are essentially single-user. Furthermore, the DEM is visualized in 2D, causing some degree of confusion to new users when imagining the DEM shape in 3D. In this paper, we propose a novel approach to the collaborative modeling of DEMs on mobile devices. Our approach uses Augmented Reality (AR) to help collaborators to easily understand the DEM's 3D representation and provides them with basic editing tools to modify the DEM shape in an intuitive manner. In addition, we implement an object sharing scheme, in order to support face-to-face interaction in real-time. By means of this approach, it is possible to create an original collaboration setting, in which a group of collocated colleagues, each carrying a mobile device, can concurrently create and modify the same DEM, while visualizing it using AR-technology. As shown by our results, the workload perceived by the users of our DEM editor is small.

Keywords: Real-time face to face interaction · Edition of 3D surfaces · Object sharing scheme · AR-based applications

1 Introduction

There exist several commercial terrain editors and 3D design applications, but very few are mobile-based and practically none of them are both collaborative and AR-based. In the case of new users who lack previous training on 3D design, most of these 3D modeling applications have inherent drawbacks, from which we mention those relevant to our work:

– It is difficult to learn how to interact with the User Interface (UI) of the application, as the editing tools are numerous and not enough intuitive.

© Springer International Publishing Switzerland 2016
T. Yuizono et al. (Eds.): CRIWG 2016, LNCS 9848, pp. 21–36, 2016.
DOI: 10.1007/978-3-319-44799-5_3

- The visual feedback given to the user is based on 2D views of the 3D object, which are taken from the viewpoint of several virtual cameras. Consequently, it is difficult to understand the 3D shape and structure of the object only from the views, as well as to precisely move and point the virtual cameras towards the intended location in the 3D virtual space.
- The editing process is single-user.

In this work, we show that our approach greatly improves the user experience by solving the aforementioned drawbacks as follows. The first problem is addressed by designing a minimalistic UI that is shown along with the DEM graphical representation using AR. In this manner, we obtain a potentially bigger virtual space to place UI elements without cluttering the screen or obstructing the workspace, independently of the device size. We say the UI is minimal because we only offer the four most essential operations to edit the DEM, and their options are few and straightforward. Also, the interaction with the UI is performed using intuitive touch gestures.

In the traditional 3D interaction paradigm, the user sees the scene through several virtual cameras. Usually, there is a perspective camera that the user can translate and rotate to get the desired point of view, and also there are other implicit cameras used to see the scene from fixed directions (top, front, and side). In some cases, the user is not quite aware of the different virtual cameras. First hand experience with freshmen shows us that they do struggle while switching virtual cameras or pointing the perspective camera to the desired location, and their views can get easily lost in the 3D virtual space.

However, nowadays, most users are quite familiar with pointing a digital camera or mobile device towards all sorts of subjects and objects of interest in the real world. Thus, when using AR, they can easily point the device towards the virtual object from different perspectives. The application no longer requires many different virtual cameras to have different perspectives. Instead, the user naturally manipulates the real device camera, in the usual way through the physical space. As the virtual object is perceived inside the real environment from any desired viewpoint, the user gets a better understanding of its shape and geometric structure in 3D. In this way, AR helps to solve the second problem by giving a better sense of location, shape, and scale of the virtual object.

During a multi-user editing session of a single 3D object, normally only one collaborator works on the modeling task, while the rest of the group waits or observes. At some point, the other collaborators can suggest editions to the one in control of the application, and they occasionally take turns to do their respective portions of the common work. This behavior is because the application does not allow the participants to work at the same time, or it does not preserve data consistency when trying to share the model data. In some stages of collaborative work, it is clearly more productive to have the participants working simultaneously, instead of taking turns. Hence, we tackle the third problem by designing and implementing an object sharing scheme that allows a group of collocated users to concurrently modify a DEM.

The main purpose of our work is to develop mobile applications for 3D digital content creation, aimed at groups of users, who might not have previous training on 3D modeling. Our approach is based on applying the advantages of both Augmented Reality (AR) and Computer Supported Cooperative Work (CSCW) research areas to the task of concurrently editing a 3D object. In this work, the kind of digital content we focus on is the 3D representation of DEMs. The application we describe is the second iteration of our mobile DEM editor. Based on the lessons learned with the previous version of the editor, we have performed several interesting modifications on the UI design and the whole architecture. Using AR technology along with our object sharing scheme constitutes an approach with a great potential to improve the productivity of the collaborators and to make the editor easier to use. Up to our knowledge, there does not exist any other application capable of supporting multi-user editing of DEMs while using AR. We show promising results from tests conducted with users working simultaneously on our DEM editor.

This paper is organized as follows: after presenting related work in Sect. 2, we provide a description of the DEM model in Sect. 3. Several design considerations are described in Sect. 4, namely: the UI design, the editing operations, and the object sharing scheme used to concurrently edit the DEM. Implementation details of the improved version of the editor are given in Sect. 5, where we mention some particularities of Unity while adding the desired behaviors to the virtual objects in the 3D scene. An evaluation of the perceived work load while using our terrain editor is given in Sect. 6. Finally, in Sect. 7, we conclude this work and provide some ideas of future extensions.

2   Related Work

In Computer Graphics, the most common use for DEMs is to represent the shape of terrains. For this reason, it is frequent to implicitly consider a DEM as almost the same as a terrain. We can divide the terrain creation programs in two types: terrain generators and terrain editors.

The terrain generators are mainly based on the procedural synthesis paradigm [1], in which the terrain is synthetized, in a global way, using several algorithms. Thus, the control over the final result is very limited. Depending on the type of algorithms used, we can distinguish between two types of methods for terrain generation: (1) fractal-based [2,3] and (2) simulation-based [4,5]. There exist hybrids of these.

As examples of terrain generators, we mention the works by Belhadj as well as by Kamal and Uddin. The former work presents a fast fractal-based algorithm [6] that reconstructs DEM data, according to sparse given constraints. In the latter work, a parametrically controlled fractal algorithm [7] is proposed, in order to create a single mountain while satisfying given properties, such as location, height, and spread of the base. On these both examples, the authors made an attempt to achieve more local control on the resulting terrain, in spite of the global nature of the terrain generators.

On the other hand, the terrain editors use the *painting with brushes* paradigm, also called *interactive brush-based sculpting*. On this paradigm, the system provides a tool that works using a brush metaphor, i.e., the user *paints* over an object and locally applies changes on one of its properties, such as color, texture, or shape. The painting operation is applied only on the region swept by the brush, not over all the terrain as in algorithmic synthesis.

Also there exists research on hybridizing global terrain generation with local edition. Here we mention the work by de Carpentier and Bidarra, in which they present *procedural brushes* [8], a method that combines the strengths of both approaches: interactive brush-based sculpting and algorithmic synthesis. As well as other procedural approaches, this hybrid method requires large calculations. Thus, they propose to use a GPU to perform at interactive rates on desktop computers.

In the market, there exist several highly polished 3D landscape generators, which run on desktop computers and are single-user. Two of the most popular packages of this type are *Bryce* [9] and *Vue* [10]. These allow the user to create and edit DEMs employed as virtual landscapes, and to populate them with grass, plants, trees, rocks, lakes, clouds, fog, soil textures, and even characters and buildings. In our work, we mainly focus on concurrently editing the DEM values, but we do not add landscape-related features.

There are also game engines and level editors, such as *Unity* [11], *Ogre* [12], and *Unreal* [13], which include several tools to create 3D environments used in video games. Some environments are based on terrains created by means of DEMs. As is the case of previous landscape creators, these packages only run on desktop computers and are single-user.

Beside games, DEMs are also useful to model environments for digital animations and artistic compositions. There are many 3D creation suites for desktop computers, which are single-user and have terrain modeling capabilities. From these suites, *Maya* [14] and *Blender* [15] deserve special mention.

The *WebGL*-based online *Terrain Editor* [16] is a project for terrain modeling on a browser. It has four editing operations, the same as our editor, but it is single-user. None of the aforementioned terrain editors uses AR. Instead, they offer the user a view projection of the terrain's 3D representation, and the user can rotate it by dragging the mouse pointer.

LandscapAR [17] is a single-user mobile application that uses computer vision algorithms to track and scan a height map drawn on a piece of white paper. First, the user draws a set of level curves using any thick black marker. Then, the application generates the 3D representation of the depicted terrain and shows it using AR over the paper. Finally, the application allows the user to publish snapshots of the created terrains on social networks. In this manner, the user can create terrains from drawings, but the generated terrains cannot be directly modified. Instead, the user has to physically edit the drawing, and later the application will create the new corresponding terrain.

Currently, there are several mobile AR applications, such as *Layar* [18] and *Metaio* [19], which offer cloud-based services for publishing digital content on printed media. This kind of services is mostly oriented to advertising, and the applications that use them are generally single-user.

However, there exists a classroom application that uses the geolocation-based AR capabilities of *Wikitude* [20] along with Google Maps to share map locations and visualize them *in situ*. Although it is claimed that these shared maps provide collaborative AR, they allow the users neither to modify the augmented content in any way nor to interact with each other. Only one author can publish locations, while the other users can just watch them. Hence, the users merely share content, but they neither collaborate nor edit maps.

The *Magic Book* [21] project augments a physical book with shared 3D scenes, on which collocated users can see the same content and virtually *travel* inside the scenes, changing from AR to VR (Virtual Reality) display. When the users enter the VR mode, the system shows them as little avatars to the other users, in order to get them aware of their location in the scene. The immersed users can also see those outside the scene as *big heads* looking down from the sky.

The *Invisible Train* game [22] is the first multi-user AR application running on handheld devices. They designed a setting for four players, who control virtual trains running on physical tracks, allowing them to compete with each other.

ARprism [23] is a desktop application that supports face to face collaboration on geographic data visualization tasks. The system augments a tabletop map with different layers of topographic data, e.g., coordinates, elevation, soil, hydrology, and subsurface structure. The 3D representations of the terrain are previously modelled using VRML (Virtual Reality Modeling Language) and cannot be modified by the users.

Back in the early days of AR development [24], running from 1998 up to roughly 2001, most of the AR applications required the use of relatively cumbersome HMDs connected to desktop computers or laptops carried on backpacks. In 2006, Billinghurst et al. [23] mentioned that it would be more user friendly to replace the uncomfortable HMDs with portable LCD displays equipped with small Web cameras, thus avoiding *simulator sickness* and reducing interference in the inter-user communication and the field-of-view isolation. Nowadays, with the advent of powerful mobile devices, this is the preferred configuration for affordable AR applications.

Nam et al. [25] present a collaborative AR-based workspace for synchronous distributed product reviewing that uses tangible synchronized turntables and virtual shadows to support awareness of remote collaborators. This system allows two remote participants to examine a shared 3D object, to talk to each other via voice, and to communicate the object rotation, in order to help focussing the discussion at some part of the model. The synchronized turntable was successful, but the use of virtual shadows was not very much, mainly because it was difficult to point in a 3D space using only 2D shadows.

Finally, *Second Surface* [26] is a mobile application that allows the user to create and virtually situate digital contents on the surrounding 3D space of everyday objects, such as trees and walls, taken as AR markers. The application also allows the user to share the created contents with other collocated users in real time. In this case, the shared content cannot be modified by other users, so it does not achieve the same level of collaborative edition we offer with our approach. However, *Second Surface* is the first attempt to provide a mobile collaborative AR experience for shared content creation.

We found that the idea of fusing AR with CSCW is not new at all. Efforts have been focused on sharing and interacting with previously made 3D objects, or on sharing 3D content with others, but not allowing them to perform modifications. Practically, there are no other reported works with our focus: to concurrently create and edit digital assets using AR.

3   DEM Model

We understand a terrain of the real world as a patch of land or territory, which can contain geometric features defining its shape. Examples of such features are mountains, craters, canyons, valleys, cracks, riverbeds, lake basins, and plains.

The simplest way to abstract the shape of a terrain into a model is to give the height value for each point on its surface, measured with respect to an agreed reference, e.g., the sea level. We can describe a terrain using a continuous function. However, in computer applications, we use instead a discrete terrain representation, which is a discrete function:

$$h : \mathcal{R} \to \mathcal{F},$$

where $\mathcal{R}$ is the rectangular region $[1, m] \times [1, n] \subset \mathbb{N}^2$ for given integers $m, n \in \mathbb{N}$ and $\mathcal{F}$ represents the domain of floating point numbers that can be stored in a computer. In this manner, we store a DEM as a rectangular floating point array of size $m \times n$. In Fig. 1, we show the plot of points composing a DEM. In our editor, we graphically represent the DEM data array as a 3D surface, by using a polygonal mesh.

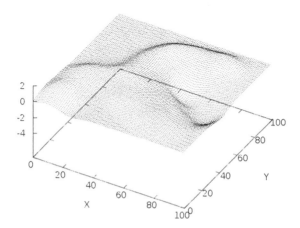

Fig. 1. Example of a DEM, in which there exists a discrete height value for each point in the discrete domain.

Given that h is a function, it cannot represent all the details of a real terrain, such as caves and overhangs. However, this representation suffices for most of the practical applications.

4   Design Principles of the DEM Editor

This new version of the DEM editor was built using Unity, a game engine widely used to create many kinds of multi-platform 2D and 3D applications, deployable on desktop computers and mobile devices. We also use Vuforia, a development library that allows us to add AR capabilities to iOS, Android and Unity-based applications. Vuforia uses computer vision algorithms to recognize some previously loaded marker and augment virtual objects aligned with it.

The architecture of our DEM editor is shown in Fig. 2. The editor is built within the Unity engine. The mesh representation of the terrain and the UI widgets are placed inside a 3D scene. Using the Vuforia plugin, we show the scene to the user with AR over the marker. When the user interacts with the UI widgets, the editing operations are triggered using RPCs (Remote Procedure Calls) via the *Data Sharing Module* that relies on the Network View functionality provided by Unity to create multi-user applications. The editing operations are broadcasted to other participants and are applied locally to the DEM data structure using the *Modeling Module*, which also updates the terrain mesh in real-time.

Some of the benefits of using AR in 3D editing applications are to give users a more natural way to manipulate the perspective from which the virtual scene is observed and to give them an improved perception of the 3D shape of virtual objects. However, the use of AR also has some drawbacks. If the mobile device is very large or heavy, it can be tiresome to hold it with a single hand while using the other to paint on the terrain. We have previously observed from our users that they use their dominant hand to perform the drawing touches, while holding

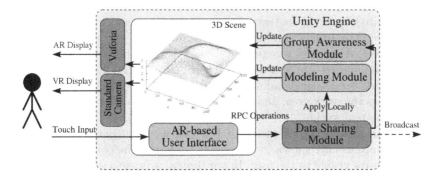

Fig. 2. Architecture of the DEM editor.

the device with the other, which is usually weaker. So, our users frequently got this hand numbed and juggle the device to switch hands. Also, if the user's hand is shaking, it becomes hard to perform the strokes in a precise manner.

Another interesting behavior we found by observing the users while testing the first version of our editor is that they tended to keep standing on a spot while editing the terrain, instead of walking around the marker to get different perspectives. Therefore, they did not completely exploit the AR main advantage. This could be caused by the lack of previous experience with AR systems.

There are also technical drawbacks. While using AR, the device must keep the camera turned on all the time, reducing the battery duration. Also, the use of marker-based AR reduces the mobility of the device, as it is bounded to the physical marker. Let us think for example what happens when the user had lost or forgot the marker, or when the editor is used in a reduced space, like inside a car. In this situation, the user simply cannot hold both the device and the marker, while performing touch operations. Three hands would be needed.

Considering all of these, we included inside the application two modes of the 3D scene: one using Vuforia (AR mode) and the other using a normal camera (VR mode). At launch, the user chooses one of these modes.

Another important improvement we added to the second version of the editor is the *Group Awareness Module*, which is in charge of informing the local user about the actions performed by the other members of the group. For the terrain editor, we do not need to show to the local user the positions and viewpoints of other participants, because they are collocated. Instead we show the points on the terrain where the collaborators are painting and what operations they are applying. We also show a small rectangular box for each participant, which acts as an avatar located in the coordinates of the terrain where the participant applied an operation, along with a label showing the participant name and the operation.

4.1   User Interface

When working on mobile devices we cannot afford to waste much screen space with many windows, buttons, and menus, as with conventional UIs. This problem can be alleviated by using contextual menus, that the user can show and hide at will, or when the application somehow determines the user would need them or not. However, AR brings a natural way to deal with this problem and seizes the most of the limited size of a device screen. AR applications are executed in full screen mode on a single window, without borders, scrollbars, or menus. The screen becomes the work area, and the content is shown as part of the captured scene from the real world.

In some cases, there is a need to add UI elements, such as buttons, sliders, and labels, which are usually shown in a separate layer over the content, in order to keep them always visible to the user. In our design, we take a different approach by placing the UI elements along with the content. One advantage is that the space available to place UI elements becomes potentially bigger than the screen size. Another advantage is that the UI elements are always virtually available,

Fig. 3. Snapshot of the UI of the DEM editor. The terrain mesh, tool selection widget and brush sprite are indicated.

although they are not drawn all the time, but only when the user points the camera to the spatial region where they are expected to be. This approach is far more intuitive than having to call some hidden menu to perform frequent interactions.

We designed the DEM editor by selecting a small number of tools and placing a minimum of UI elements on the workspace, using a simple and uncluttered layout (see Fig. 3). In the center, we show the graphical representation of the terrain, modeled as a polygonal mesh of 100×100 squares.

To directly manipulate the terrain, we propose four different operations, which are described in Sect. 4.2. To select one of these operations, the user taps on the corresponding button of the tool selection widget shown at the left side of the terrain. Only one tool can be active at a time. So, if the user selects another tool, the previous one is automatically deselected,

We designed the icons shown in Fig. 4 to clearly convey what kind of operation will be applied on the terrain with the currently selected tool. When a tool is selected, its button is highlighted and its corresponding icon is shown in the widget.

When applying an operation on the terrain, the users employ a digital brush to *paint* on the regions they want to modify. At the right side of the terrain, we placed a *sprite* with the shape of a brush. The sprite size corresponds with the brush size, and its transparency is related to the stroke strength.

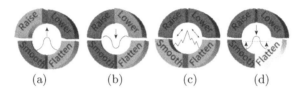

Fig. 4. Icons for the four tools: (a) Raise, (b) Lower, (c) Smooth, and (d) Flatten.

The user can change the brush strength and size by using the corresponding sliders. This sprite representation helps to give the user a precise idea of the terrain portion that will be affected when painting on it.

In the previous version of the editor, we found that the users were looking for a way to rotate the terrain, apart from walking around the marker. Thus, we added a rotation widget (the white sphere in the lower left corner in Fig. 3) which works like a trackball that rotates the terrain around two axes. This widget is also useful when the editor is visualized in VR mode. Along with an additional slider to zoom in the terrain mesh, the user can watch its shape from any desired perspective.

4.2   Brushes-based Operations

Our DEM editor works under the *painting with brushes* paradigm, that is inspired by the process of painting a surface by applying paint with a brush. This is the *de facto* standard for existing DEM editors, such as *WebGL Terrain Editor*.

In analogy with a real brush, with which we can apply different colors on a surface, using a digital brush we can apply different kinds of editing operations on the terrain. To easily manipulate the shape of the terrain, we chose to implement four editing operations, whose effect is as follows:

– **Raise:** It raises the terrain by incrementing the height values of the points inside the region of the DEM swept by the brush stroke. The effect of this operation is accumulative as it adds over the previous values.
– **Lower:** It lowers the terrain inside the swept region of the DEM by decrementing its height values. Its effect is also accumulative as it subtracts from the previous values.
– **Flatten:** It flattens the terrain inside the swept region by shifting the value of its points towards a certain height, given by the user. Its effect is accumulatively destructive, since it overwrites the former height values after repeated applications of the operation over the same region.
– **Smooth:** It reduces abrupt changes in shape inside the swept region by shifting the height values towards the average of the heights in the selected circle. As with the previous operation, this one also overwrites the height values after repeated applications on the same region.

When we apply an editing operation over a region of the terrain, its effect depends on the brush properties: shape, radius, and strength. There are several shapes a brush can have, e.g., circle, square, or triangle. Currently, we only offer the two most basic circular brush shapes: a hard brush and a soft brush. The brush shape is used to mask the effect of the operation applied to modify the terrain.

Each operation is applied inside a circle centered at the terrain coordinates given by the user with a touch on the screen. The radius of this circle is the radius of the brush sprite. The amount of change applied to each point inside the circle depends on the brush shape and also is multiplied by a strength factor, selected using a slider. When the user draws a stroke on the screen, the different touch events triggered at several coordinates perform successive editions on the DEM, giving as a result the edition along the path of the touch gesture.

The brush size and strength properties are set using their corresponding sliders. Also, to switch between the hard and soft brush shape, the user can employ a checkbox or make a double tap gesture on the brush sprite. In the case of the *Flatten* operation, the desired height value needs to be provided by the user. To set this value, our DEM editor implements a third slider aligned with the vertical axis of the screen and moves an indicator plane to the selected height, in order to provide visual feedback to the user.

4.3   Data Sharing

In order to allow several collocated users to share the data structure of a DEM, we implemented a data sharing scheme based on data replication, i.e., each instance of the application holds a local copy of its data structure. Our target scenario corresponds to the *face to face collaboration* classification [27], which refers to a group working together in the same place and at the same time. The proposed data sharing scheme relies on a client-server architecture, which is the architecture of the multi-user communication support provided by Unity.

Let us suppose that we have n instances of the application. So each one can establish a communication channel with another by creating two one-way sockets. But instead of creating $n(n-1)$ sockets to connect every pair of instances, we only create $2(n-1)$. The instances of the application are connected with the server via a WiFi network. The server (also called the Session Coordinator) manages the connections among participants, and any instance of the application can potentially become the Coordinator for each session, but it needs to have a public IP address, in order to be found by the rest of instances over the network. In our case, the server is executed on a desktop computer that allows the mobile instances to perform the NAT (Network Address Translation) punch-through protocol, needed by Unity to connect them.

When sharing the DEM, each instance of the application holds a local copy of its data structure. Each time an editing operation is issued by the local user, the *Data Sharing Module* sends a RPC to the server, which broadcasts it to the other connected instances, so they can apply it to update their own local copies. The operations are applied in the order they arrive to each instance. In this manner, we reduce the network traffic as each instance of the application sends the minimum data required to reproduce the applied operations.

From the perspective of consistency schemes, such as *Operational Transformation* [28,29], the operations should be transformed before their application, in order to avoid inconsistencies among the different instances. In a previous work, we assessed the need of transforming editing operations by experimentally measuring terrain differences among users on several editing sessions. We found that the measured inconsistencies where negligible.

5   DEM Editor Implementation

All the figures shown in the 3D scene of Unity are instances of the class GameObject, which contains all the properties needed to locate the object inside the scene, such as position, orientation, and scale. It also has associated the class Mesh that stores the mesh data used to render the object on the screen, such as vertices, faces, and texture. Unity also has the class MeshCollider to determine whether a touch gesture hits the object and on which point that happens. We can add other classes to GameObject to define additional behaviors, depending on the application we want to implement.

In a collaborative editor, it is needed to keep track of the state of other participants during a collaborative session. We have mentioned in Sect. 4 that we use small avatars to show the touches from other participants. These avatars are instances of GameObject, and they have also associated the class PlayerState that holds the user name and other properties that define the selected operation and the brush shape of its particular participant, as shown in Fig. 5. The methods in this class allow us to easily create and resize a dynamic array, called mask, which is used as digital brush in the application, while the properties change in run-time.

When a new participant connects to an editing session, we use the Prefab mechanism, provided by Unity, to create clones of GameObject. We created Player-Prefab to use it as a template to create instances of participant avatars.

Besides the participant avatars, in the scene there are other instances of GameObject that compose the editor: the graphical representation of the DEM and the UI widgets. To these instances, we added their corresponding behavior classes to manage how they must react to user touches.

As shown in Fig. 5, the in-scene terrain representation is an instance of GameObject, which in turn has associated the class MeshCollider that manages the collision of the touch events with the object mesh.

To manage the response of the terrain to the applied touches, we added the class PaintScript, which is responsible for mapping the touch coordinates to the correct index in the DEM array. PaintScript receives touch events from MeshCollider and triggers operations through the class TerrainManager. This class stores the DEM array and has all the functionality to apply editing operations on this array, using any participant state stored in players, which is an array of PlayerState instances. Also, TerrainManager holds a reference to the Mesh instance of the terrain and updates the Z coordinate values of its vertices using the DEM data in the array, changing the shape of the terrain in real-time.

It is possible to create multi-user applications in Unity using the class Network-View associated with GameObject. Using this class, each instance of GameObject can update its own instance of Transform and can also trigger RPCs on all connected instances of the application. The avatars of connected participants use this mechanism to update their positions and to change their own PlayerState instance. The terrain (an instance of GameObject) also uses NetworkView to perform editing operations via RPCs, calling applyOp() with the correct PlayerState in all connected instances.

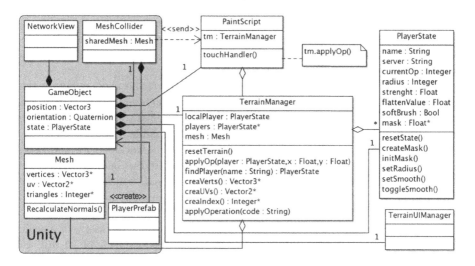

Fig. 5. Participant creation and terrain edition diagram.

In Sect. 4.1 we have described the UI design for the DEM editor, which is composed of four buttons, three sliders, a checkbox, a spherical widget, and a sprite. All these widgets are implemented as instances of `GameObject` and instead of adding a behavior class for each widget, we created the class `TerrainUIManager` to manage all of them.

The sliders and the checkbox were used as provided by Unity. While the user interacts with them, the corresponding methods from `TerrainUIManager` are called in order to change the desired `PlayerState` property for the local user, namely, the brush radius, strength, and smoothness; and also the height value for the *Flatten* operation. The buttons were created from `GameObject` instances to which we added the `TapGesture` behavior from `TouchScript` classes, in order to register when the user taps over the buttons. To implement the spherical widget, we used a sphere shape and added the class `PanGesture` to register the dragging over the sphere. This dragging action triggers the rotation over the terrain (an instance of `GameObject`). Finally, the sprite is implemented as a plane (an instance of `GameObject`) with two transparent image textures associated: one for showing a smooth brush and the other for a hard one. To this plane, we added the `DoubleTapGesture` and `PinchGesture` behaviors with which we call the methods of `TerrainUIManager` that change the smoothness and radius of the brush.

6 Perceived Workload Tests and Results

In our experiments, we got up to four devices connected via WiFi, due to the limited number of testing devices available. Theoretically, our system can support more participants, but we have not yet explored the limitations to this respect, such as the maximum user capacity or the performance decay versus the number of connections.

We measured the perceived workload for eight users of our terrain editor, using the *NASA Task Load indeX* [30]. This is a subjective assessment tool that uses six scales, also called dimensions, to measure the perceived workload by an individual or a group in the execution of some task.

The test is composed of two sections. In the former, the users evaluate the task in the following scales: *mental demand, physical demand, temporal demand, performance, frustration,* and *effort.* For each scale the user selects a value in the interval $[0, 100] \subset \mathbb{N}$ with ticks of 5 units, giving 21 possible qualifications.

It is important to say that we want to measure the workload for the task, so a big value means a lot of workload, that is considered as bad. On the other hand, a small value close to zero means a small workload, which is good.

In the latter part of the test, each user assigns a custom weighting for the six scales with which the final pondered rating is calculated.

The average rating for the *perceived workload* given by eight users, in a scale from 0 to 100, was $\mathbf{23.67 \pm 8.29}$, which gives the interval $[\mathbf{15.38, 31.96}]$. In Fig. 6, we show this average rating and its corresponding interval that gives us an approximate idea about how good was the perception of the users about the editor UI.

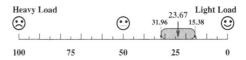

Fig. 6. TLX result for eight users of the DEM editor: the average rating was $\mathbf{23.67 \pm 8.29}$.

7   Conclusions and Future Work

The contribution of this paper was a novel AR-based approach to the multi-user modeling of 3D objects using mobile devices. New users who lack previous training on 3D design can obtain three main advantages from this approach: (1) the interactive visualization of the changes applied to the virtual model in the real 3D space, (2) an intuitive and easy UI, augmented along with the model, and (3) the concurrent sharing of the 3D objects among several collocated users. Moreover, the proposed DEM editor is a multi-platform mobile application and does not require extra equipment. By relying on AR technology, users can obtain an improved sense of structure, shape, and size of the DEM in the 3D space, which makes the DEM editor engaging and easy to use. This design aspect, along with a minimalistic and intuitive design of the UI widgets and editing operations, greatly improves the user experience. The result of the NASA TLX assessment tool shows that our users perceived a low workload while using our prototype, even though most of them were using a 3D modeling tool for the first time.

The data sharing scheme we propose allows a group of collocated users to perform interactive and concurrent editing on a shared DEM, while perceiving its shape evolution in the real space and in real-time, through the camera of their respective mobile device. This feat, up to our knowledge after a thorough research, has not been achieved to this day or, at least, it has not been published yet in the literature. In this work, our focus is on Computer Graphics design tools, where small inconsistencies can be accepted, as long they are not visually obvious. For other more demanding practical applications, where data consistency is a major concern, it would suffice to implement a more strict data consistency scheme, such as Operational Transformation.

This research opens a wide range of opportunities for further development and improvement. We plan to build a development framework based on the design principles of our DEM editing approach. In order to improve the multi-user functionality, this framework should provide mechanisms for supporting latecomers and distributed collaboration settings. In addition, adequate protocols should be designed to guarantee consistent saving for all editor instances and prevent packet loss on a busy network. With respect to the editing functionality, the framework should support more complex distributed operations (e.g., undo, reset, and erase) and a wider variety of brush shapes. Finally, it could be useful for users to have the possibility of changing the appearance of the terrain mesh (e.g., rendering it in wireframe, with mountain textures or color gradients) and exporting the DEM in several 3D formats (e.g., OBJ, VRML, and DAE).

References

1. de Carpentier, G.J.P.: Effective GPU-based Synthesis and Editing of Realistic Heightfields. Delft University of Technology, The Netherlands (2008)
2. Mandelbrot, B.B.: The Fractal Geometry of Nature, vol. 173. Macmillan, USA (1983)
3. Perlin, K., Hoffert, E.M.: Hypertexture. ACM SIGGRAPH Comput. Graph. **23**(3), 253–262 (1989). ACM Press
4. Musgrave, F.K., Kolb, C.E., Mace, R.S.: The synthesis and rendering of eroded fractal terrains. ACM SIGGRAPH Comput. Graph. **23**(3), 41–50 (1989). ACM Press
5. Belhadj, F., Audibert, P.: Modeling landscapes with ridges, rivers: bottom up approach. In: Proceedings of the 3rd International Conference on Computer Graphics and Interactive Techniques in Australasia and South East Asia, pp. 447–450. ACM, November 2005
6. Belhadj, F.: Terrain Modeling: a constrained fractal model. In: Proceedings of the 5th International Conference on Computer Graphics. Virtual Reality, Visualisation and Interaction in Africa (AFRIGRAPH 2007), pp. 197–204. ACM Press, Grahamstown, South Africa (2007)
7. Kamal, K.R., Uddin, Y.S.: Parametrically controlled terrain generation. In: Proceedings of the 5th International Conference on Computer Graphics and Interactive Techniques in Australia and Southeast Asia (GRAPHITE 2007), pp. 17–23. ACM Press, Perth (2007)
8. de Carpentier, G.J.P., Bidarra, R.: Interactive GPU-based procedural heightfield brushes. In: Proceedings of the 4th International Conference on Foundations of Digital Games (FDG 2009), pp. 55-62. ACM Press, Orlando (2009)

9. Bryce. http://www.daz3d.com/bryce-7-pro
10. Vue. http://www.e-onsoftware.com/products/vue/
11. Unity. http://unity3d.com/
12. Ogre. http://www.ogre3d.org/
13. Unreal. https://www.unrealengine.com/
14. Maya. www.autodesk.mx/products/maya/overview
15. Blender. www.blender.org
16. WebGL-based online Terrain Editor. www.chromeexperiments.com/experiment/webgl-terrain-editor
17. LandscapAR. https://play.google.com/
18. Layar. https://www.layar.com/
19. Metaio. http://www.metaio.com/
20. Wikitude classroom application. http://www.wikitude.com/build-wikitude-world-google-collaborative-maps/
21. Billinghurst, M., Kato, H., Poupyrev, I.: The MagicBook: a transitional AR interface. Comput. Graph. **25**(5), 745–753 (2001). Elsevier
22. Wagner, D., Pintaric, T., Ledermann, F., Schmalstieg, D.: Towards massively multi-user augmented reality on handheld devices. In: Gellersen, H.-W., Want, R., Schmidt, A. (eds.) PERVASIVE 2005. LNCS, vol. 3468, pp. 208–219. Springer, Heidelberg (2005)
23. Billinghurst, M., Kato, H., Hedley, N.R., Postner, L., May, R.: Explorations in the use of augmented reality for geographic visualization, presence: teleoperators and virtual environments. MIT Press J. **11**(2), 119–133 (2006)
24. Arth, C., Gruber, L., Grasset, R., Langlotz, T., Mulloni, A., Schmalstieg, D., Wagner, D.: The History of Mobile Augmented Reality: Developments in Mobile AR over the last almost 50 years, Institute for Computer Graphics and Vision, Graz University of Technology, Technical Report ICGTR2015-001, Graz, Austria (2015)
25. Nam, T.J., Sakong, K.: Collaborative 3D workspace and interaction techniques for synchronous distributed product design reviews. Int. J. Des. Natl. Taiwan Univ. Sci. Technol. **3**(1), 43–55 (2009)
26. Kasahara, S., Heun, V., Lee, A. S., Ishii, H.: Second Surface: multi-user spatial collaboration system based on augmented reality. In: SIGGRAPH Asia 2012 Emerging Technologies, pp. 1–4. ACM Press, Singapore (2012)
27. Ellis, C.A., Gibbs, S.J., Rein, G.: Groupware: some issues and experiences. Commun. ACM **34**(1), 39–58 (1991)
28. Sun, D., Sun, C.: Context-Based operational transformation in distributed collaborative editing systems. IEEE Trans. Parallel Distrib. Syst. **20**(10), 1454–1470 (2009)
29. Saucedo-Tejada, G., Mendoza, S., Decouchant, D.: F2FMI: a toolkit for facilitating face-to-face mobile interaction. Expert Syst. Appl. **40**(15), 6173–6184 (2013). Elsevier
30. NASA TLX. http://humansystems.arc.nasa.gov/groups/tlx/

A Wearable System with Individual Cuing for Theatrical Performance Practice

Ryosuke Takatsu[1(✉)], Naoki Katayama[1], Tomoo Inoue[2], Hiroshi Shigeno[3], and Ken-ichi Okada[3]

[1] Graduate School of Science and Technology, Keio University, 3-14-1, Hiyoshi, Minatokita-ku, Yokohama, Kanagawa, Japan
{takatsu,katayama,shigeno,okada}@mos.ics.keio.ac.jp
[2] Faculty of Library, Information and Media Science, University of Tsukuba, 1-1-1, Tennodai, Tsukuba, Ibaraki, Japan
inoue@slis.tsukuba.ac.jp
[3] Faculty of Science and Technology, Keio University, 3-14-1, Hiyoshi, Minatokita-ku, Yokohama, Kanagawa, Japan

Abstract. In theatrical performance, actors are required to understand the libretto as they act. However, actors often make mistakes in their actions in early stages of practice when they still do not understand the libretto. This stops the flow of the practice. In order to learn action, it is necessary to coordinate a smooth group practice. We propose a system that supports actors in grasping the action. This system detects the actor's speech, and cues the order of actions for each actor. In the evaluation, both mistakes in order and in speech were decreased. We confirmed that this system can support theatrical performance practice efficiently.

Keywords: Acting order · Theatrical performance · Cueing individually · Smart watch · Wireless socket

1 Introduction

Theatrical performances have been common for people throughout the world for hundreds of years. The theatrical performances are collaborative work, which each person has different role. The most theatrical performances are played according with librettos. Librettos usually have detail instructions, about lines, gesture and who acts it, in timeline format. There are many steps in the development of a performance. In each step, actors have to remember a lot of things, in addition to the lines of speech–movement, standing position on stage, and flow of acting. To grasp these factors, so much practice and time is necessary. However, in many cases, it is very difficult to provide enough opportunities, because of costs and schedule coordination. Correspondingly, actors compensate for the lack of resources by practicing privately. Actors can understand their own actions, speech and movement, although it can be difficult to grasp their

© Springer International Publishing Switzerland 2016
T. Yuizono et al. (Eds.): CRIWG 2016, LNCS 9848, pp. 37–49, 2016.
DOI: 10.1007/978-3-319-44799-5_4

relationships with other actors. So, actors have to hold many group practices to understand their interactions. By supporting the efficient group practice, understanding is reached more quickly, costs are reduced, and the quality of performances improves.

There are many supporting roles that help create theatrical performances. There is support involved in set-making, as well as directing. However, few studies have provided any support for understanding relationships, and especially, there is no report that focuses on ordering of action in a performance. It is very important to grasp the ordering of action. Actors cannot understand order if they just practice alone. To know when their own turn comes in the action, actors have to grasp the other actors' actions that take place before and after.

In this paper, we focus on the supporting actors and their understanding of the ordering of action. We target the situations related to group-thorough-practice. The system we implemented detects an actor's speech and provides cues in the proper order for each actor. The cues are different for each actor depending on their roles. The librettos are stored in the system in advance. Using this system, actors can better understand the flow of the scene and concentrate on their own actions.

We evaluate whether this system functions well, and confirm a decrease in both of action mistakes and speech mistakes. We confirm this system can support theatrical performance practice efficiently.

2   Theatrical Performance

2.1   Theatrical Performance Practice

At first, we describe how the flow moves from the librettos to the final rehearsal. The purpose of practice is to enhance the quality of performance right up until the recital. First, actors get together and read the librettos. Each actor reads his or her own speech in order. This is called a "read-through." In this step, actors have librettos in their hands, and they usually sit on chairs. They can grasp a rough image of the story.

In the second step, actors stand up. They actually move as they speak the libretto. They confirm their own moves and standing positions. This is called the "run-through" step. At last, they have "rehearsal" right before the eventual recital. During the rehearsal, the costumes, apparatuses, illuminations and sounds are used just as they would be during the recital.

2.2   Run-Through Practice

In this section, we describe the run-through practice, which is the second step in Sect. 2.1. There are three subsidiary steps; rough run-through, extract-step and sometime-stop-step. In the first step, the actors act through the scenes roughly. Even if there are some mistakes, they act through the end of the script unless there is some extreme failure. Basically, the actors do not have librettos.

The purpose of this step is to gain a rough understanding of the entire flow. In the second step, the actors interrupt the flow of their action and practice repeatedly according to the director. In the third step, they act through as long as director does not stop them. If director notices mistakes, the actors are required to redo only those errors.

After each of these steps, the actors run through the script, but not roughly. This is based on the premise that actors understand enough of their own acting by this step.

2.3   Mistakes in the Practice

In this section, we discuss mistakes in practice as explained in Sect. 2.2. The biggest problem in these situations is unwelcome interruption caused by fatal mistakes that cannot immediately be repaired. Mistakes involving order are major. Even if actors remember their own actions well enough, if they lose the relationship with the other actors, such mistakes will happen easily. For example, if an actor speaks before scheduled, or forgets to move, this can throw off other actors. If these mistakes happen, the rehearsal is stopped, the cause is confirmed, and the scene must be replayed from a point in the script prior to the error. This is not only a waste of time, but it can cause stress for the actors. To solve these situations, support is available in the form of a "prompter". The prompter helps the acting move forward. If an actor forgets his or her own lines and stammers, the prompter shows the lines immediately. This makes the acting smoother and relieves potential stress. Other actors sometimes take on this role in their free time. Prompting at the appropriate time makes practice efficient.

2.4   Related Works

In the theatrical performance field, many kinds of works have been researched. Kato et al. proposed an automatic scenario-making system using the information about character and things that have been drawn in preliminary pictures [1]. Sugimoto et al. proposed a scenario making system called "GENTORO" which uses robots and a handy projector [2]. Additionally, there are animation systems called "Pixel Material" [3] for children. In this regard, there is much research supporting story creation.

Much work has also been done on staging. For example, there are systems for presentation apparatuses and illumination on the PC [4], as well as presentation renditions for actors [5]. Kakehi et al. proposed "Tablespace Plus" with which a user can interact with stage information by moving objects [6] A derivative application focuses on the actors' standing positions. In addition, there is a system that deals with 3-dimensional position information [7]. In most of the systems that support staging, computer graphics are used.

In terms of performance planning support systems, there are many types of software being sold. "WYSIWYG" by CAST company [8] focuses on setting stage illumination and spotlights. "Matrix3" by Meyer Sound company [9] supports sound needs. Furthermore, there is some research for multi planning collaboration in face-to-face [10] and remote situations [11].

Although not specifically designed for theatrical performances, there is the presentation system for a chairperson, activated by using a wearable device. However, this system is only for one chairperson, and not for multiple users.

As described above, various research supports theatrical performance. However, we cannot find one that focuses on the ordering of action in the theatrical field. Moreover, in the field of collaborative work, the same is true.

3   Supporting Actors Understanding Acting Order

3.1   Actors' Action Management

Actors can train to perfect their own acting skills, such lines and movement. However, action in relationship to other actors is difficult to understand in solo training. We decided to take the libretto into the system and management actors' ordering of action. This means actors can act without understanding other actors' actions. Actors just act when they are cued by the system, and they can always act in the right order.

3.2   Efficiency of Run-Through Practices

As mentioned in Sect. 3.1, to grasp the acting order is difficult in private practice, and mistakes in order will happen frequently. These mistakes have enormous impact on practice. Mistakes interrupt run-through practice and cause stress for the actors. So, it is necessary to be efficient with the available practices. Actors can more easily experience the flow of acting when supported.

3.3   Hands Free and Individual Cuing

In the run-through practice, actors confirm their moving and standing positions. When they do this, having the libretto in their hands can hinder appropriate training. Furthermore, each actor has a different role, speaks different lines and moves differently. So, the information they need is unique to each actor. It is therefore necessary to present appropriate information to each actor individually under hand- free circumstances. In addition, in the theatrical performance, the timing of the actors' is determined by the actions of other actors. So, when system cues are created, the clock is also determined by actors' actions.

3.4   The Cuing System for Theatrical Rehearsal

We propose a system that cues actor individually. We use wearable devices to keep the system hands free. Basically, the vibrations of the wearable devices provide cues. Using this method, actors do not have to see the device's display in order to know the order. The system cues according to the uploaded libretto, and it communicates to each actor individually. The information provided corresponds to what the individual actor needs to know. In addition, actor's speech triggers the cues. With this system, the clock can offer relative rather than absolute time. To use this system for run-throughs, actors can concentrate on their own acting and grasp the flow in the early stages of practice.

4 Implementation

In this chapter, we describe implementation of the prototype system for supporting run-throughs. The anticipated outcome includes actors being able to practice without librettos or mistakes in acting order. The system provides cues for the acting order uniquely to each actor according to each role. In this prototype, we used three actors.

4.1 Hardware Configuration

The system configuration overview is shown in Fig. 1. Actors wear the smart watch (Samsung Gear Live) which is used to notify them of their cues. It has Android Wear installed, and it can connect with smartphones or tablets that also use Android. The input is performed mainly by voice and touch display, and the device has a vibration function. With the use of wearable devices like smart watches, the system can keep actor's hands free, and when vibrations are used to notify them of cues, actors do not have to look at the display to confirm the cues. This means actors can concentrate on their own acting, especially their movements. In order to realize this system, synchronization of the devices is necessary. To accomplish this, we prepare a PC as a server. We input libretto information in advance. We also prepare tablets (Nexus7) between the server PC and smart watches in order to control the watches. We implement these with Android SDK (Android 5.0, API21).

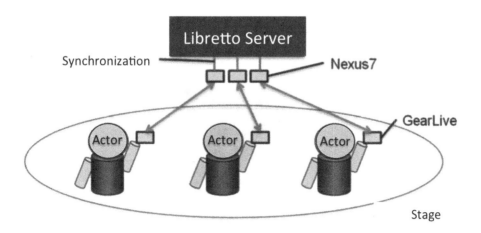

Fig. 1. System configuration overview

4.2 Connect Devices

We use wireless sockets to connect the server PC with tablets, and Bluetooth to connect the tablets with smart watches. The smart watches are synchronized via tablets and PC.

Fig. 2. First screen of a Gear Live

We show the home screen of a Gear Live after connection in Fig. 2. "Voice," "Copy Select," and "Actor Select" are the buttons. The user can select the libretto by touching the "Copy Select" button, and select the role by touching the "Actor Select" button. In Fig. 2, the libretto is selected as No.3, and the role is selected as the "Actor A" part. The "Voice" button means ready for practice. When all watches have "Voice" activated, "practice mode" starts.

4.3   Practice Mode

In the practice mode, three types of screens are presented for each actor, as shown in Fig. 3. The watches present the stand-by screen (Fig. 3-1). Before the actors are to speak, the screen changes to lines. And, when it is time to speak, the screen changes to voice input. Although the system cues with vibrations, if the screens are similar in appearance, it confuses the actors, so we apply clear color coding.

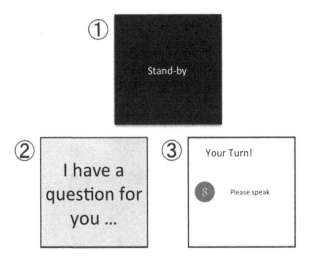

Fig. 3. 1: Stand-by screen, 2: Lines' screen, 3: Voice input screen

The lines screen (Fig. 3-2) is presented for the actor who speaks next, while the actor just before is speaking. When practicing with this system, the actors do not have librettos. This screen, much like a prompter, offers the actor the first lines of the next speech. When the watch display changes this screen, it vibrates. So, actors do not have to see this screen to be reminded of the next lines. We set a max of 15 Japanese characters on the screen in a large font, so that the actor can recognize it in a moment. And, we set the presentation time to two seconds.

The voice input screen (Fig. 3-3) is displayed when the actor speaks, two seconds after the lines screen is displayed. The watch also vibrates when the screen changes to the voice input screen. So, actors receive vibration twice for each speech. While this screen is displayed, the smart watch accepts voice input. When the actor speaks, the smart watch detects it and sends information to the server. This detection does not mean recognition, per se. The system does not judge the correctness of the speech; it just detects whether the actor who should speak is speaking. In many cases, actors do not speak perfectly according to the libretto. They are usually more concerned about whether the intention is correct. Judging intention with a computer system is very difficult. So, we decided that the system would just detect the utterances of actors.

The vibration in this step is not related to the timing of speech, but only with alerting an actor of his or her "next turn". The proper timing of speech is the actors decision, based on the previous action. That the actor, not the system, determines the detailed timing is important to more natural acting. If the system were to specify the detailed timing, it could cause unnatural moments.

For the implementation of voice detection, we use "RecognizeIntent" in the Android.Speech package.

4.4 Timelines of Speech Detection and Processing

To detect the utterances, some time is required for processing. We used the preliminary experience to evaluate the accuracy and time lag of the utterance detection process. We had five participants. Each one wore a smart watch and spoke lines. We checked whether the system could detect the utterance (accuracy), and the time lag from one participant speaking to another smart watch receiving its cue (time lag). We used five librettos and all participants read them.

As a result, we confirmed accuracy of 76 % and time lag of 3.1 s. From this experiment, we found that quiet or garbled speech was hard to detect. So, we can say that this prototype doesn't work with quiet pieces. The time lag represents a total lag in voice detection, connecting with the server and cueing for another smart watch. This delay may cause problems, so we devised a timing process that was related to the smart watches. In particular, we assigned the processing time for another actor speaking. This reduced influence of lag on practice. We describe this in the next section.

4.5   Flow of Practice with the System

We describe the flow of practice with the timeline (Fig. 4). There are three actors named "actor A," "actor B," and "actor C." The horizontal axis represents time. The blue line represents the lines screen (Fig. 3-2), the white line means the voice input screen (Fig. 3-3), and the red line represents system processing time. The portion with no lines represents the stand-by screen (Fig. 3-1). We explain situations (1) to (8) as follows.

1. The system shows the lines screen for all actors. The actors can confirm the first lines of the libretto.
2. Cueing for Actor A, and he/she starts speaking. In the meantime, the lines screen is displayed for Actor B, and the stand-by screen for Actor C (Fig. 5).
3. Actor B's lines screen finishes in two seconds and changes to the voice input screen.
4. Actor A finishes speaking, and Actor A's watch starts processing. Actor B confirms that Actor A is finishing and starts speaking.
5. After the processing of Actor A's watch, it shows the stand-by screen for Actor A. And, the system shows the lines screen for Actor C (Fig. 6).
6. Actor C's lines screen finishes in two seconds and changes to the voice input screen.
7. Actor B finishes speaking, and Actor B's watch starts processing. Actor C confirms that Actor B is finishing and starts speaking.
8. After processing by Actor B's watch, it displays the stand-by screen for Actor B omitted below.

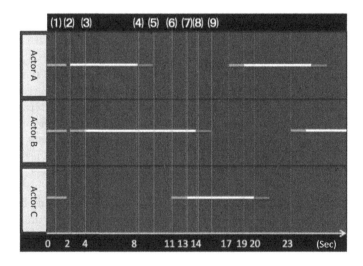

Fig. 4. An example of the timeline (Color figure online)

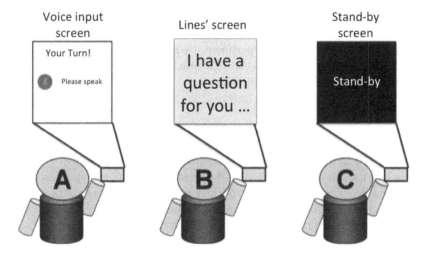

Fig. 5. Screen of smart watch at the time of 2.

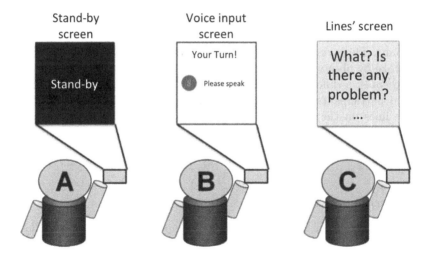

Fig. 6. Screen of smart watch at the time of 5.

Assigning a lag time between the actors' speaking parts cues the next actor after next, and the influence of mistakes on practice can be reduced. The actor scheduled to speak next receives a cue after the first actor finishes speaking. This prototype does not is not ideal for the exchange of short conversations, such as those shorter than processing time.

This prototype assumes three actors. However, as long as the local server can process it, we can extend the number of actors for lager group practices.

5 Evaluation

In this chapter, we describe the experiment used to evaluate whether this system can improve the efficiency of run-through practice. We focused on mistakes in the order of action and mistakes in lines.

5.1 Evaluation Method

Participants were 24 university and graduate students. They made up 8 groups consisting of 3 participants each. All participants had little experience with theatrical performances. We prepared 16 librettos for the experiment. Participants took on the roles of actors and tried to speak the lines according to the librettos.

All librettos were about one and a half minutes long, with three parts and 10 to 20 lines per actor. This represents an average setting for actual scenes in theatrical performance. The comparison environment was rehearsal without systems. All participants experienced both environments. To counteract order factor, half of the participants used the system first and secondarily practiced without the system, and the other half practiced without the system first, and secondarily used the system.

We focused on ordering of action and speech in this report. So, in this experiment, we assumed the number of acting order mistakes and line mistakes as evaluation items. This system has no function for mistake recognition. We counted each mistake by observing the participants' acting. The definition of a line mistake is to speak a different meaning clearly. We did not count as mistakes the times that participants spoke with little variation in wording. This system displays the lines on the smart watch. We wanted to evaluate the line mistakes under the same conditions. So, in this experiment, we told participants not to look at the smart watch display, and if they did so, it was counted as a line mistake.

5.2 Experimental Procedure

First, we explained the experiment to the group. Next, we explained how to use the system, and participants tested it for a short time. Then, we explained that they were to enunciate clearly in order to be detected by the smart watch. After this, we choose librettos at random and handed out the librettos on paper. We entrusted participants to casting. As preparation before the experiment, we gave them 5 min to memorize the lines in private. In this step, we did not limit their methods for memorization, such speaking the lines or writing on the libretto. Next, the group members gathered and read through the libretto one time. Finally, we gave them 3 min to review. The time settings were prepared on the basis of advice from an actor with theater experience.

After that, the participants tried to act out the libretto relying on their memories. There was only one opportunity to act each libretto. If a fatal mistake were to happen and stop the acting, they resumed from the previous line. After finishing the first libretto, we changed librettos and environment (using system or not) and repeated the same steps. Each group, therefore, experienced these flows twice with different librettos and environments.

5.3   Result

The number of mistakes per libretto is shown in Fig. 7. the vertical axis shows the number of mistakes. The error bar represents standard deviation. From this graph, we can say that both acting order mistakes and line mistakes decreased when participants used the system. As demonstrated by the t test, the acting order mistakes: $t = 5.351$, $df = 7$, $p < 0.05$, as line mistakes: $t = 5.019$, $df = 7$, $p < 0.05$, so both of them demonstrated significant differences at a level of 5 %. From this, we confirmed that this system increases the efficiency of rehearsal.

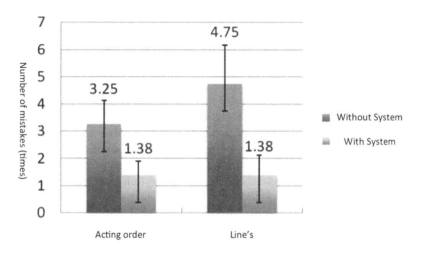

Fig. 7. Number of mistakes per libretto

5.4   Discussion

Discussion of Result. From the results, we can confirm that the system can reduce the number mistakes in both acting order and lines. This is due to the system cueing proper order for the actors. With this system, in order for actors to act in the proper order, they need only follow the vibration cue. If the system can cue perfectly, there should be no mistakes in order. However, the results did demonstrate some order mistakes. These were caused by the low accuracy of the smart watch's voice input. So, in this experiment, the results showing order mistakes represent the system's voice input mistakes. As we mentioned Sect. 4.4, in order for utterance to be detected by the smart watch, it must be clear. Although we asked the actors to speak clearly, actors sometime tend to act quietly per the libretto's atmosphere.

In terms of line mistakes, we confirm a large difference in results dependent on whether or not the system is used. In circumstances without the system, actors have to remember both the acting order (the relationship with other actors) and their lines. However, in order to use the system, actors only have to remember their own lines only. So, in this experiment, they were able to concentrate on their own lines, and the number of mistakes as reduced. This system which cues actors as to order can support their memory of lines.

Significance of This System. We assume that this system is for the rehearsal step, not for performance. It would be unnatural for actors to wear the smart watch on the performance stage. The significance of this system is it leads to efficient practice. This system can allow actors to concentrate on their own acting during rehearsals. We can expect actors' skills to improve in this step. And, actors can start learning the flow of acting earlier with the help of the system.

Future Work. In theatrical performances, actors have to memorize a lot of information in librettos. In order to grasp the order of actions and line delivery, actors have to understand not only their own acting but also their relationships with other actors. So, we proposed a system that supports actors in remembering the proper order. This system cues the order for each actor individually. In the experiment, we confirmed decreases in both order mistakes and line mistakes with the use of this system. In this system, we can expect actors can concentrate on their own acting and grasp the acting flow in the early stages of rehearsal. We can say that using this system is effective in the rehearsal process.

6   Conclusion

In the theatrical performance, actor have to memory a lot of information in libretto. Especially, to grasp the acting order, actors have to understand not only own acting but also relationships with other actors. So we proposed the system supports actors acting in properly order. This system cues the order for each actor individually. In the experiment, we confirmed the decrease both order mistake and lines' mistakes to use this system. In this system, we can expect actors can concentrate for own acting and grasp the acting flow in the early step. We can say that there is effectiveness for using this system in the through practice.

References

1. Shigeru, K., Takehisa, O.: The support system for story creation using pictures. In: Proceedings of the 2006 International Conference on Game Research and Development, pp. 141–148. Murdoch University (2006)
2. Masanori, S., Toshitaka, I., Tuan, N.N., Shigenori, I.: Gentoro: a system for supporting children's storytelling using handheld projectors and a robot. In: Proceedings of the 8th International Conference on Interaction Design and Children, pp. 214–217. ACM, New York (2009)

3. Tal, D., Michal, R.: Pixel materiali: a system for creating and understanding pixel animations. In: Proceedings of the 6th International Conference on Interaction Design and Children, pp. 157–160. ACM, New York (2007)
4. Matthew, L.: Bowen virtual theater. In: ACM SIGGRAPH 2003 Web Graphics, pp. 1–1. ACM (2003)
5. Mel, S., Howell, J., Steed, A., David-Paul, P., Maia, G.: Acting in virtual reality. In: Proceedings of the Third International Conference on Collaborative Virtual Environments, pp. 103–110. ACM, New York (2000)
6. Yasuaki, K., Takeshi, N., Mitsunori, M.: Tablescape plus: interactive small-sized vertical displays on a horizontal tabletop display. In: Second Annual IEEE International Workshop on Horizontal Interactive Human-Computer Systems, TABLE-TOP 2007, pp. 155–162. IEEE (2007)
7. Kim, H., Takahashi, I., Yamamoto, H., Kai, T., Maekawa, S., Naemura, T.: MARIO: Mid-air Augmented Reality Interaction with Objects. In: Reidsma, D., Katayose, H., Nijholt, A. (eds.) ACE 2013. LNCS, vol. 8253, pp. 560–563. Springer, Heidelberg (2013)
8. Cast Group of Companies Inc. http://www.cast-soft.com/wysiwyg/overview
9. Meyer Sound Laboratories Inc. http://www.meyersound.com/
10. Daiki, N., Yousuke, H., Tomoo, I., Kenichi, O.: Diamond theater: a system for suproting creative activities. Inf. Process. Soc. Jpn. J. **51**(12), 2396–2408 (2010)
11. Christian, D., Denis, L.: Avatar: a virtual reality based tool for collaborative production of theater shows. In: The 3rd Canadian Conference on Computer and Robot Vision, p. 35. IEEE (2006)

Support Communication and Intercultural Adjustment of Exchange Students Based on the AUM Theory

Gustavo Zurita[1], Nelson Baloian[2(✉)], José A. Pino[2],
and Sergio Peñafiel[2]

[1] Management Control and Information Systems Department,
Universidad de Chile, Santiago, Chile
gzurita@fen.uchile.cl
[2] Department of Computer Science, Universidad de Chile, Santiago, Chile
{nbaloian,jpino,spenafie}@dcc.uchile.cl

Abstract. People who have to insert and adapt themselves to a different culture than the one where they grew up usually experience feelings related to anxiety and uncertainty. This is exactly the situation of the students who decide to go abroad to continue their education or make an internship in a foreign country. The number of these students has been constantly increasing during the last years. In order to better adapt themselves to the new culture they are confronted with the Anxiety/Uncertainty Model, states that they have to manage the levels of anxiety and uncertainty in order to communicate effectively with local students and teachers. According to the literature, an effective communication and intercultural adjustment of the foreign students has a direct impact on their academic performance. Therefore, it is a relevant task to support them in this process. This work introduces a geo-collaborative application called EMHC (for Exploring My Host Country) which run son mobile devices and allows exchange students to access contextual information as well as information about cultural behavior which could help them to manage their anxiety and uncertainty levels, thus improving their ability to adapt themselves to the new cultural environment. A preliminary evaluation of the EMHC was performed with a small number of exchange students of a Business School, obtaining encouraging results.

Keywords: Geo-collaboration · Collaboration through social media · Intercultural adjustment

1 Introduction

The rise in internationally mobile students reflects growing university enrolment around the world. In 2013, over 4.1 million students went abroad to study, up from 2 million in 2000, representing 1.8 % of all tertiary enrolments or 2 in 100 students globally. Central Asia, home to the most mobile student population, has experienced a steady rise in the number of students studying abroad. This group grew from 67,300 in 2003 to 165,542 in 2013, with the outbound mobility ratio more than doubling from

© Springer International Publishing Switzerland 2016
T. Yuizono et al. (Eds.): CRIWG 2016, LNCS 9848, pp. 50–64, 2016.
DOI: 10.1007/978-3-319-44799-5_5

3.5 % to 7.6 %, [1]. This means that an increasing number of students need to acquire, experiment and practice social abilities which will help to adapt themselves to the culture of the host county. These abilities are very much the same which are required to any professional of the 21st century [2–4].

Among the abilities of the 21st century [3, 4], a very important one is the ability to communicate and interact in intercultural situations, which are the same needed by foreign students in order to achieve the intercultural adjustment in the host country. Particularly, business and management schools around the world largely agree that the development of communication, interaction, teamwork and intercultural adjustment are important competences. Due to this, they have been included in the international standards of accreditation by Association to Advance Collegiate Schools of Business (AACSB), [5]. In 2013 the AACSB [4], defined standards for undergraduate and graduate programs in for developing the following abilities: (a) communicating with others (locals or foreign) and teamwork in intercultural settings; and (b) being successful in the intercultural adjustment with the aim of acquiring knowledge and skills to perform in today's globalized world.

Effective communication and intercultural adjustment of foreign students are full of challenges: cultural aspects associated to communication patterns, language barriers, feelings of isolation and loneliness, and even discrimination are just a few example of the experiences which hinder the communication with local people (including their teachers), achieve an intercultural foreign student may face when trying to perform successfully in the new environment [6]. According to [7], there is a positive correlation between the intercultural adjustment and the academic performance of a foreign student, which means, the better the adjustment of the student to the culture of the host country, the better will be the academic performance. Some studies suggest that having good friends with mates of the same culture as well as the foreign one help to reduce homesickness feelings [8]; also integrating a student association, fraternity or sport team positively impacts the student's social integration and intercultural adjustment, which leads to a better academic performance [9].

For all these reasons we consider supporting effective communication and intercultural adjustment of foreign students a relevant task.

Gudykunst [10, 11], introduced his Anxiety/Uncertainty Management (AUM) theory, which states that anxiety and uncertainty are critical factors influencing communication and intercultural adjustment. The theory states that certain levels of anxiety uncertainty are necessary in order to awake the interest of an individual to discover a new environment and culture but not high enough to scare her/him.

Based on our previous experience developing collaborative application for supporting decision [12], urban planning [13], learning activities in real contexts (situated learning) [14, 15], all them using geo-referenced information over maps, we developed an application based on the AUM theory called "Exploring My Host Country" (EMHC). The application basically supports the foreign students' process of adaptation to the host country by providing her/him with important and accurate geo-referenced information which is contributed collaboratively by other foreign or local students. Some of this application's characteristics are mobility (since it can run on Smartphones and Tablets), and positioning (using the device's GPS). The main differences this platform has with other tourism-oriented social networking sites (like TripAdvisor) is that this one stresses the communication among users, not only in terms of allowing dialogues between two or chats between many users but also helping the user to find contributions from people they would trust better or are more keen to ask questions. For example, one may prefer contributions from local people while another would prefer people of the same age, gender or nationality. Communicating with people they trust (which may be different when searching for one or another kind of information) can reduce the uncertainty and anxiety while trying to get acquainted with a new culture and environment.

The rest of the paper is organized the following way: Sect. 2 reviews the relevant literature about collaborative applications using geo-referencing in order to state that this problem has not been tackled using this approach yet. It also shows the relevance of geo-localized information to improve the communication. Section 3 explain the AUM theory in detail, especially how it is used to overcome the intercultural adjustment of people living in a foreign culture. Section 4 uses the axioms of the AUM theory in order to identify the basic design principles and functionalities of the EMHC application. Section 5 describes the application in detail. In Sect. 6 we present a preliminary evaluation of the application and Sect. 7 concludes the paper.

2 Geosocial Media and Collaboration

According to [16], a Geographic Information System (GIS) is viewed as an inherently interdisciplinary endeavor in which disciplines operated with a variety of scientific paradigms. It may involve collaborative exploration or mapping meaningful representations and/or interpreting geographically related data, or making geospatial decisions collaboratively in various situations like crisis management [17], decision making [12], collaboratively planning [13], collaboratively defining strategies [18], or conducting collaborative educational activities by geo-referencing information in authentic contexts and physical locations, where students can establish significant cognitive relationships between what was understood inside the classroom and what is visualized in a real context [13–15, 19]. Among the wide range of self-stated purposes for the GIS initiatives examined, Elwood et al. [20] discerned three primary groupings: initiatives primarily oriented toward mapping user-contributed information (geovisualization, 14 %); initiatives oriented toward capturing, compiling, and integrating geotagged content, data generated through location-based services, and geo-locational information for place names (geoinformation, 51 %); and initiatives that allow users to share geo-located media with others in their professional or social networks (geosocial, 35 %).

Budhathoki and Haythornthwaite [21], showed in a comprehensive study which criteria increase the contributor motivation in geosocial media projects; they identified intrinsic motivations as altruism, recreation, learning/personal enrichment, self-expression; and extrinsic motivations as social reward/relations, career, personal reputation, community.

According to [22], the ubiquitous usage of location-enabled devices, such as smartphones, allows citizens to share their geographic information on a number of selected geosocial media applications over maps in online portals, in order to mark and annotate the geographical characteristics or to add geographic location information to

4 Design Principles of EMHC Based on AUM Theory

The design principles of EMHC identified in this section are based on the "basic causes" and "superficial causes" of the AUM theory. EMHC has been designed with the aim of facilitating the generation of geo-referenced contextualized and relevant information. This information will be shared by the foreign and local students in order to maintain the levels of anxiety and uncertainty of foreign students at adequate levels to achieve the intercultural adjustment.

Table 1 shows the most relevant axioms of the AUM theory which were used to state the principle designs of EMHC, and consequently, identify the relevant functionalities (RF), which are described in detail in Sect. 5. From our point of view other axioms could also have been selected to be associated with design principles and functionalities,

Table 1. "Basic causes" and "superficial causes" axioms of the AUM theory [10], used to state the design principles of EMHC classified as relevant functionalities (RF) described in Sect. 5. "Basic causes": Ax. 38, 29, and 40 for "anxiety, uncertainty, mindfulness and effective communication". "Superficial causes": Ax. 66(19) for "Social Categorization of Hosts", Ax. 26, 27, 28 and 30 for "Situational Processes", Ax. 34, 35, 36 and 37 for "Connections with Hosts".

Axioms	EMHC design principles
Ax. 38. An increase in our ability to gather appropriate information about hosts will produce an increase in our ability to accurately predict their behavior	**RF2. RF3. RF4. RF5.** The generated, shared or commented information about customs of local people together with the search functionalities should improve the capacity to predict the behavior of local people
Ax. 39. An increase in our ability to describe hosts' behavior will produce an increase in our ability to accurately predict their behavior	**RF2. RF3. RF4.** The information generated by local and foreign people regarding the behavior of local people will improve the prediction ability of foreigners about the behavior of locals
Ax. 40. An increase in our understanding the host culture's stocks of knowledge will produce an increase in our ability to manage our anxiety and our ability to accurately predict hosts' behavior	**RF2. RF4. RF6.** The information contextualized with geo-localization (through check-in functionality, see Sect. 5) along with brief explanations to better understand the meaning of certain customs in specific places will lower the anxiety of foreigner students
Ax. 34. An increase in the quantity and quality of our contact with hosts will produce a decrease in our anxiety and an increase in our ability to accurately predict their behavior	**RF2. RF4. RF6.** The generation, review, classification of the geo-referenced and making comments about the published information should produce a decrease in our anxiety and an increase foreign students' ability to accurately predict their behavior. The check-in functionality should increase the precision and therefore the quality of the information

(Continued)

Table 1. (*Continued*)

Axioms	EMHC design principles
Ax. 35. An increase in our interdependence with hosts will produce a decrease in our anxiety and an increase in our confidence in predicting their behavior	**RF1, RF2. RF3. RF4.** Creating sessions where students can share information with locals, as well as generating and reviewing, rating, and alert other students about the comments associated to the information decrease anxiety and an increase confidence in predicting locals' behavior
Ax. 36. An increase in the intimacy of our relationships with hosts will produce a decrease in our anxiety and an increase in our confidence in predicting their behavior	**RF4. RF6.** The comments made to the information posted by other local or foreigners may serve to express personal points of view increasing the intimacy of the relationships
Ax. 37. An increase in the networks we share with hosts will produce a decrease in our anxiety and an increase in our confidence in predicting their behavior	**RF1. RF2. RF3. RF4.** Sharing information with locals and other foreigners will promote foreign students to be part of local networks, promoting positive and active attitudes among them
Ax. 66(19). An increase in our understanding of similarities and differences between our culture and host' culture will produce an increase in our ability to manage our anxiety and our ability to accurately predict their behavior	**RF2. RF3. RF4.** The shared information concerning cultural patterns could in some cases allow comparing and evaluating similarities between local and foreign customs
Ax. 26. An increase in the complexity of our scripts for communicating with hosts will produce a decrease in our anxiety and an increase in our confidence in predicting their behavior	**RF4.** The information about behavior patterns of local people posted by locals will offer foreign students scripts for communicating with hosts
Ax. 27. An increase in the informality of the situation in which we are communicating with hosts will produce a decrease in our anxiety and an increase in our confidence in predicting their behavior	**RF4.** Comments associated to the geo-referenced information posted by local and foreign people will allow an informal communication between them which should decrease in anxiety and an increase in confidence in predicting their behavior
Ax. 28. An increase in the cooperative structure of the goals on which we work with hosts will produce a decrease in our anxiety and an increase in our confidence in predicting their behavior	**RF1. RF2. RF3. RF4.** The information shared between foreign and local students generates a collaborative process, expected to result in an increase in the confidence of foreign students in predicting locals' behavior
Ax. 30. An increase in the percentage of members of our culture present in a situation when we interact with hosts will produce a decrease in our anxiety	**RF1.** Collaboration (through creating, commenting, and sharing information) between users identified as coming from the same country; will allow exchange students decrease their anxiety, as they share their experience with members of their own culture

however, they would not generate other functionalities than those already identified and therefore are not mentioned in this paper.

4.1   Content of the Generated, Shared and/or Commented Information

EMHC will contain geo-referenced information about the host city about attractions, such as places to stay, restaurants, entertainment, transport, services, shopping, etc.; on which it is expected to describe (both by foreigners and the local) how to proceed in certain circumstances, explain basic communication patterns, reporting specific locations, make recommendations, etc.

By accessing this information, foreign students will be aware of the existence of relevant aspects to know in order to predict the behavior of local people. Foreign and local students can comment on the geo-referenced information iteratively and openly share it with all members invited to a session. Members of a session are invited by the creator of the session which may be foreign or local students. In EMHC, users can create multiple sessions for various purposes, each of which may have different members; for example, to share information on local customs, recreational areas, recommended to eat, of aspects related to studies or general purpose sites.

While posting comments, EMHC users can create alerts for specific persons who they think will be interested in that post. Comments with alerts can be used to address questions to certain people or share information with foreign students which they know are interested in the information posted. Through comments to the geo-referenced information, foreign students can meet their levels of awareness and/or understanding of what usually happens or do in certain places, achieving mindfulness; i.e. foreigners achieve optimal levels of uncertainty and anxiety leading to their intercultural adjustment.

4.2   Format of the Information to Be Generated, Shared and/or Commented

The geo-referenced information will be delivered in capsules of information, e.g. a microblogging style, in order not to overwhelm students with long texts, which could cause even more anxiety. EMHC implements a reward system since users will be asked to rate the usefulness of information with a scoring system. It is expected that this feedback will motivate local and foreign users to use of the application. The geo-referencing of information will be assisted by the use of GPS devices where the application runs. Also, the geo-localized information to be shared may be associated with the record that it was produced in the same place through the "check-in" option. This option is implemented because information generated with the "check-in" option has a greater context value than the geo-referenced information produced remotely, as it has a record that can be associated with greater veracity and accuracy.

5   Description of the EMHC Application

EMHC application has been developed with HTML5, thus users only need a device (Smartphone, Tablets) with any browser and an Internet connection to run it. Users may generate a geo-referenced information at the same place (using mobile devices) or remotely (using desktop computers, notebooks or laptops). After the information is published by its author, all users participating in the session can see, associate comments and/or rate it. The application has been designed for supporting foreign exchange students at a Business Faculty in a University.

This section describes the six relevant functionalities (RF) of EMHC, which were derived using the "basic causes" and "superficial causes" of the AUM theory described in the previous section.

RF1. Create Sessions. In EMHC users may participate in a public session which has been foreseen to be managed by staff members dedicated to support foreign people in an institution, which in the case of our scenario is the office in charge of supporting exchange students. Staff members publish information of general interest for these students like locations of important services, where to buy at convenient prices, or where are the students' amusement quarters. Foreign or local students may create

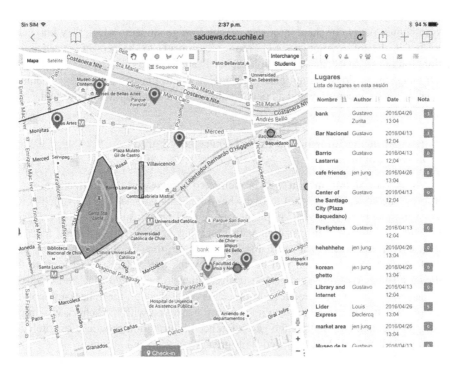

Fig. 2. The EMHC interface as shown when running on a Tablet, Desktop Computer, Notebook, or Laptop. The figure shows the georeferenced places over the map and the associated information of each one on the table listing them at the right. The green mark on the map displaying the label "bank" means the user has currently selected it. (Color figure online)

sessions for special interests, like for students speaking a certain language or practicing a certain sport, or a certain hobby to share information about that. Figure 2 shows a session called "Interchange Students" (written on the label at the upper-right corner of the map shown by the application's interface) which contains information created by the support staff for a prelaminar evaluation of the application.

RF2. Generating Geo-Referenced Information. Users may create geo-referenced marks, regions or paths on a map corresponding to locations of interest with information to share with all members of a session. The added information added should contain at least a title. An associated description and images are optional. The published information may also be associated to one or more categories accommodation, restaurant & coffee, commerce, culture, sports, entertainment, foreign, family, finances, properties, religion, health, security, public services, transport, tourism, public utility, volunteering.

It is possible to "fine tune" the location of marks when they are close to a Street thanks to Google-Maps' Street-View. By activating Street-View (inside the application) users can see 360° images of the streets and the buildings nearby, including the mark that they have put on the map, which can be conveniently moved to pose it on a certain building entrance, statue, corner, bench, etc. thus giving in this way more context information to the post.

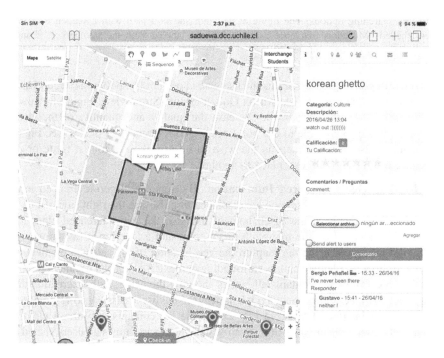

Fig. 3. The EMHC interface as shown when running on a Tablet, Desktop Computer, Notebook, or Laptop. The figure shows a polygon geo-referencing an area currently selected by the user. At the right the information associated to this element is displayed: title ("korean ghetto"), a description ("watch out"), and a couple of comments emitted by other users. The stars allow users to rate the contribution assigning 1to 7 stars. In this case it has 0 starts, which means it has not been rated yet.

Fig. 4. View of EMHC user interface running on a Smartphone. The figure left shows information searching options. The figure at the right shows a path with a sequence of three entries labelled "Museums Sequence". The points are labeled with the numbers 1, 2 and 3 showing the order of the sequence.

In order to geo-reference regions the user can chose circles, polygons, rectangles or lines. However, these are not shown on Google-Maps' Street-view. Figure 3 shows a geo-referenced polygon. In order to increase the quality and quantity of the shared information it is also possible to use polylines to geo-references of places (see Fig. 4). This option is useful when there is the wish to inform about a tourist route or recommend a way to go from one place to another.

RF3. Reading Geo-Referenced Information. By default, all geo-referenced inputs made by users of the current session are displayed as a list (see the right side of Fig. 2). When clicking over the name of an item of this list, the geo-referenced element is immediately displayed on the map with green color and a label on it (as shown with "bank" on Fig. 2), centering the map on the geo-location of the selected element and zooming to show the element and its surrounding context. The list can be shown in three different ways: (a) the list contains all entries showing their title, author, creation date, rating obtained and category to which it belongs (see the list of places geo-referenced to the right of the interface EMHC in Fig. 2), (b) the list contains only those elements created by the user showing their title, creation date, number of times all users visited the geo-referencing, the assigned rating, the number of comments made, and whether it was created with the check-in functionality; (c) the list contains all elements created by all users in the current session, showing title, creation date, the number of times that all user visited the geo-referencing, the average rate, the number of comments received by all users, and whether it was or not created with the check-in functionality.

For the three variants the lists may be ordered by any of the attributes shown, that is, the title, date, rating, comments received, etc.

RF4. Commenting on, Rating and Alerting about Contributions. For entering a comment associated to a certain geo-referenced element it must be selected either using the list or the map. Comments may include pictures. The length of the comments is limited in order to avoid having large entries which would discourage people to read them. All users of the session may comment and/or answer to previous entered comments (see right of Fig. 3). Contributions can be rated with 1 to 7 stars, with 7 being the highest score according to the usefulness and accuracy of the information provided. The rate shown for each entry corresponds to the average of all ratings received.

Optionally, alerts may be sent to one or more users of the session every time a user posts a comment. These alerts are reported to the receiver user with a number on the menu item icon with the shape of an envelope (see Fig. 3.); which when activated, displays a list of all received alerts (which are marked with a number corresponding to the number of alerts received). By choosing one of these alerts, all information corresponding to the associated element is displayed, along with its location on the map.

RF5. Information Search in EMHC and Google-Maps. Searching for contributions having certain information which the user is looking for may be done in two ways: (a) by navigating on the map, supported by zoom-in and zoom-out options; that is, a search for geo-referenced elements by location; (b) through the simple and advanced search options which implement a query-by-example interface allowing the search based on the entries' attributes like author's user name, gender, nationality, language (or languages) that the author speaks. It also possible to search for contributions made within a range of dates (see EMHC interface on the left of Fig. 4).

RF6. Check-in Functionality and Comments. The check-in option can be optionally used by a user in order to communicate she was in (in case of areas) or very near (in case of marks and lines) the position of a geo-referenced contribution. It can also be used to by a user to communicate that she was on site when making a comment associated to a geo-referenced contribution. When the check-in button located at the bottom of EMHC is pressed, the generated geo-referenced contribution acquires the geographical location information of the place where this was created.

6   EMHC Initial Evaluation

There are several dimensions in which this tool could be evaluated, such as usability and suitability, but also from perspectives such as technology adoption. Of course, it is also a matter of available resources, since a comprehensive evaluation may be very expensive [25].

An opportunity for initially trying and evaluating EMHC was an international school organized by the Faculty of Economics and Business of the University of Chile in Santiago in 2016. A large number of graduate students from a variety of countries attended that school. So, it appeared natural to test a system prototype with those students.

Therefore, a few days after the students had arrived to Santiago, they were invited to a session in which the system was presented. Then, the students could play with EMHC installed in some computers. Finally, they were asked to fill a questionnaire. Five students from Europe, two from North America and one from Asia answered the questionnaire. We analyze their answers below.

Half of the students felt they had some difficulties to interact with people from the host country. This confirms one of the assumptions of our research. By contrast, all the respondents found "easy" or "very easy" to interact with their classmates.

Concerning their initial opinions on the prototype, 3 students answered the application had some value, 3 said the application should be useful, and one student said it would be very useful. All students also said they would read contributions made by peers. However, about half of the students did not think they would make contributions.

Another question concerned the utility of the geographic localization of comments. There were four options to answer: very useful, somehow useful, not too useful, a nuisance. About half of the students answered "very useful" and the other half said it was "somehow useful".

Finally, the questionnaire had a space for giving open opinions. Some of the students mentioned they would have liked to have the phone version of the system available (they just tried the PC prototype). One student mentioned the system should look similar to other systems (like Google reviews or TripAdvisor) in order "not to discourage people who are not tech friendly"; we see here a technology adoption oriented advice.

All in all, the respondents had a positive initial evaluation of the prototype. However, we should take into account they are young educated adults, who typically are users of technology. The results could have been different with senior adults, for example. On the other hand, perhaps senior adults would have more anxiety about a foreign country than young adults. We certainly need additional evaluation and with the smartphone version as well.

7   Conclusions

The reviewed literature shows there is transient problem with people arriving to visit a new country: the anxiety and difficulties concerning the relationships with local people at the beginning. Different culture, language, way of interaction, etc. are typical barriers to a relaxed life during that period. We propose a technological support based on a kind of social network: people in similar situation sharing their tips on how to visit a city. People who have already passed the same experience can also join the network as well as good willing hosts. The design of our technological support, EMHC, incorporates geo-localization as a way of simplifying and making comments and suggestions more visually-oriented.

The initial evaluation of the tool shows a group of graduate students in a situation like the target of this research found it appropriate and useful. However, further validation is needed and with other types of visitors.

Acknowledgement. This paper was partially funded by Fondecyt 1161200.

References

1. Unesco: Global Flow of Tertiary-Level Students (2016). http://www.uis.unesco.org/ Education/Pages/international-student-flow-viz.aspx. Accessed 2 June 2016
2. ACARA: General Capabilities in the Australian Curriculum (2014). http://www.australian curriculum.edu.au/generalcapabilities/pdf/overview. Accessed 07 April 2016
3. Griffin, P., McGaw, B., Care, E.: Assessment and Teaching of 21st Century Skills. Springer, Netherlands (2012)
4. AACSB: Standard 9. Curriculum content is appropriate to general expectations for the degree program type and learning goal. (2013). http://www.aacsb.edu/accreditation/ standards/2013-business/learning-and-teaching/standard9.aspx. Accessed 20 April 2015
5. AACSB: Teaching Design for Creativity and Innovation 2015. http://www.aacsb.edu/en/ events/Seminars/curriculum-development-series/design-thinking.aspx. Accessed 20 April 2015
6. Lee, J.: International student experiences: neo-racism and discrimination. Int. High. Educ. **44**, 3–5 (2015)
7. Rienties, B., et al.: Understanding academic performance of international students: the role of ethnicity, academic and social integration. High. Educ. **63**(6), 685–700 (2012)
8. Hendrickson, B., Rosen, D., Aune, R.K.: An analysis of friendship networks, social connectedness, homesickness, and satisfaction levels of international students. Int. J. Intercultural Relat. **35**(3), 281–295 (2011)
9. Russell, J., Rosenthal, D., Thomson, G.: The international student experience: three styles of adaptation. High. Educ. **60**(2), 235–249 (2010)
10. Gudykunst, W.B.: Applying anxiety uncertainty management (AUM) theory to intercultural adjustment training. Int. J. Intercultural Relat. **22**(2), 227–250 (1998)
11. Gudykunst, W.B., Nishida, T.: Anxiety, uncertainty, and perceived effectiveness of communication across relationships and cultures. Int. J. Intercultural Relat. **25**(1), 55–71 (2001)
12. Antunes, P., et al.: Integrating decision-making support in geocollaboration tools. Group Decis. Negot. **23**(2), 211–233 (2014)
13. Zurita, G., Baloian, N.: Mobile, collaborative situated knowledge creation for urban planning. Sensors **12**(5), 6218–6243 (2012)
14. Zurita, G., Baloian, N.: Context, patterns and geo-collaboration to support situated learning. In: Bravo, J., López-de-Ipiña, D., Moya, F. (eds.) UCAmI 2012. LNCS, vol. 7656, pp. 503–511. Springer, Heidelberg (2012)
15. Zurita, G., Baloian, N.: Using geo-collaboration and microblogging to support learning: identifying problems and opportunities for technological business. In: Antunes, P., Gerosa, M.A., Sylvester, A., Vassileva, J., de Vreede, G.-J. (eds.) CRIWG 2013. LNCS, vol. 8224, pp. 215–232. Springer, Heidelberg (2013)
16. Mark, D.M.: Geographic information science: defining the field. Found. Geogr. Inf. Sci. **1**, 3–18 (2003)
17. Folino, G., et al.: A grid portal for solving geoscience problems using distributed knowledge discovery services. Future Gener. Comput. Syst. **26**(1), 87–96 (2010)
18. MacEachren, A.M., et al.: Enabling collaborative geoinformation access and decision-making through a natural, multimodal interface. Int. J. Geogr. Inf. Sci. **19**(3), 293–317 (2005)
19. Silva, M.J., et al.: Sensing the schoolyard: using senses and sensors to assess georeferenced environmental dimensions. In: Proceedings of the 1st International Conference and Exhibition on Computing for Geospatial Research and Application. ACM (2010)

20. Elwood, S., Goodchild, M.F., Sui, D.Z.: Researching volunteered geographic information: spatial data, geographic research, and new social practice. Ann. Assoc. Am. Geogr. **102**(3), 571–590 (2012)
21. Budhathoki, N.R., Haythornthwaite, C.: Motivation for open collaboration crowd and community models and the case of OpenStreetMap. Am. Behav. Sci. **57**(5), 548–575 (2013)
22. Neis, P., Zielstra, D.: Recent developments and future trends in volunteered geographic information research: the case of OpenStreetMap. Future Internet **6**(1), 76–106 (2014)
23. Croitoru, A., et al.: Geosocial gauge: a system prototype for knowledge discovery from social media. Int. J. Geogr. Inf. Sci. **27**(12), 2483–2508 (2013)
24. Caldwell, K.: Sprechen sie… What? Anxiety/Uncertainty Management in a German American School (2012)
25. Antunes, P., et al.: Structuring dimensions for collaborative systems evaluation. ACM Comput. Surv. (CSUR) **44**(2), 8 (2012)

Remote Collaboration Support on Physical Tasks: Exploring Handheld and Hands-free Setups

Frâncila Weidt Neiva[✉], Vinicius Bittencourt, Wallace Ugulino,
Marcos R.S. Borges, and Adriana S. Vivacqua

Postgraduate Program in Informatics, Universidade Federal do Rio de Janeiro (UFRJ),
Rio de Janeiro, Brazil
fran.weidt@gmail.com, vbb@ufrj.br,
{ugulino,mborges}@ppgi.ufrj.br, avivacqua@dcc.ufrj.br

Abstract. Collaborative work involving teams and individuals distributed across the globe is an inevitable trend. Because of that, the expertise is getting increasingly distributed and we have seen a growing need for technologies to support remote collaboration. Despite this need, the differences of technologies used to support remote collaboration are unknown, especially considering different kinds of physical tasks, such as analytical tasks and construction tasks. In order to better understand their impact on collaborative behaviors, perceptions, and performance, we conducted a lab setting study to evaluate two different arrangements of technology: a handheld model and a hands-free model. These models were compared for both, analytical and construction tasks. Our results suggest us that hands-free setting is more suitable for analytical tasks, while the handheld setting is more suitable for construction tasks. These differences among technological setups for remote collaboration on physical tasks motivate additional studies, especially long-term studies in natural settings, which could investigate aspects of collaboration that may not have been explored on our lab setting study.

Keywords: Remote collaboration · Handheld · Hands-free · Physical tasks

1 Introduction

Remote collaboration technologies allow professionals to work together when they are geographically distributed [1]. Because of that, expertise is increasingly distributed, and there is a growing demand for this kind of technology [2]. One example of a situation where remote collaboration is beneficial is the occurrence of a natural disaster: in that case, experts at a far away distance may communicate with assistants supported by mobile or wearable while located closer to the place of the disaster. Assistants can even send pictures and videos directly from the field. Enabled by technology, experts can share their opinions and support the local group in analyzing and evaluating damages, for instance [3]. In the case of a disease outbreak, through collaborative technologies support, the right procedures can be taken in time, because the best experts in the globe can use these technologies to collaborate with local professionals [4, 5]. Furthermore,

© Springer International Publishing Switzerland 2016
T. Yuizono et al. (Eds.): CRIWG 2016, LNCS 9848, pp. 65–80, 2016.
DOI: 10.1007/978-3-319-44799-5_6

the poorest or most isolated parts of the planet that suffer with the lack of doctors, teachers and other experts, for example, may benefit from remote collaboration [3, 5].

Collaborative tasks often involve novices, assistants, or people with little experience. Experts' supervision is necessary for these situations [2] (among others). It supports professionals in avoiding critical mistakes that can compromise the task and also supports its completion. However, such expertise is often limited in supply and not always available locally [2]. Mobile and Wearable technologies allow experts collaborate remotely, cut costs and speed up the process in comparison to having an expert physically present [6]. In this way, research has been conducted to investigate how to support a task performed by novices or assistants having the remote guidance of an expert, such as [1, 7]. The problem is that most current research addressing remote collaboration are designed to support group activities that can be performed without reference to the external spatial environment [1]. The question of how to support collaborative physical tasks has been less investigated. By definition, collaborative physical tasks are those ones that involve two or more individuals working together to perform actions on concrete objects in the three-dimensional (3D) world [1]. This definition was adopted in this paper.

This article investigates how different technological setups can influence different kinds of physical tasks. The technological setups considered in this research involve a handheld tablet and a hands-free head-mounted camera. The kinds of physical tasks considered in this research were construction and analytical tasks. Through this experiment, this paper aimed at increasing the body of knowledge related to remote collaboration on physical tasks.

Despite the growing demand for technologies to enable remote collaboration on physical tasks, the suitability of different technologies to support this context is not well explored in the literature. According to [7], little research has been conducted in this research field. This is especially true when we look for research that investigates the impact of handheld and hands-free setups to support collaboration considering different kinds of physical tasks, namely analytical tasks and construction tasks. In literature, there are few works investigating construction tasks [7] or analytical tasks [8]. However, reference [7] investigates how tasks with different levels of mobility influence in the suitability of technological setups. Reference [8] proposes a mediated reality head mounted device to support analytical task. This paper contributes with a different perspective by investigating the impact of different technological setups in these different types of physical tasks.

In order to perform the investigation, we conducted an experimental study that aimed at establishing how different technological setups and the different kinds of physical tasks affected collaborative outcomes such as: how collaborators behave, perceive the collaboration, and perform collaborative tasks.

In the remainder of this paper, Sect. 2 presents the related works. Related works include research related to remote collaboration for supporting both construction physical tasks and analytical physical tasks. Section 3 presents the research model used. The research model includes hypothesis definition and method of investigation. Section 4 presents the results of the experiment performed based on the research model described in Sect. 4. Results from our experiments give us a clue on how the different technological setups and different kinds of physical tasks did affect outcomes from collaboration. Section 5 brings a discussion about the results obtained from the empirical study we conducted. Finally, conclusion and future works are presented in Sect. 6.

2 Related Work

Some technologies are already being used with the purpose of allowing remote collaboration on physical tasks. Among these wearable technologies, the most widespread setups to support collaborative physical tasks involve (i) smartphones and tablets and (ii) head-mounted devices (like cameras or displays) [8, 9]. The former setup is classified as a handheld setup, while the latter is classified as a hands-free setup.

Regarding collaborative physical tasks, we can also identify two categories: (i) construction physical tasks [10] – those ones that involve collaborative building of a real world object, and (ii) analytical physical tasks [8] – those ones that involve the analysis of objects in real world such as, measurements and identification of properties.

Previous works on remote collaboration have shown that different mobility requirements in a construction task influence which is the most suitable technology arrangement to support it [2]. For example, in [7], evidence pointed that in construction tasks that require low levels of mobility (static tasks), perceptions of collaborative success were significantly lower when participants used a hands-free model based on Google Glass compared to a handheld model with a tablet. On the other hand, hands-free setup provided a more fluid collaboration than handheld setup considering construction tasks that require high levels of mobility (dynamic tasks).

Another study [1], also focused in construction tasks comparing different technological setups. The collaboration was investigated using audio only, head-mounted camera,scene camera and side-by-side setups. The completion time of proposed tasks was evaluated and results have shown that regarding side-by-side setup, the tasks proposed were completed faster. When side-by-side setup is not possible, evidence suggested that head-mounted camera and scene camera setups are better than audio-only. Besides that, scene camera with wide-angle view had better results than the head-mounted camera where mobility was not necessary. The combination of head-mounted camera and scene camera together did not enhance the results. This may be due difficulties to distribute participants' attention between cameras.

Also considering tasks involving mobility, [10] evaluated the remote users feeling of presence through a robotic telepresence system. In this system, a participant appears on a tablet display mounted in a robot. Using this robot, the participant collaborated with another to perform low and high mobility tasks. Evidence pointed that in high-mobility tasks, the presence feeling of the remote user was higher than in low-mobility task.

A robotic telepresence system was also investigated in [6] through an exploratory study. In this work, the telepresence robot was designed to support collaboration between a field worker and a remotely located expert. The authors concluded that field work, for example considering industrial environments, frequently involves moisture, dust and heat. In this way, a telepresence robot must be resistant. Also, the robot must be able to deal with obstacles, such as heavy doors, stairs, etc. Telepresence robots must meet a range of requirements before they become completely suitable for field work in industrial environments.

Regarding analytical tasks, [8] have used a mediated reality system to support remote collaboration in crime scenes. The authors were motivated by a real problem of the Netherlands local police. Netherlands local police are, in a first moment, responsible for crime scene investigation. However, the local police are frequently supported by experts from Dutch Forensic Institute to analyze crimes. The process to contact these experts and bring them to the crime scene is expensive. To face this problem, the authors used a head-mounted device to build a 3D map of the environment in real-time. In this way, remote users were able to virtually join and interact together with the local participant in the scene.

In summary, there are works in literature investigating remote collaboration on construction physical tasks [2] and analytical physical tasks [8] and also, works investigating handheld setups and hands-free setups [7]. However, none of the reviewed works in literature have investigated the effects of a handheld setup and a hands-free setup to support different kinds of physical tasks, namely analytical and construction physical tasks.

In this way, this paper investigated the influence of a handheld setup and a hands-free setup to support analytical and construction physical tasks. The next section describes this investigation.

3   Research Model

By reviewing literature, we found that a scene camera with wide-angle view was more effective than a head-mounted camera setup to perform a collaborative construction task, where mobility was not necessary [1]. In [7], the authors concluded that the head-mounted camera setup improved collaborative behaviors and collaborative performance (effectiveness and efficiency) considering construction tasks. During collaboration tasks, effectiveness and efficiency were measured by means of error rate and completion time respectively, in different research [7, 11]. Based on these studies we formed our hypothesis on how different technological setups and the different kinds of physical tasks (analytical and construction) will affect collaborative outcomes—how collaborators behave, perceive the collaboration, and perform. We expect that different technological setups will be suitable for different kinds of physical tasks.

We imagine that analytical and construction tasks have different features and thus, they have different requirements. Through an experiment we intend to observe these differences and analyze if they result in a different optimal model (hands-free or handheld) of wearable technology for performing these different types of tasks.

In this way, the evaluation scope was defined based on GQM method [12] as following:

Analyze a handheld and a hands-free technological setup **for the purpose of** evaluation **with respect to** behavioral, perceptual, and performance dimensions of collaboration **from the point of view of** participants when performing analytical and construction physical tasks **in the context of** remote collaboration.

3.1 Hypothesis

Based on the defined scope, the hypothesis was formulated. It was defined a null hypothesis and an alternative hypothesis as follow:

- (H^0) Hands-free and handheld technological setups will not generate differences on behavioral, perceptual, and performance dimensions of collaboration outcomes regarding construction and analytical tasks on physical objects.
- (H^1) Hands-free and handheld technological setups will generate differences on behavioral, perceptual, and performance dimensions of collaboration outcomes regarding construction and analytical tasks on physical objects.

3.2 Method

In order to test our hypothesis, we designed empirical studies in which different participants had to perform two kinds of physical tasks using two proposed arrangements of technology. In this way, we had four scenarios to investigate. For each study, we had pairs of participants where one of them performed the role of remote peer and the other performed the role of local peer. The local pair is defined by the participant that is physically co-located with the 3D object that will be manipulated.

Participants. We recruited 26 participants to take part in this study. Participants were Brazilian, 18 males and 8 females, aged 18 and over (23y.o. in average, StdDev = 2.3) and all have access to Internet. Participants were recruited in pairs and we previously identified the one with more expertise in each task to perform the role of remote participant. In this way, we had 13 pairs that participated in the studies. Each pair participated in only one of the four proposed scenarios. It is important to state that we balanced the number of pairs through the scenarios.

Once pairs participated only in one scenario, we avoided the testing effect that could happen due to the learning resultant from the first experience in other scenarios. Also, we avoided that fatigue in doing multiple tasks could affect results. Before the study, we performed training with participants to familiarize with technologies and concepts involved in the proposed task.

Study Design. We designed a study with two independent variables: technology type (handheld or hands-free) and physical task type (construction or analytical).

Based on prior studies observations [1, 6] and [7], we have decided that a wide-angle camera would be the best camera option for a head mounted hands-free setting. Therefore, we chose a GoPro Hero 3 + camera, considering it as an example of a modern and widespread camera that already has the ability to broadcast video using Wi-Fi ad-hoc connection (Fig. 1).

Fig. 1. Head mounted - hands-free setup.

For the local participant in the handheld model, we decided to use an Android tablet due to its massive use in world (Fig. 2). When performing a task with the handheld setting, users communicated using Google Hangout app. In the hands-free setting, the helpers saw the broadcasted video using GoPro official app. Audio communication was performed using extra cell phones due to the fact that the GoPro wireless broadcast does not transmit live audio.

Fig. 2. Tablet - handheld setup.

Regarding physical tasks, the construction task consisted in building a LEGO ship, where the local participant had the pieces without the instructions and the remote participant had the full instructions manual with schematics images (Fig. 3). On the other side, the analytical tasks consisted in identifying issues on a computer case, where the remote participant had to ask the local participant to identify characteristics of the computer asked and instructed by the remote participant. The remote participant had to complete a report about the computer case status.

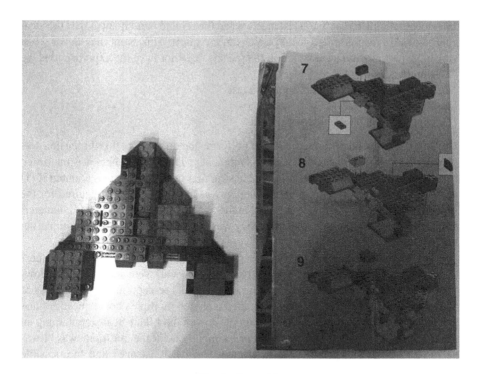

Fig. 3. Lego ship

Setup and Materials. In both tasks, the remote and local participants were located in different rooms, without any type of communication besides the technological setups proposed. All rooms had a table and a chair to participants perform their tasks.

For the analytical task, above the table of the local participant, there were a toolbox and a computer case; above the table of the remote participant there were a list of questions he/she had to answer about the computer and a schematic figure of the location of the components inside the computer case.

For the construction task, above the table of the local participant there was a set of LEGO pieces; above the table of the remote participant there was an instructions manual with schematic figures showing how to build a ship step-by-step.

Analysis. The analyses were based on [7]. In this vein, we analyzed the behavioral, perceptual, and performance dimensions of collaboration during the task.

In order to collect data considering the *behavioral dimension*, the experiment was video recorded and direct observations were performed during the experiment. The material produced was analyzed to identify the following events:

- Remote participant proactive assistance – when the remote participant offered his/her assistance without being asked. This event may occur when remote participant is able to realize that local participant needs his/her assistance. In other words, the remote participant is aware of the local participant needs.

- Remote participant reactive assistance – when the remote participant assists the local participant in response to a local participant's request. This event may occur when the local participant face a situation that he/she does not have the expertise to solve for him/herself.
- Remote participant questions about the task
- Local participant questions about the task
- Difficulties in technological setup used.

In order to collect data considering the performance dimension, this dimension was divided into two metrics: effectiveness and efficiency. The effectiveness was measured as the number of errors in the task. In the construction task, an error was counted if (1) a part that wasn't required for the construction was used or (2) a part required for the construction was used in the wrong place. In the analytical task an error was counted if a result of an analysis is wrong. The efficiency was measured in both tasks as completion time.

In order to collect data considering the perceptual dimension, two follow-up questionnaires, one for each experimental role (remote and local) were applied. The follow-up questionnaires were designed to capture participants' perceptions of the success of their collaboration. Besides, the questionnaires included multiple choice questions and open questions. The multiple choice answers followed the Likert Scale, containing an intermediate level as suggested by [13]. For example, one of the questions was "I was able to help my partner every time he/she needed my assistance" and the possible answers were: completely disagree, disagree, neither agree or disagree, agree or completely agree. The questionnaire is available at https://goo.gl/yDbnm9.

4   Results

The results were divided into behavioral, perceptual, and performance dimensions of collaboration. These dimensions were analyzed considering four different scenarios, (1) construction task using handheld setting, (2) construction task using hands-free setting, (3) analytical task using handheld setting and, (4) analytical task using hands-free setting.

4.1   Behavioral Dimension

In order to investigate the behavioral dimension, we recorded the experiments in both remote and local participant sides. In order to do that, we captured and saved the videos broadcasted by the tablets' built-in camera and the GoPro camera. We also performed direct observations during experiments conduction.

Scenario 1. In this scenario, we could notice that remote participants were more reactive than proactive during collaboration. This is probably due to the fact that in this handheld setting the remote participant did not see all the time what the local participant was doing. Instead, the remote and local participant engaged a face to face conversation.

The local participant frequently asked questions about the task progress and remote participant gave constant feedback to local participant.

Sometimes, local participants left tablet on table in order to connect the pieces in the construction task. Because many pieces were small, there were moments in which participants could handle both the tablet and the piece with his/her hands. However, if the proposed task required both hands participant would have to leave the tablet over the table all the time and, therefore, losing the character of a handheld setting.

When local participants wanted to show to remote participants the construction status, they had to point the camera to the right place. This experience was sometimes difficult and required remote participant feedback to assess the camera direction.

Finally, we realized that local and remote participants had to adapt a system of words and gestures to identify pieces and actions. In the beginning of collaboration process, we frequently notice a struggle to understand and be understood. Because local and remote participants established a common and shared system of gestures and keywords to identify pieces and actions, collaboration became easier.

Scenario 2. In this scenario, once remote and local participants established a language to specify pieces and positions and a good adjust of the camera in local participant's head, collaborations becomes more intense. As remote participants can see the task progress during all the experiment time, they were more proactive. We could notice that once the local participant could not see the remote participant, the gesture system to identify pieces and actions that was established in scenario 1 did not happen. The identification of pieces and actions had to be performed only using conversation which increased complexity.

We observed that the quality of the broadcasted video could be a great differential to this kind of task. Since the camera is fixed to the worker's head and there is no way to zoom-in, we observed that remote participants had more difficult to see if the local participants were placing the pieces correctly and they frequently complained about the low resolution. However, all participants were able to complete the task successfully.

The fisheyes lenses, which we decided to use to provide a wide field of view to remote participants, as suggested in [1] and [6, 7], were very criticized by participants, which claimed that distortion hinders the view.

Scenario 3. In this scenario, remote participants were more reactive than proactive. Considering local participants had to use both hands to analyze the 3D object, there were several times that they had to let the tablet over the table, letting the camera pointed to another place rather the analyzed object. This fact may evidence that, a handheld setting lost its character in these moments because participants had a considerable need to maintain their hands free for work.

In that way, we observed that remote participants asked the questions they had to answer in their report based on the local participant analysis. Also, remote participants waited for local participants' response, sometimes without seeing what they were doing in the computer case. During this process, they only interacted when local participants had doubts, asking the remote participants for more information or if they were analyzing the correct piece. When this happened and local participants have to show the pieces inside the 3D object (computer case) to the remote participants, the handheld setting was useful since the tablet could be placed very near to the point of interest, so the helper could validate the process. However, to point the camera to the right place was not always an easy task. Therefore, this model of technology can make this kind of task feasible, but there is no proactivity.

Scenario 4. Different from scenario 3, in this scenario we could notice that remote participants were more proactive than reactive during collaboration. This is probably due to the fact that in hands-free setting the helper was able to frequently see the local participant analyzing the 3D object involved in proposed task. In this way, remote participant frequently asked questions to local participant.

Furthermore, we also can notice that in an analytical task the focus changed from local to remote participant in comparison with a construction task. In the construction task, the local participant was responsible for the construction and the remote participant played the role of an advisor. However, in the analytical task, the remote participant was responsible for giving a final decision about analysis questions, while local participant managed the 3D object to obtain the information needed for a proper analysis.

In the hands-free setting, a camera was fixed in local participant's head. Remote participants had no control of the camera and then, they frequently asked local participant to position his/her head in a different way.

In all scenarios, the video quality was pointed as a complicating factor. Video quality hindered a more satisfactory experience. However, because it was a common factor in all investigated scenarios and there was no limitation time to complete the proposed tasks, this factor could be circumvented.

Our hypothesis (H1) claims that these two technological setups (hands-free and handheld) induce differences in all three dimensions investigated in this paper regarding construction and analytical tasks on physical objects.

Considering the results above presented, in behavioral dimension, evidence pointed that there are differences in hands-free and handheld setups to perform construction and analytical tasks. In summary, hands-free setting was more suitable for the proposed analytical task, while handheld setting was more suitable for the proposed construction task.

4.2 Perceptual Dimension

In order to investigate the perceptual dimension, we applied follow-up questionnaires to capture participants' perceptions. The questionnaire contained questions related to perception of collaboration success. In this study, the questionnaire questions were answered after participants had accomplished the proposed task.

Since the questionnaire questions followed the Likert Scale, containing an intermediate level as suggested by [13], we assigned a score for each answer option ranging from 1 to 5. The score is the average of five questionnaire items in remote participant questionnaire and five questionnaire items in local participant questionnaire (Part 3 - https://goo.gl/yDbnm9). A score close to 1 indicates non success in collaboration, while a score close to 5 indicates success in collaboration. After the analysis of all the questions from all questionnaires, the results were (Fig. 4):

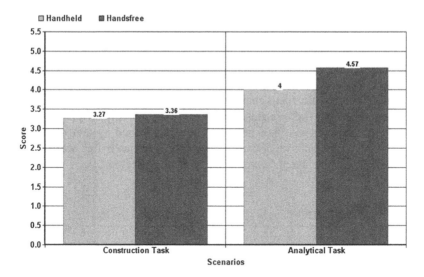

Fig. 4. Perceptual dimension

As can be seen in Fig. 4, in construction task, the handheld setting (scenario 1) achieved a slightly lower score than hands-free setting (scenario 2). In analytical task, the handheld setting (scenario 3) achieved a lower score than hands-free setting (scenario 4).

In the handheld setting, collaboration occurred through a Google Hangout app that was used for supporting a face-to-face conversation. In this way, remote participant rarely saw what the local participant was doing. As noticed in behavioral dimension, this fact could hinder the perception of success considering the handheld setting. This situation is different in hands-free setting, because the remote participant can check more frequently the task progress and inform about the correctness to local participant than in handheld setting.

Considering the results presented in perceptual dimension, our evidences pointed to differences in hands-free and handheld setups for performing construction and analytical tasks. In summary, using a hands-free setting participants considered the collaboration more successful than using a handheld setting regarding both kind of physical tasks. The collected data generated evidence to accept our alternative hypothesis (H1).

4.3   Performance Dimension

In performance dimension we collected two measurements. The time spent and the correctness to perform tasks in each scenario. The time spent was used to measure efficiency, while correctness was used to measure effectiveness.

Considering efficiency measurement (Fig. 5), we noticed that, by the means, the time spent to perform the construction task was about 23 % lower using handheld setting (scenario 1) comparing to hands-free setting (scenario 2). In analytical task, the time spent was about 51 % lower using hands-free setting (scenario 4) in comparison with handheld setting (scenario 3). These results can be explained by the evidence collected in behavioral dimension. For example, during construction task, the hands-free setup did not allow participants to establish a more sophisticated system of words and gestures to identify pieces and actions, as occurred in the handheld setup. In analytical task the focus changed from local to remote participant in comparison with construction task. In this way, the remote participant played a role of advisor. In this case, it was not necessary a sophisticated system of words and gestures among participants as in construction task. The hands-free setup was beneficial to participants manage the computer case in analytical task.

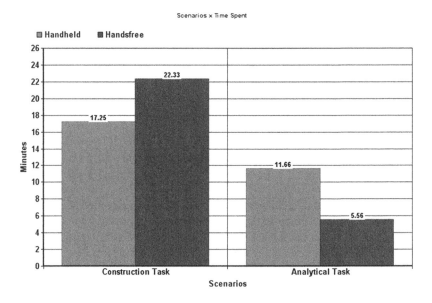

Fig. 5. Performance dimension (Efficiency)

The evidence pointed that behavioral differences influenced time completion regarding the use of distinct technological setups in distinct kinds of physical tasks.

Considering effectiveness measurement, participants had around 100 % percent of correctness in proposed tasks. This happened because participants had unlimited time to complete tasks, so they keep trying until they properly complete task steps.

In conclusion, evidences collected in behavioral dimension reflected in performance dimension. In behavioral dimension analysis, hands-free setting was more suitable for proposed analytical task. This fact was witnessed in performance dimension through a more efficient task completion. Handheld setting was more suitable for proposed construction task, which was witnessed in performance dimension. Hands-free setting was more efficient regarding analytical task completion.

5   Discussion

In general, we could notice that image quality was an issue that hindered a better collaboration in all scenarios analyzed. Despite this fact, the tasks were completed and results could be collected and analyzed.

Analyzing all dimensions, we conclude that evidence collected in this study pointed that hands-free setting was more appropriate to analytical task, while handheld setting was more appropriate to construction task. A summary of the more appropriate technological setup considering the kind of physical task and the collaborative dimension, can be seen in Table 1. The performance analysis reinforces this conclusion. Analyzing means, we could notice that considering efficiency, the time spent to perform the construction task was about 23 % lower using the handheld setting. In the analytical task, the time spent was about 51 % lower using hands-free setting.

Table 1.   Suitable setup considering the kind of task and collaborative dimension.

Task type	Behavioral dimension	Perceptual dimension	Performance dimension
Construction	Handheld Setup	Hands-free Setup	Handheld Setup
Analytical	Hands-free Setup	Hands-free Setup	Hands-free Setup

As stated by our alternative hypothesis (H1), data collected suggested that these two technological setups (hands-free and handheld) induced differences in behavioral, perceptual and performance dimension regarding construction and analysis tasks on physical objects.

In **construction task using the hands-free setting**, we observed some difficulties in the communication. As the camera is fixed at the head and cannot be zoomed, the remote participants sometimes had problems to identify if the placing of pieces were completely correct. At least one time in each experiment, the local participant asked if he or she was doing it correctly and the remote participant answered that didn't know because it was hard to see. However, as the participants had no time limitations to complete the task, each pair created their own "code" to specify the pieces, distinguishing them by size, height and color; and also the position where the pieces should be placed based on a referential. All participants completed the task correctly. In the questionnaire, despite every participant agreed about the success in performing the proposed task, only 50 % percent said it was easy to perform.

A positive fact that we observed is that remote participants were more proactive compared to the handheld model, since they could see the construction in the camera view all the time, while the other ones could only see when local participants hold the tablet and pointed to the construction. This can indicate that if we had a better resolution for real-time video transmission in this arrangement, the results could be better.

To conclude, 33 % of participants said they partially agreed that this technology is appropriate, while 16 % partially disagreed and 50 % didn't agree nor disagree. In the comments, participants said again that the idea is very good, but the low quality of broadcasted video is a very negative point that has to be improved. Some suggested a video monitor to the local participants, so they can see what they are transmitting.

In the **analytical task using the hands-free setting**, we observed that people completed the task easily. With the hands being free, the local participant could hold cables inside the computer and get to the information they had to find very quickly. Remote participants were very proactive, seeing if their peers were doing the task correctly and indicating where they should get the information needed to proceed with the task. Regarding participants, 66 % totally agreed that they could easily complete the task, 16 % partially agreed and 16 % didn't agree nor disagree.

The results indicated that even with lower quality of real-time video streaming, this arrangement was appropriate for analytical task. Asked if they think this technology is appropriated, 66 % partially agreed and 33 % didn't agree nor disagree.

In the comments, participants said it is very useful model of technology and makes feasible to perform the task, but also that the camera resolution has to be improved. Remote participants said it is important to see what the local participant is doing in real-time.

Considering the **handheld setting in analytical and construction tasks**, we also observed some difficulties in communication. In both task types, we noticed that in different moments the remote participant have difficulties to point the tablet camera to the right point in physical 3D object. In Hangout app, as in main conferences apps, the application was built to maintain a face to face conversation using the frontal camera. In this way, when the remote participant wanted to see the 3D object in the local participant side, he/she had to ask and guide the local participant to point the frontal camera to the right place. At this moment, the worker could not see the remote participant anymore which increases the complexity of the setup used.

In analytical tasks, there were also situations where the local participant asked if he or she was doing it correctly and the remote participant answered that didn't know because it was hard to see. The more inexperienced was the local participant considering the task and/or technologies involved the greater became image quality problem. Because, more dependent the local participant were on the remote participant and more dependent on the image quality seen by the remote participant.

Despite communication problems, participants were able to complete the proposed tasks. The questionnaires indicate that participants were more confident on task success considering construction task than analytical task. In analytical task, 66 % participants completely agree and 33 % didn't agree nor disagree that task was correctly completed. In construction task, 75 % participants completely agree and 33 % agree that task was correctly completed. The results also indicate that in participants' perception, remote participant supported better the local participant in construction task. In analytical task, the most common frequencies indicated that 33 % participants completely agree and 33 % didn't agree nor disagree that remote participant was able to support the local participant. In construction task, 62 % participants completely agree and 50 % that remote participant was able to support the local participant.

Asked if the handheld arrangement was appropriate for analytical task, 33 % of participants strongly disagree that the arrangement was suitable. No participant strongly disagree that the arrangement was suitable in construction task.

6   Conclusions

In this paper we presented an experiment to analyze the effects on collaborative behaviors, perceptions, and performance when a handheld tablet setup and a hands-free head-mounted camera setup were used to perform different kinds of physical tasks, namely analytical tasks and construction tasks. Our experiment generated evidence that hands-free and handheld settings, when used to perform different kinds of physical tasks (construction and analytical tasks), induced different outcomes regarding behavioral, perceptual and performance dimensions.

This experiment was mainly motivated by the lack of studies in literature investigating how distinct technological setups can affect collaboration processes. Despite this lack of studies, some technologies (e.g. wearable) have been pointed as potential tools to support remote collaboration. In its turn, collaboration activities are an essential part of our day and a huge number of potential users and domains can benefit from remote collaboration support. In this way, this paper contributed to increase our understanding on the suitability of different technological setups to perform different kinds of physical tasks. In summary, our study generated evidences that hands-free setup was more suitable for analytical tasks, while handheld setup was more suitable for construction tasks.

This experimental study presented some limitations. During the experiment, the participants knowledge on collaboration tasks proposed may influence the outcomes. In order to reduce this threat, remote participants received, before the study, a training for acquiring the necessary knowledge for the proposed task. Also, a characterization questionnaire was used to select participants. The low number of participants does not allow generalizing results obtained. However, this paper presents important contributions to remote collaboration on physical tasks and increases the scarce body of knowledge of this research field.

As future works, the conduction of experiments with lager subjects sample and considering real collaboration situations can generate contributions to allow generalizing results obtained in this paper. Different devices to create new hands-free and handheld setups can be investigated. Based on evidence generated in this work, technological setups for remote collaboration can be investigated and proposed to be applied in specific domains, such as health, learning and business. Apps that interoperate with proposed setups to allow control the camera (e.g. zoom-in and zoom-out) can also be investigated in order to address some limitations reported by participants in experiment.

Acknowledgment. Frâncila Weidt Neiva and Wallace Ugulino are partially supported by CAPES. Marcos R.S. Borges is partially supported by grants No. 484030/2013-2, and 308149/2015-7 (CNPq), and grant # E-05/215.285/2015 (FAPERJ). Adriana S. Vivacqua is partially supported by grant No. 309171/2015-6 (CNPQ) and grant # E-26/202.753/2015 (FAPERJ). The authors also thank the participants in the experiment for their patience and cooperation.

References

1. Fussell, S.R., Setlock, L.D., Yang, J., Ou, J., Mauer, E., Kramer, A.D.: Gestures over video streams to support remote collaboration on physical tasks. Hum. Comput. Interact. **19**(3), 273–309 (2004)
2. Huang, W., Alem, L.: HandsinAir: a wearable system for remote collaboration on physical tasks. In: Proceedings of the 2013 Conference on Computer supported Cooperative Work Companion, pp. 153–156 (2013)
3. De Greef, T., Oomes, A.H. Neerincx, M.A.: Distilling support opportunities to improve urban search and rescue missions. In: International Conference on Human-Computer Interaction, pp. 703–712 (2009)
4. Fraser, H.S., Jazayeri, D., Nevil, P., Karacaoglu, Y., Farmer, P.E., Lyon, E., Fawzi, M.K.C.S., Leandre, F., Choi, S.S., Mukherjee, J.S.: An information system and medical record to support HIV treatment in rural Haiti. BMJ **329**(7475), 1142–1146 (2004)
5. Ozdalga, E., Ozdalga, A., Ahuja, N.: The smartphone in medicine: a review of current and potential use among physicians and students. J. Med. Internet Res. **14**(5), 128 (2012)
6. Vartiainen, E., Domova, V., Englund, M.: Expert on wheels: an approach to remote collaboration. In: Proceedings of the 3rd International Conference on Human-Agent Interaction, pp. 49–54 (2015)
7. Johnson, S., Gibson, M., Mutlu, B.: Handheld or hands-free?: remote collaboration via lightweight head-mounted displays and handheld devices. In: Conference on Computer Supported Cooperative Work & Social Computing, pp. 1825–1836 (2015)
8. Poelman, R., Akman, O., Lukosch, S. Jonker, P.: As if being there: mediated reality for crime scene investigation. In: Proceedings of the ACM 2012 Conference on Computer Supported Cooperative Work, pp. 1267–1276 (2012)
9. Prgomet, M., Georgiou, A., Westbrook, J.I.: The impact of mobile handheld technology on hospital physicians' work practices and patient care: a systematic review. J. Am. Med. Inform. Assoc. **16**(6), 792–801 (2009)
10. Rae, I., Mutlu, B., Takayama, L.: Bodies in motion: mobility, presence, and task awareness in telepresence. In: Conference on Human Factors in Computing Systems, pp. 2153–2162 (2014)
11. Neiva, F.W., David, J.M.N., Braga, R., Campos, F. and Freitas, V.: PRIME: Pragmatic Interoperability Architecture to Support Collaborative Development of Scientific Workflows. In: Brazilian Symposium on Components, Architectures and Reuse Software (SBCARS), pp. 50–59 (2015)
12. Van Solingen, R., Basili, V., Caldiera, G., Rombach, H.D.: Goal Question Metric (GQM) approach. In: Encyclopedia of Software Engineering (2002)
13. Laittenberger, O., Dreyer, H.M.: Evaluating the usefulness and the ease of use of a web-based inspection data collection tool. In: Proceedings IEEE Software Metrics Symposium, pp. 122–132 (1998)

Rambla: Supporting Collaborative Group Creativity for the Purpose of Concept Generation

Johann Sell[✉] and Niels Pinkwart

Department of Informatics, Humboldt-Universität zu Berlin,
Unter den Linden 6, 10099 Berlin, Germany
{sell,pinkwart}@informatik.hu-berlin.de
https://cses.informatik.hu-berlin.de/

Abstract. Asynchronous participation in volunteering social systems is mainly based on various communication and collaboration tools. Supporting creativity in such groups during the process of concept generation is one major challenge to reach high quality working results. This paper presents a collaboration tool supporting the creative process of concept generation. The solution focuses the support of a concrete social system with loose structures and that aims open participation, as discussed in a case study. At the end, the paper shows an evaluation of the solution itself with regards to the described social system.

Keywords: Socio-technical system · Collaboration · Creativity · Concept generation · Loosely structured social systems · Open participation

1 Introduction and Motivation

Ideas, the results of creative cognitive processes of individuals, are volatile and difficult to communicate. These problems are even more important if the context of the creative cognitive process is a collaborative working process that uses the resulting idea. The communication of ideas inside a collaborative working process is a crucial step to archive the shared goal [1,10]. What can be done to record an idea in that way every person in the group could understand it? A common solution is the creation of a concept that expresses the idea.

While there are a lot of tools supporting such a creation of concepts for professional business organisations as shown in Sect. 3, there exists less research with regards to loosely structured voluntary organisations as mentioned in Sect. 2. So, the presented work will focus such organisations and introduces characteristics of them that have to be considered, if a support for collaboration has to be designed.

Furthermore, this paper shows how to develop a tool supporting the collaborative process of concept generation for such organizations. The developed tool will also try to help reaching high quality for the created concepts. The results of a socio-technical walkthrough (STWT) motivated the technical system [8].

© Springer International Publishing Switzerland 2016
T. Yuizono et al. (Eds.): CRIWG 2016, LNCS 9848, pp. 81–97, 2016.
DOI: 10.1007/978-3-319-44799-5_7

The Workshop was held to analyse the working processes of the non-governmental organisation Viva con Agua de St. Pauli e.V. that is mainly based on volunteering. The STWT itself will not be presented here, but the work shown in this paper is based on its outcomes. The results of the STWT are asserting that missing or insufficiently described formalized concepts are a main reason for unsuccessfully realized ideas. So, it is an important issue for the organisation to support the voluntaries in the creation of well-described concepts. This can be done by the design of an appropriate support tool.

The next section describes a case study that the results of this paper are based on. That will be followed a presentation of the state of the art for the support of creativity and concept generation in a collaborative setting. The requirements section describes a possible solution for the above-mentioned issue. Afterwards, the implementation of the system Rambla will be shown that fulfils the requirements. Finally, the results of an evaluation and the open possibilities for future research will be sketched.

2   Case Study

The non-profit association Viva con Agua mainly based on volunteering. A decentralized network of local units organizes the voluntary people. The organisation describes itself as "a network of people and organisations commit[t]ed to establish access to clean drinking water and basic sanitation for all humans worldwide."[1] This aim should be achieved by the generation of awareness for the issues Water, Sanitation and Hygiene (WASH) using creative and joyful activities. In the end, this characterisation of the activities provides an adequate explanation for the rapid growth of the social system. Starting at the mid of the 2000s with few volunteering people, currently there are more than 12,000 volunteers.

Such a huge network of decentralized units requires a lot of self-regulated coordination and communication to ensure the creative character of the activities, but also to guarantee the conformance to the legal requirements. Focusing young adults for volunteering, the organisation becomes a magnet for digital natives using various software products to coordinate themselves. Additionally, the social system of Viva con Agua defined itself as very open in participation. That means it is possible to decide to get oneself involved in some activity this day and to veer away from it the next day. Following this the social system describes itself as based on flat hierarchies. So, implementing complex hierarchies in the social system can not solve the problem of self-coordination, as it is often done by companies which expanded in such a way. These were the major motivations for the association to implement a central coordination tool, named "Pool".

This technical system helps some specific recurring tasks and the social system uses it in a way that can be described as a socio-technical organisation in the meaning of Kunau [11], but it has no support for creative activities.

---

[1] http://www.vivaconagua.org/home, visited on 2016-05-02.

Furthermore, there is no communication support implemented yet. These circumstances motivated the young volunteering digital natives to try a lot of third-party products during their working processes. Such approaches mostly failed, because some tasks, roles and aspects like the open participation of the social system were not taken into account (cf. [11]). Furthermore, during the development of a technical component for such a socio-technical organisation it is important to prevent cognitive overload, because the users are volunteers. For the process of adoption this could be crucial, because not only the users are volunteers, but also their usage of the system is by choice. Additionally, a high cognitive load will impede the participation by new members.

As mentioned before, companies and other close structured organisations, like institutions of education, establish complex social systems and their collaboration systems have to consider these circumstances. So, there is little applicable support for organisations like Viva con Agua. That was the reason why the organisation started a collaboration with the Humboldt-Universität zu Berlin in 2014 using STWTs to survey requirements for technical systems supporting the social character of Viva con Agua. The results of the first of these workshops are the base for the requirements of the collaboration tool given in Sect. 4.

3   Related Work

Next the basic terminology will be explained, followed by models of the creative process and identified problems of the creative (group) task. Subsequently, a subsection presents established support methods and some tools to give an overview of the state of art. Each subsection focuses the support of loose structured organisations during the creative group process of collaborative concept generation.

Also it will be interesting to take a look at argumentation support methods like IBIS [12] or tools like GRADD [3] or ArguMed [18]. These methods and tools are mainly based on the principle of explicitly modelling arguments using predefined templates. For the use case described in Sect. 2, these methods and tools might put too high demands on users and might thus not be applicable – yet, empirical research will be needed to substantiate this.

3.1   Terminology

It is hard to define the widely spread term "concept", because it is often used in different contexts and integrated into the everyday speech. So, for the following explanations, a concept will be defined as a structured presentation of all aspects of an idea. These aspects can be understood as sub-ideas, following the same goals as the main-idea, but imply some concrete effects. For example: If someone has the idea to inform people about the concept of "virtual water" on a special event, the kind of information, the use of special material or some entertainment would be possible aspects. So, the term concept does not mean the mental representation of the idea as often used by cognitive science, but a special form of externalization of the idea. This externalization serves as a possible communication base between people.

Supporting the collaborative and creative process of concept generation requires a clear comprehension of creativity. Csikszentmihalyi [6], Asimov [2] and Herrmann with regards to Sternberg [9,17] can be summarized by the following characterisation of the term: Creativity is the "...ability to produce work that is novel... and appropriate..." [17]. The social context of the idea evaluates its novelty and appropriation [9]. Csikszentmihalyi complements that such a common evaluation is often influenced by individual expert assessments [6]. Additionally, Csikszentmihalyi and Asimov [2] recognize that really novel and appropriate results are mostly outcomes of so-called collaborative creativity. This means a group of people, following their individual creative processes, share their individual results. This way the members could increase the knowledge base of the whole group and stimulate effects of synergy. One group member can come up with a novel and appropriate result that would not be possible without the results of creativity of the other group members.

Such an understanding of creativity will also match the "search for ideas in associative memory" (SIAM) model [15]. The model describes the creative process as based on a set of ideas inside people's memory. During the process only those ideas with a strong relation to the current thoughts are activated. If multiple ideas became active, the resulting thought will be creative, if the ideas were loosely or not linked before. Also Link et al. [13] recognize that the definition of creativity given above implies the possibility to evaluate a tangible result of the creative process. The next section will give an understanding of the structure of creative processes.

3.2 Creative Processes

Liu et al. describe different phases of the creative process [14]. They distinguish between divergent and convergent working steps. There are many other possible descriptions for the creative process, but the one mentioned by Liu et al. is commonly used [9]. The divergent working steps produce a huge number of concept alternatives, while creative people merge or sort out some concepts during the convergent steps. Liu et al. aimed to support the creation of promising concepts. On the one hand, this implies the generation of a huge amount of concept alternatives to prevent overlooking a valuable possibility. On the other hand, such a huge amount of concept alternatives reduces the clarity. It becomes harder to recognize valuable concept alternatives and also to evaluate and select some of them. So, next to the creation of a huge amount of concepts, the generated set has to be held manageable.

Herrmann describes four characteristics of creative processes [9]: playfulness, iteration, back and forth considerations and "aha-moments". Due to the fact that creative processes should produce novel ideas, some free space is needed to follow extraordinary thoughts. This is meant by the term playfulness. Iteration is important for walking on and going back between the phases. Additionally, forward considerations allow to refine thoughts during the creative process.

Also creative people can do a consideration backwards, if they identify ideas as not novel or not appropriate. Results of creative processes are often marked by moments of realization, if the creative person appreciates the new insight. This is called "aha-moment".

Next to phases and process descriptions, some characteristics of the social system have to be mentioned, which are required for an effective and creative collaboration. Asimov noticed the importance of a relaxed and open-minded social context [2]. Herrmann pointed out that a consensus has to be built up inside the collaborative group to change the current working phase [9]. Additionally, he mentioned that creative thoughts are often very complex and so it is hard to communicate them. The main problems that motivated this work and that were introduced in Sect. 1 are very similar to this one. Herrmann noticed that this kind of problem will arise more frequently in distributed collaboration.

3.3   Existing Support Methods

In this subsection some established approaches and methods supporting goal-oriented creative working procedures will be presented that are based on the understanding of creative processes given above.

Liu et al. introduce an approach to work in a creative manner for concept generation in their work. As anticipated, they described a divergent phase followed by a convergent one. These phases consists of different working steps which could also be classified as divergent or convergent. Furthermore, they decided to follow the idea of multiple layers of abstraction. This implies that a result of the creative process of concept generation will be reached by a step-by-step detailing of the concept alternatives. The innovation described by the approach of Liu is the ordering and weighting of the working steps. Both are defined by the current phase of the creative process. That means, during the divergent phase the corresponding working steps will be followed by a quick convergent step to keep the set of concept alternatives small. Also, for the convergent phase quick divergent working steps will precede the convergent ones.

Another method of concept generation is called "KJ-Method". Yuizono et al. use this method to order a chaotic mass of information [19]. It aims at the generation of ideas and a following transformation of them into concepts. Additionally, the engaged people always work in a cooperative manner. The "KJ-Method" consists of four steps. At first, all participants are suggesting ideas using so called "tags" (a small chit of paper could be used), which are placed on a shared desk. The participants place their "tags" at the same time. This will be repeated multiple times, so the suggestions can inspire other group members. Next, the ideas will be grouped into "islands". This is done during a discussion of the similarity of the "tags". Afterwards, the participants create relations between the islands and as a last step, they write a conclusion.

This methods have influenced the development of several tools, which will be described in the following subsection.

3.4 Tools

The Idea-Thread-Mapper (ITM) developed by Chen et al. [5] has to be considered, because the supported process of enquiry might be equal to creative concept generation. A timeline containing the collaborative working steps of enquiry visualizes the process of knowledge generation. It consists of chronologically-ordered discussion inputs focusing a shared issue. In that way the development of knowledge becomes visible. So, this kind of visualisation helps the users to contextualize their knowledge by using the timeline for asynchronous communication.

Liu et al. also implemented their approach [14] and the resulting system is called "FuncSION". It allows the creation of concepts by the usage of so-called "Building Blocks". These are detailed parts oriented at components as used in their domain mechanics. The composition of such "Building blocks" has to follow given rules that reduces the set of possibilities. Obviously, "FuncSION" follows their approach, if at first a set of alternative concepts will be generated.

Both tools based on the creation of a huge amount of concept alternatives, which will be reduced by procedures of evaluation and merging. Link et al. [13] implemented a system using a more detailed view on ideas. Their approach of an anchored discussion supports the explicit creation of relations between a discussion input and a part of an idea description. The users are able to split an idea during the idea creation process to reduce the complexity, although the authors mentioned the possible problem of missing context, if the users describe the idea only by its different aspects.

The possibilities of supporting creative processes shown above have to be used to extend the existing socio-technical organisation Viva con Agua. The referenced papers exhaustively evaluate all tools and methods, especially the approach of Liu et al. Mostly the authors have chosen a study setting that forced the participants to use the system in specific working procedure. Additionally, the systems are developed for organisations with a complex structured social system. So, they are not applicable for the purpose of such an organisation of volunteers as described in Sect. 2. The usage of the mentioned methods considering the explained problems and steps during the collaboration will be shown in the next sections, focusing a volunteering organisation.

4   Requirements

The Sects. 2 and 3 imply that the system has to support a varying set of group members, specially the integration of new members into the working process. Additionally, the open participation requires that it should guide the users to select the correct working steps during the process, instead of supporting some special steps as done by several other tools.

In contrast to the implementation of their approach by Liu et al. [14] the creation of multiple alternatives by the users should be prevented, to reduce the cognitive load as mentioned by Link et al. [13]. The users have not to evaluate and merge different concepts for a following analysis of the details of the resulting concept. Following the guidelines of Herrmann [9], the users can start their working process by manipulating different details of the concept or with a general discussion of the topic. So, the creation of different alternatives corresponds to the definition of aspects of the idea, instead of the definition of whole concepts. It should be ensured that the discussion will focus on the aspects and their influences into the concept as a central theme. The documentation of influences of aspects can be interpreted as a kind of convergent working phase, while the discussion about the influences and aspects could be described as a divergent phase.

It becomes apparent that the divergent and the convergent phase are intertwined, so it is really important to support communication between the working group members by the system. Additionally, the decentralized character of the social system as mentioned in Sect. 2 implies spatially and temporally asynchronous communication, so the social system also requires a special support of communication by the technical system (Req. R1).

A confusing discussion could result in cognitive overload, as described in Sect. 3. Following this, for the purpose of ordering and sorting discussion input a possibility to assign the input to explicit aspects of the idea should be created (R2). Afterwards, the user could limit the discussion input by the aspects of an idea (R3). This will reduce the cognitive load and helps new people to focus on interesting aspects of the discussion. Such an implementation of functions will also follow Link et al. [13]. Furthermore, the Idea-Thread-Mapper (ITM) [5] recommend an ordering of the discussion input by its creation date (R4).

For the purpose of transforming the contents of the discussion into sketched influences inside the formalized concept, the system will provide the possibility to assign such values at a connection between the concept and the aspect. In this way it will be possible to separate the influences and filter the concept's content (R5). Thus, the system supports the user in getting an overview of the described influences and new users will get easy access, as forced by the social system described in Sect. 2. Additionally, the influences of the aspects can be aggregated automatically to reduce the cognitive load of the users (R6).

With regards to the four characteristics of creative processes identified by Herrmann, specially the iterations and back and forth considerations, the system implements a function to exclude described and formalized influences of aspects from the concept (R7). Such a function will help if users have to remove the described influences, which is an error-prone proceeding. Also, the possibility to re-include such influences will help during forward considerations.

As Herrmann suggested the system should support a dynamic switch between discussion and working on the shared material [9]. This is extra required, because the system should guide the users working like the approach of Liu et al. The first implication will be the parallel visualisation of the discussion and the shared material (R8). Additionally, the system has to allow the user to work inside the discussion, but his/her actions influence the concept and the other way around (R9). A clear, syntactical separation of discussion input, explicit aspects of the idea and the described influences inside the concept should be extra help for the users to keep the overview of the system contents (R10).

The definition of the term "concept" given in Subsect. 3.1 allows the implementation of a type of concept known in the social system of Viva con Agua. Such a concept will be structured by a set of key-value pairs (R11). A key could be understood as a pair of aspect and influence label, while a value would be the concrete description of an influence affected by the aspect. It follows, that an aspect could have multiple described influences, identified by an influence label. Additionally, all influence labels can be grouped by so-called sections (R12). For the example of Sect. 1, the special event to inform people about the thoughts of "virtual water", it would be possible to describe an influence as labelled by the term "costs" and the value "100 Euro", given by the aspect "entertainment". Secondary, the section "input" could categorize the influence labelled by "costs". Obviously, the different aspects of an idea could be described by a structured set of influences. Such a kind of description will satisfy the definition of the term concept given above. Following the guidelines given by Herrmann in [9], the shared material should always be malleable. So, the affiliated influences and specially their labels have to be an open set. In relation to a function that aggregates all values of a influence label (already mentioned by (R6)), it is required to implement a possibility for the users to dynamically add new influence labels, but also values (R13).

At least, the system needs to be highly accessible, because the social system requires less or no barriers for the integration of new volunteers (R14). There will be users accessing the system multiple times a week and others who will use it only a few times in a year. So, the acceptance of the new technical system by the social system depends intensively on the accessibility of it.

Taking the approach of Liu et al. into account, it seems clear that a divergent phase could be described as a generation of new explicit aspects, which can be generated only by creating discussion input. The system allows the description of influences of such explicit aspects at any time, so it would always be possible to follow a divergent working step of creation of such an aspect by a convergent step. In the end, the users are free to decide whenever they like to describe the influences. The assumption is that the structure of the socio-technical organisation, the communication pattern of the social system in relation to the functions and presentation of the technical system, guides the users to work according to the approach of Liu et al.

The explanations above are relating the social context of the new technical system Rambla to the theory of creativity, collaboration and concept generation. This section has shown the details that have to be considered during the design of the technical system. In the next section the concrete implementation will be sketched and after that an evaluation will be described.

5   Design and Architecture

Following (R14), Rambla is designed as a Rich Internet Application (RIA) [4], accessible via a Uniform Resource Locator (URL) using a modern web browser. Additionally, a broad selection of mobile clients is possible. The technical system

"Pool", introduced in Sect. 2, is also designed as a RIA and already adopted by the social system. So it can be suggested that a RIA implementation has the potential to become adopted.

As described above, the collaboration using Rambla requires a lot of interaction between the user and the shared material. Consequently, the system will produce a high communication ratio between the clients in order to keep the shared material synchronized. For the purpose of preventing blocked states of the system for the users, the communication with remote computers should be reduced to the required ones. So, the client-side is handling the events and inputs at first. Only after detecting the requirement of synchronisation the client will initialize a communication.

For the purpose of implementing the communication between clients as forced by (R1), the central server has to be mentioned, which is implicitly given on a RIA based on HTTP, HTML, CSS and JavaScript. The server always has to reroute the communication. Preventing the effort to create a connection each time a communication has to be done, the system initiates WebSockets. So, if a client system decides to synchronize the results of a user interaction with all other clients, it uses an open WebSocket connection to send the results to the central server. The server uses the WebSocket connections to all other clients to propagate the updates.

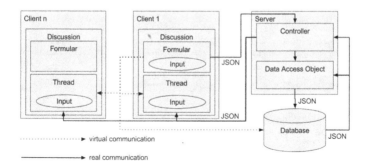

Fig. 1. Virtual communication between the clients for the purpose of sharing one consistent state.

Figure 1 shows the realization of the virtual communication, exemplified by the synchronisation of the discussion. The client sends entered input to the server that saves it into the database and supplements it by information unknown to the creating client. The server sends the completed input to all clients, including the creating one. The clients add the new content into the discussion thread, which shows all input in a chronological order.

The client implementation is realized using the JavaScript Framework *react*.[2] This allows to separate the different functions and areas into components and

---

[2] https://facebook.github.io/react/index.html, visited on 2016-04-14.

helps during the development process. Particularly, the implementation of a highly reactive user interface using WebSockets becomes manageable by the differed *react* components. The system uses the components in a hierarchical form, following the composite pattern [7]. Thus, a form and a thread compose a discussion (R1), as shown in Fig. 1.

Figure 2 presents the user interface of Rambla. The three basic elements, discussion, concept and the set of explicit aspects will be shown using three different components next to each other (R10). While the discussion will use the left side, the concept and the set of explicit aspects will share the right side of the website (R8). The system implements functions for adding, editing and deleting inputs for the discussion (R1) and connects this functions with the equivalents for explicit aspects (R2). Also, discussion input will be ordered by its creation date (R4). Furthermore, it is possible to add new influences by adding a label (R13) at first and assigning a value afterwards (R5). For the latter function the user has to select the label of an influence and an explicitly described aspect. A new form allows to add a value will replace the form at the bottom of the concept. The entered value is saved at the relation between the aspect and the influence label (R11). These labels are grouped by predefined sections (R12).

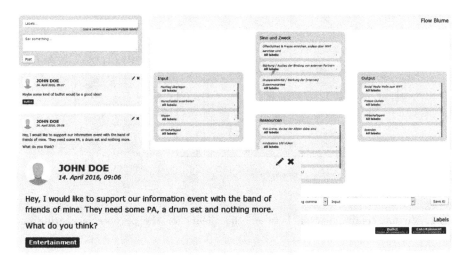

Fig. 2. The user interface of Rambla, showing the layout. For reasons of readability one discussion input is zoomed in.

In addition to the functions described above, it is possible to change the name of aspects and to define if the aspect should be excluded (R7). For this purpose, the user has to select the aspect, which she/he wants to change and a form will be shown in the bottom of the aspects area, which allows the editing.

By the selection of an aspect, the discussion will be shortened to the set of input, which are assigned to the selected aspect (R3). Also the selection of an aspect changes the visualisation of the concept (R9). While by default, the concept shows for each influence label its aggregated value, after the selection of an aspect its special influence will be shown below the aggregated value.

Such a detailed view of influence values can be displayed for all influence labels, by selecting them. A users click on it presents a list, whose items consist of the aspects name and the specific value given by the aspect. This list will also be shown below the aggregated value. Such an aggregated value of all values described by some aspects is shown inside the concept for every influence label (R6).

6   Evaluation

The following section presents a system's evaluation, showing that the system is implemented in such a way it will motivate the users to work on a process like the approach of Liu et al. [14]. The usage of the approach implies that the working procedure of the users shows the patterns of divergent and convergent working steps as described in Subsect. 3.3. So, the system is an example case for supporting a loosely structured organization of volunteers executing the complex task of concept generation.

6.1   Hypothesis and Data Collection

In this paper one hypothesis will be examined, while much more was investigated during the study. The detailed results are available in [16]. Here, the following hypothesis will be analysed: The system is designed in such a way that the users will adopt the approach of Liu et al. without any external assistance. As mentioned in Sect. 4 the social system requires the consideration of this approach for the purpose of adoption and participation of new members. So, this seems to be one major step to integrate the new technical system Rambla into the social system. The set of available system functions and their presentation to the user will be investigated by evaluating this hypothesis. This way the evaluation outlines to what extent the system fits the needs of a loosely structured organization performing the task of collaboratively generating concepts.

Focusing on the approach during the development is the base for the given assumption and Sect. 5 shows that the system allows working procedures following that approach. But whether users select the working steps in the right order can only be examined by a qualitative analysis of the users behavior. Additionally, the qualitative analysis will be underpinned by a questionnaire, which is analyzed in a quantitative manner.

The qualitative analysis is based on a chronologically sorted list of logged user actions. These actions were classified as a divergent or convergent activity and the resulting sequences were interpreted in the context of the approach. The system saves every action inside the database to generate a set of data that could be used for this purpose.

Focusing the presented system Rambla, the detailed development and discussion of aspects can be understood as the divergent phase, while the description of the influences of the aspects inside the concept marks the convergent working phase. The divergent steps are the creation and editing of aspects and discussion input. The convergent ones are the assignment of aspects to discussion input, the change of the status of aspects (included or excluded) and the creation of influence labels and values. The deletion of aspects and discussion input can also be described as a kind of convergent step, but this would imply that the function of exclusion for aspects is not being used. So, it is case-sensitive to decide if an activity of deletion will be a divergent or convergent working step. This meets the definition of divergent and convergent steps, while the functions described as divergent ones will always expand the set of aspects or extend the detailed description of an aspect. The functions that have been described as convergent working steps, will always imply a kind of analysis and cognitive load. Additionally, they are used for the purpose of clustering the set of input as well as reducing or extending the descriptions of influences by values inside the concept. The decision if the working procedure is following the approach was driven by the ordering and weighting of the working steps.

The underpinned quantitative analysis is based on a questionnaire that is designed as a set of items which could be assessed by a five-points-likert scale. Additionally, a closing free-text field for extra comments on the system and an input field for the users name is prepared. The latter is used to associate the questionnaire with the user's actions for the purpose of estimating its validity. The combination of both methods has been chosen with regards to the other objectives of the study. Some of them can be examined only by the qualitative approach, others only with the quantitative one. Table 1 lists the items of the questionnaire those have been used for the quantitative analysis of the described hypothesis. It has to be noted that these items determine the subjective impression of the participants. This will support the qualitative analysis of their working steps with regards to the difference between the noticed interaction with the system and the real done interaction. This way it becomes possible to identify

Table 1. Items of the questionnaire with regards to the evaluated hypothesis.

1	Before I changed the concept, I had reflected about this amendments
2	The discussion input of other users and their amendments of the concept have not influenced my activities with regards to the system.
3	If I had an idea for the concept, I have always recorded it inside the concept.
4	What I have done inside the system was always based on the actions of other users.
5	I have always discussed a theme, before I reflected about its influences to the concept.
6	If a theme occurred during the discussion, I always noted some possible impacts inside the concept

the influence of the system itself to the chosen working procedure. After using the system, the participants were requested to fill out the given questionnaires.

6.2 Study Setting

The task of the participants was to develop ideas for an action that is common for Viva con Agua. In the end, they have to transform the ideas into influences described inside a concept.

As mentioned in Sect. 4 and 5, the implemented type of concept is already known by the members of the social system. Nevertheless, the participants already had some experiences in working with this kind of concept, because in the context of this study they would not have enough time to learn the basic principles. Research focusing the work of inexperienced people can be part of the future perspective. So, eleven people which have or had roles inside the social system by which they often mingle with the used kind of concept, agreed to become participant for the study. Groups were formed under the condition that every group contains people which know each other and people which are unknown for the rest of the group. This should ensure real communication without a communication only based on implicit context information. Additionally, the groups should have the same size, so two groups of four members and one group with three members have been established. Such grouping supports the comparability of the results to reduce the influence of external factors as a cause for identified problems or findings.

The eleven participants had to work with the system during two weeks. As usual for the organisation they did it in their free time and got less instructions about the usage of the system and the working procedures. Preventing a time consuming process of initial ideation and decision-making inside the given group constellations, an initial frame was given. The participants had to create a concept for an event concerning the "World-Water-Day". This day is widely known inside the social system and a huge set of events were scheduled at this day during the last years. Therefor, it can be assumed that the participants had not to inform themselves about this day and mostly they will have a real interest in creating a concept for an event at this day. Additionally, the ideas of the last year can be used as a base by the participants.

6.3 Results

First of all, it was possible to identify both phases of divergent and convergent activities in the correct order, by a qualitative analysis of the logged user actions. The actions classified in Sect. 6.1 mostly followed the ordering described in Sect. 3.3. So the users initially worked in a divergent phase of intensive discussion, naturally a group activity. During the divergent phase the users have always assigned an explicitly described aspect to each discussion input. This means they have done a divergent working step (creation of input) followed by a convergent one (assignment). Mostly, the assignment of an aspect was not done during only one step. The users often added or edited aspects, assigned one and removed the assignment. So the alternating switch of divergent and convergent working steps is observable. For example, one participant added a discussion input to suggest alternative possibilities for the realization of a "Flash mob". This divergent working step was followed by a convergent one, assigning the existing aspect "Flash mob" to the new input, although the system allows to do this in one step. Mostly, the users changed their assignment between a new discussion input and existing aspects after they had saved their initial thoughts. So they performed a fast convergent action after they had seen the resulting discussion thread presented by the system. That means the distribution between divergent and convergent steps followed the approach of Liu et al. [14] and is influenced by the systems presentation of the input.

However, the convergent phase can not be characterized as a group activity. This second phase was also entered by some participants, but it was never more than one group member. So the convergent phase was not entered by the whole group. It turns out that the support of collaboration by the system has to be extended. Most of the groups run into trouble while they try to reach a group consensus about the current working phase, because making such a coordination decision is not supported. Also the decision was made using the discussion thread, as exemplified by a participant (translated from German): "So, we've collected some ideas. Should we start to play around with 1–2 concrete suggestions?" Furthermore, it was possible to observe that the changes the users made during the convergent working phase were not noticed by the other group members.

Finally, the divergent phase follows the approach of Liu et al. and this is influenced by the system's design. Additionally, all groups tried to enter the convergent phase as a group activity. Their decision-making processes for this purpose were all initiated after reaching an acceptable set of ideas during the divergent phase. Also users initiating a convergent working phase did it always following a divergent one. So the ordering of the phases follows the approach. The analysis showed that the convergent phase did often not contain a divergent step. This is an issue that could be addressed in future research and development. Considering that the results of the divergent phase are by definition necessary for entering the convergent phase, the ordering of the phases is more influenced by the method itself than the new tool.

Next to the qualitative analysis of the users' working steps, the results are underpinned by the quantitative evaluation of the questionnaire. The evaluation of the first item shows that the users rarely planned their actions using the system. Following this, the motivation of the users to work by the approach of Liu et al. can be taken as a success of the system's presentation of functions. Additionally, the results of the items two and four implied that the users tried to orientate their own actions towards the group consensus. So the system has to motivate the whole group working by the approach. The behavior of one participant exemplified that the system supports the motivation of the whole group. She opened a discussion with one input and multiple aspects. Following this she added several influence descriptions to the concept. Afterwards, when the other group members restricted their interaction to detailed discussion, the participant also limited herself to the discussion and the creation of aspects. The proceeding itself was not discussed during this process of decision making inside the group. So the awareness about the others' behavior inside the system motivated the user to align her behavior to that of the group.

The items three, five and six are focusing the concrete sequence of working steps. The evaluation of item three is inconsistent with the observed behavior. The concepts are mainly not described, but the participants mentioned that they recorded every idea inside the concept. The item seems to be unclear. Following item five, some participants noticed that they have discussed an aspect before they thought about potential influences, others did it the other around. This finding underpins the result that the construction of a group consensus has to be supported. At least the participants agree with each other that they try to discuss at first, followed by a description of the aspect's influences inside the concept.

As shown above, the results of the qualitative analysis of working steps are underpinned by the qualitative evaluation of the questionnaire.

7   Discussion and Future Opportunities

The presented work shows the development of a collaborative tool supporting creative concept generation. In Sect. 2 the collaborating social system is described and its impact to the tools design is sketched. This is followed by an overview of related work, the requirement and the implementation of the tool. Afterwards, a study evaluating the tools design shows that the approach on creative processing of Liu et al. [14] will be supported. Additionally, it is shown that the system helps the user in selecting the correct working steps without forcing them into a specially designed working procedure.

The most problematic part of the evaluation is the notice that the convergent working phase of the creative process was not entered as a group activity. As a reason has been identified the missing possibility to define the group phase by the collaborating people. So, the implementation of coordinating functions will be a crucial step to bring the system in production. Especially, an explicitly support of the decision making process has to be created. Additionally, the implementation of an awareness system was only rudimentary given, because of the different focus of this work. So, making users aware of the changes inside the concept would help to communicate the process phase a user has entered. Furthermore, the transfer of discussion content into explicit influences inside the concept has to be analyzed. Currently, a detailed concept results in much scrolling, because the lists of influence labels are very long. Functions have to be designed that overcomes this limitation and helps the user to see changes very fast.

At least an interesting proposal by a study participant has to be mentioned. It was observed that a kind of a history function will help to note every change that was done in the users absence. This way, it will be possible to detect working steps of the convergent phase done by other users and to respond to it. Such a way, the users can define the currently entered group activity without explicitly decision making. Instead they can use the principle of a critical mass of users entering a phase of the working process to define the current group activity.

Next to the implications given by the discussion of the results above, there are some more possible future developments. It will be interesting to try the system for the purpose of organisational knowledge. Next to well implemented search and categorisation features the implementation of a recommendation system can solve the task. Graph structures using aspects of concepts as nodes and discussion content as arcs between nodes enable the recommendation of the consideration of aspects based on discussion of other concepts.

References

1. Appelt, W., Busbach, U., Koch, T.: Kollaborationsorientierte asynchrone Werkzeuge. In: Schwabe, G., Streitz, N., Unland, R. (eds.) CSCW-Kompendium, pp. 194–203. Springer, Berlin (2001)
2. Asimov, I.: How do people get new ideas? (2014). https://www.technologyreview.com/s/531911/isaac-asimov-asks-how-do-people-get-new-ideas/
3. Becker, K., Bacelo, A.P.T.: The evaluation of GRADD: a GDSS supporting asynchronous and distributed meetings. In: Proceeding of CRIWG 2000, pp. 19–26. IEEE (2000)
4. Bozzon, A., Comai, S., Fraternali, P., Carughi, G.T.: Conceptual modeling and code generation for rich internet applications. In: Proceedings of ICWE 2006, pp. 353–360. ACM, New York (2006)
5. Chen, M.-H., Zhang, J., Lee, J.: Making collective progress visible for sustained knowledge building. In: Proceedings of CSCL 2013, vol. 1, pp. 81–88. ISLS, Madison (2013)
6. Csikszentmihalyi, M.: Creativity: Flow and the Psychology of Discovery and Invention. Harper Perennial, New York (1997)
7. Gamma, E., Helm, R., Johnson, R., Vlissides, J.: Design Patterns: Elements of Reusable Object-Oriented Software. Addison-Wesley, Westford (2010)
8. Herrmann, T., Kunau, G., Loser, K.-U., Menold, N.: Sociotechnical walkthrough: designing technology along work processes. In: Proceedings of PDC 2004, vol. 2, pp. 132–141. ACM, New York (2004)
9. Herrmann, T.: Support of collaborative creativity for co-located meetings. In: Randall, D., Salembier, P. (eds.) From CSCW to Web 2.0: European Developments in Collaborative Design, pp. 65–95. Springer, London (2010)
10. Holmer, T., Haake, J., Streitz, N.: Kollaborationsorientierte synchrone Werkzeuge. In: Schwabe, G., Streitz, N., Unland, R. (eds.) CSCW-Kompendium, pp. 180–193. Springer, Berlin (2001)
11. Kunau, G.: Facilitating computer supported cooperative work with socio-technical self-descriptions. Universität Dortmund (2006)
12. Kunz, W., Rittel, H.W.J.: Issues as elements of information systems. Working Paper 131. Inst. Urban and Regional Devt., Univ. Calif. at Berkeley (1970)
13. Link, G.J.P., Siemon, D., de Vreede, G.-J., Robra-Bissantz, S.: Evaluating anchored discussion to foster creativity in online collaboration. In: Baloian, N., Zorian, Y., Taslakian, P., Shoukouryan, S. (eds.) CRIWG 2015. LNCS, vol. 9334, pp. 28–44. Springer, Heidelberg (2015)
14. Liu, Y.-C., Chakrabarti, A., Bligh, T.: Towards an 'ideal' approach for concept generation. Des. Stud. **24**(4), 341–355 (2003)

15. Nijstad, B.A., Stroebe, W.: How the group affects the mind: a cognitive model of idea generation in groups. Pers. Soc. Psychol. Rev. **10**(3), 186–213 (2006)
16. Sell, J.: Konstruktion eines technischen Systems zur kollaborativen Gruppenkreativität im Kontext der Konzepterzeugung. Diploma thesis, Humboldt Universität zu Berlin (2016)
17. Sternberg, R.J.: Handbook of Creativity. Cambridge University Press, Cambridge (1999)
18. Verheij, B.: ArguMed - a template-based argument mediation system for lawyers. In: Proceedings of JURIX 1998, pp. 113–130 (1998)
19. Yuizono, T., Munemori, J., Kayano, A., Yoshino, T., Shigenobu, T.: A proposal of knowledge creative groupware for seamless knowledge. In: Negoita, M.G., Howlett, R.J., Jain, L.C. (eds.) KES 2004. LNCS (LNAI), vol. 3214, pp. 876–882. Springer, Heidelberg (2004)

Effectiveness of Tabletop Interaction Using Tablet Terminals in a Shared Virtual Workspace

Naoto Ito, Hideyuki Takada$^{(\boxtimes)}$, and Ian Piumarta

Faculty of Information Science and Engineering, Ritsumeikan University,
1-1-1 Noji-Higashi, Kusatsu, Shiga 525-8577, Japan
htakada@cs.ritsumei.ac.jp
http://www.cm.is.ritsumei.ac.jp/~htakada/index_e.html

Abstract. In this paper we present an empirical study of the effectiveness of tablet-based interaction for users of a tabletop shared virtual workspace. We built a tabletop interaction environment in which tablet terminals present sliding windows onto a larger, shared virtual workspace, allowing multiple users to view and manipulate objects within the workspace. The environment offers a physical paradigm to support groupwork within the shared virtual space, providing users with good situational awareness of their viewing position with respect both to the viewing positions of other users and to the location of content within the large virtual workspace. We conducted experiments to compare 'tablet scrolling' with a more traditional 'swipe-scroll' paradigm for the ease remembering the positions of objects, locating the viewable area within the overall workspace, and communicating locations between users during groupwork. The results show that the tabletop interaction environment enables workers to communicate more effectively than 'swipe-scroll' paradigms, although difficulties associated with scrolling and physical movement may decrease the efficiency of individual work.

Keywords: Collaborative work · Tablet-based interfaces · Tabletop computing · Shared virtual environments

1 Introduction

Tablet terminals, such as Apple's iPad, are now common elements of our personal computing environment. A major use of these terminals is content delivery, including browsing the Web, watching movies, reading books, and playing games. Productive work is also supported to some extent by word processing, spreadsheet, and media editing tools. This type of tool, however, still offers limited support for direct collaboration between several concurrent users. Apple's Air-Drop, for example, only supports the exchange of website URLs and photos. Google's online 'office suite' enables users to simultaneously edit the same document, but does not convey awareness of the particular part of the document on which each user is working. These limitations are fundamental to the traditional style of using a tablet terminal as a personal, hand-held device.

© Springer International Publishing Switzerland 2016
T. Yuizono et al. (Eds.): CRIWG 2016, LNCS 9848, pp. 98–114, 2016.
DOI: 10.1007/978-3-319-44799-5_8

Given the form factor of tablet terminals, we can consider another style of use. Placing a tablet terminal on a tabletop allows multiple users to interact simultaneously with it. Searching web pages, watching movies, or editing documents using the terminal become shared activities. This style of interaction provides users with awareness of each other's working situation; they can directly share features of interest within the content, and physical pointing becomes an effective mode of communication. A problem remains, however, in that the screen size is not large enough to support more than two users.

One possible solution is to extend the shared workspace virtually over a tabletop surface, and then use multiple tablet terminals each of which provides a smaller *window* onto the larger virtual workspace. Such an environment gives an interface similar to a tabletop display except that users can see only that portion of the workspace over which the tablet terminals are placed, instead of displaying the whole workspace on a large display. The environment is expected to provide users with good situational awareness of their viewing position as we can find it on a tabletop display.

In the present work we build an interactive tabletop environment exposing a large virtual shared workspace via tablet terminals and investigate aspects of its effectiveness for users working individually or collaboratively. As described in Sect. 2, although various kinds of system have been proposed to support interaction among users of mobile terminals, no studies appear to have been published on the effectiveness of environments in which users perform collaborative tasks within a virtual workspace projected via mobile terminals onto a tabletop surface.

The rest of this paper is organized as follows. Section 2 introduces related work and clarifies the contributions of our work. Section 3 describes the functional requirements and expected benefits along with implementation of our prototype tabletop environment. Section 4 presents experimental results on the performance of searching objects and user study of manipulating objects by multiple users, compared with a swipe-scroll based system which has been developed for this evaluation. Section 5 concludes this research and state future direction.

2   Related Work

Much attention has been paid to supporting collaboration among users with mobile terminals.

ConnecTables [10] allows users to couple two or more displays on demand. When two ConnecTable displays are placed close to each other, they form a homogeneous display area for users to work in parallel and to exchange information by dragging objects from one display to another. G-Pad [3] is a flexible workspace expansion system for idea generation letting multiple tablet devices be connected and separated. The purpose of these systems is to enlarge a shared physical display by extending it across the screens of multiple devices, whereas our system uses multiple devices as windows on a large virtual workspace that extends across any available horizontal surface.

Many ideas have been proposed to support transferring data between devices. GroupTogether [6] exploits micro-mobility of users to trigger transferring objects from one device to another among *F-formations* (the physical arrangement of people within small, focused, conversational groups). MobiSurf [9] integrates personal devices with an interactive surface to facilitate smooth transitions between individual and group work while still taking advantage of both types of device. Easy coupling methods using sensors and cameras equipped with mobile devices have also been proposed [1,4]. These focus on exchanging objects between individual devices, and there is no concept of a single shared workspace supporting multiple users.

Several groups have investigated spatially-aware computing environments. Chameleon [2] uses palmtop computers which act as an 'information lens'. The palmtop senses its position and orientation relative to a physical object, such as a wall map, and displays information relevant to that specific position. Peephole Displays [11] allows users to physically move a hand-held display around to see different parts of a larger workspace. The portable personal displays library *pizu* [5] can be used to build applications that share the same information space with spatially-aware mobile displays. These systems assume that each user holds a palm-sized device in their hand, possibly operated with a stylus pen; the potential of interaction with tablet-sized terminals is not considered. Usability studies were also limited to simple operations such as selection, viewing, and drawing.

HuddleLamp [7] supports spatially-aware, multi-user and multi-device applications for around-the-table collaboration. A desk lamp style tool tracks the movements and positions of mobile devices and hands on the table. A mobile device can act as a lens or 'peephole' to physically navigate virtual information as if it were situated in physical space. Several applications have been built using HuddleLamp to validate the design; however, the effectiveness of this style of collaboration has not been sufficiently studied.

The purpose of this paper is to present our empirical findings on the effectiveness of tabletop interaction using multiple tablet terminals to display sliding windows onto a shared virtual workspace, based on our implementation of a virtual tabletop environment. Our environment inherits the advantages of tabletop displays, such as a communal experience of the content and identification using physical pointing. In contrast with tabletop displays, our workspace is not fixed; the virtual environment is created by the tablet terminals, which require only to be placed on any available tabletop surface.

3   Tabletop Interaction Environment

The tabletop interaction environment allows users to see a virtual shared workspace extended over a tabletop through the displays of tablet terminals, and to manipulate objects within the virtual workspace by direct manipulation using gestures on the touch-sensitive tablet displays.

3.1 Functional Requirements

Only a part of the virtual shared workspace is shown on each tablet terminal, and users can change the part displayed by *sliding* the tablet terminal around on the tabletop as shown in Fig. 1. Multiple terminals can be placed on the tabletop, and each tablet will display the part of the virtual workspace that corresponds to its position. The number of terminals does not have to equal to the number of users; many users may use a few terminals, or a few users may use many terminals.

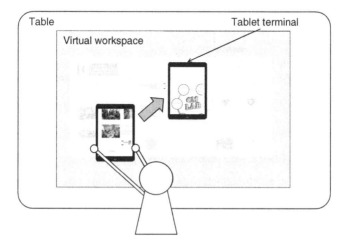

Fig. 1. Tabletop interaction using a tablet terminal

We identified that the following operations, each of which is shown in Fig. 2, must be supported for users to manipulate objects in the workspace.

Editing an object larger than the display area: Users have to be able to move the terminal while editing an object larger than the display area.

Moving an object beyond the display area: Users have to be able to move the terminal while dragging an object, if the destination position is not already visible on the display.

Searching for objects to manipulate: Users have to be able to move the terminal so that the object to be manipulated is displayed on the screen.

Manipulating an object by multiple users: Multiple users using multiple terminals must be able to manipulate a single object, of which only a portion is shown on each user's display, with immediate reflection of the manipulations they perform.

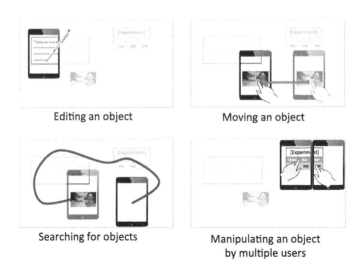

Fig. 2. Operations to be supported

3.2   Expected Benefits and Evaluation Methods

Our goal is to investigate the effectiveness of a tabletop virtual interaction environment compared with a traditional 'swipe-scroll' system, with respect to the four operations described in the previous section. The expected benefits of the virtual environment and our methods of evaluation are summarized below.

1. *Editing and moving an object*
   Yee [11] has already demonstrated the benefits of physically moving a terminal, as an alternative to swipe-scrolling, while editing or repositioning an object. (For example, one hand slides the terminal while the other hand drags the object or continues to manipulate its contents.) Since our tabletop environment has similar characteristics to Yee's environment, we do not evaluate its effectiveness for these two operations here.

2. *Searching for objects*
   We are not aware of any previous investigation of locating objects in a context similar to ours. We therefore evaluate the effectiveness of the virtual tabletop environment by comparing it to swipe-scrolling, with an experiment in which a single user searches for multiple targets placed within the virtual workspace. Compared to swipe-scrolling, the expected benefit of the tabletop environment is a reduction in unnecessary 'panning' around the search space, because users can associate the location of an object in the virtual space with a specific physical location on the tabletop.

3. *Multiple users manipulating multiple objects*

No investigation regarding the manipulation of many objects by multiple concurrent users has been done in this kind of tabletop environment. We therefore investigate the characteristics of our tabletop environment compared to swipe-scroll systems with an experiment in which multiple users classify and arrange multiple objects within the virtual workspace. Benefits of the tabletop interaction environment are expected to include easier cooperation when working on a common task because of the correspondence between virtual and physical placement providing a more intuitive understanding of the locations of objects being manipulated by a user as well as the locations of objects being manipulated by other users. The mode of interaction between users is also expected to be more natural, because of their ability to associate and indicate physical positions on the tabletop corresponding to the locations of objects.

3.3   Experimental Implementation

We now describe an experimental implementation of our tabletop interactive virtual environment. This implementation is not intended to be a fully-functional product, but rather to provide sufficient functionality to perform the experiments needed for our evaluation objectives.

Detecting Terminal Movement. The most significant function for the tabletop interaction environment is to scroll the display of the virtual space when a terminal device is moved. We therefore need to detect and measure the movement of each terminal across the tabletop.

The Apple iPad was chosen to serve as the mobile terminal in our prototype. We first attempted to measure movement using the iPad's built-in accelerometer, but were unable to achieve the accuracy required by our tabletop environment. We then tried attaching a Bluetooth wireless mouse to the side of each iPad for motion detection, but problems with data loss prevented this from being a reliable solution. A reliable compromise was finally reached by communicating motion information to the iPad indirectly via a PC.

Figure 3 shows the final communication arrangement. A Bluetooth mouse attached to the iPad is paired with a MacBook. When the iPad is moved, a corresponding cursor movement occurs on the MacBook. (If the cursor reaches the edge of the screen, it is warped back to the center to ensure continuous and unlimited motion measurement.) The cursor movement is then transmitted to the iPad over Wi-Fi using a UDP-based protocol. The iPad responds by scrolling its display in the opposite direction to its movement.

This implementation has some limitations. First, the iPad terminal cannot be rotated because the orientation of the displayed area is fixed. Second, some inconsistency occurs between terminal movement and display scrolling that can prevent precise correspondence between physical position on the tabletop and

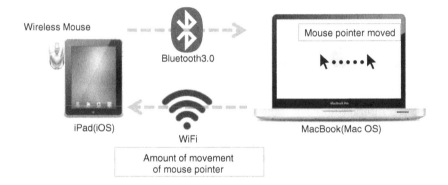

Fig. 3. Indirect tracking of terminal movement

the displayed area within the virtual workspace. This is due to a 0.2 s delay that is introduced when the mouse cursor is returned from the edge of the MacBook screen to its center; the consequent error depends on the speed of movement of the terminal. This positional error gradually accumulates because we use relative mouse movement. In order to compensate for this cumulative error, we provide a function to re-calibrate the scroll position at any time.

Basic Functions. In addition to scrolling as described in the previous section, the following basic functionality has also been implemented.

1. *Dragging an object*
   Objects can be moved around the workspace by dragging them across the screen with a finger. If the terminal is moved while a finger is dragging an object, the position of the object in the larger virtual workspace is changed according to both the dragging gesture and the movement of the terminal. In this way, changing the position of the physical screen's window within the larger workspace can be achieved at the same time as moving an object.

2. *Zooming the workspace*
   Tablet applications typically provide a zoom function to enlarge or shrink the user's view of the workspace. In our environment, zooming functionality is provided to support an overview of the workspace on the tablet screen. When a 'pinching-in' gesture is performed on screen, the display is zoomed out to display the entire virtual workspace. If the terminal is moved while zoomed out, the original magnification ratio is restored to maintain the correspondence between the displayed area and the physical position within the workspace.

Multiuser Functionality. Our tabletop interaction environment shares a single virtual workspace, overlaid on a physical table, among multiple tablet terminals. Manipulations of objects within the workspace must therefore be *mirrored* among the multiple terminals. In our prototype implementation, only the position of objects within the workspace is synchronized among terminals.

Synchronization of the shared workspace among terminals is performed using the MultipeerConnectivity framework provided by the iOS platform. At the time of starting up the application, MultipeerConnectivity peer-to-peer connections among terminals are established. When an object is moved on one of the terminals, the released position of the object is broadcast using the MultipeerConnectivity channel and the recipient terminals update the position of the object accordingly.

4 Experiments

In addition to our virtual tabletop environment (described in the previous section) we also implemented a traditional 'swipe-scroll' system. We evaluated the effectiveness of the tabletop environment by comparing it with the swipe-scroll system.

4.1 Experimental Swipe-Scroll System

The swipe-scroll system provides scrolling, dragging and zooming functionality similar to the tabletop interaction environment. This functionality is described in more detail below.

1. *Scrolling*
   The displayed area can be scrolled with a swiping gesture.

2. *Dragging*
   The position of an object can be changed with a dragging gesture. When an object is dragged to the edge of the display, the display area scrolls continuously to keep the object on the display. Dragging an object and scrolling the displayed area can therefore be performed simultaneously. This operation is synchronized among the multiple terminals; when the position of an object changes on one terminal, its position also changes on the other terminals. To mitigate conflicting inputs from multiple terminals, when a user is manipulating an object that object is hidden from all other screens for the duration of the manipulation. This is achieved by multicasting 'hide' and 'show' messages containing the object's ID to all other terminals over a MultipeerConnectivity channel.

3. *Zooming*

The displayed workspace can be zoomed in and out with a pinch gesture. Zoom can be set to any ratio, from 1:1 to displaying the entire workspace. Object manipulation and scrolling can both be performed while the workspace is zoomed out. (This behavior is different to that of the tabletop environment described in the previous section, where a 1:1 ratio is restored whenever the terminal is moved).

Two experiments were performed, comparing the swipe-scroll system to the tabletop system for object search and for collaborative manipulation. For clarity we present each experiment separately, including its results and a short discussion of them.

4.2   Object Search Experiment

The purpose of this experiment is to evaluate the effectiveness of the environment when searching for objects.

Experiment Design. The task to be evaluated is scrolling the display to make a target object visible. Participants are required to search for a series of target objects (numbered from 1 to 9) in sequence, and delete each object by double-tapping it. (The drag functionality is not used because the assigned task requires only searching and deleting. The zoom functionality is also disabled, to exaggerate relative strengths and weaknesses of the two systems when panning to find an off-screen object).

The participants were eight Computer Science students ('User A' to 'User H'), divided into two groups of four people. All of them were familiar with the swipe-scrolling operation on smartphones or tablets. Both groups performed the task twice, first using the swipe-scroll system and then using the tabletop system. Two patterns of objects were used, as shown in Fig. 4, designed so that several numbers appear in the display while searching for a target number. The first group performed the task using pattern (1) on the swipe-scroll system, and then

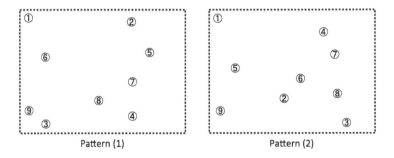

Fig. 4. Numbered object patterns

Table 1. Results of observations: time taken and pixels scrolled

Time (secs)	A	B	C	D	E	F	G	H	Mean	SD
				Users						
Swipe	22.4	30.4	33.0	25.9	43.2	35.0	44.6	41.7	34.5	7.66
Tabletop	58.9	32.4	52.0	36.4	32.5	51.0	120.7	68.1	56.5	27.11

$(p = 0.072)$

Scrolling ($\times 10^3$ pixels)	A	B	C	D	E	F	G	H	Mean	SD
				Users						
Swipe	27.8	27.8	27.3	27.0	48.2	32.1	44.7	33.1	33.4	7.834
Tabletop	62.0	28.2	22.3	34.3	26.6	34.8	56.8	44.6	38.7	13.536

$(p = 0.396)$

Table 2. Results from the questionnaire

Importance of each factor	
Easiness of scrolling	0.538
Easiness of remembering the place of numbers seen once	0.148
Easiness of grasping the current viewing area	0.314

	Weights for each factor		
	Scrolling	Remembering numbers	Grasping area
Swipe	0.805	0.432	0.401
Tabletop	0.195	0.568	0.599

Total preference	
Swipe	0.622
Tabletop	0.378

using pattern (2) on the tabletop system. The second group performed the task using pattern (2) on the swipe-scroll system, and then using pattern (1) on the tabletop system. They performed the tasks without knowing the patterns beforehand. The workspace was 74 cm wide and 49 cm high.

During the experiment we recorded the time spent searching for the nine objects, and the amount of scrolling that had to be performed. After the experiment participants were asked to answer a questionnaire based on the paired comparison method, which was then evaluated using the Analytic Hierarchy Process (AHP) [8].

Results. Table 1 shows the time spent scrolling and the distance scrolled while searching for objects in each environment. The time spent scrolling in a swipe-based system tends to be shorter than in a tabletop virtual environment,

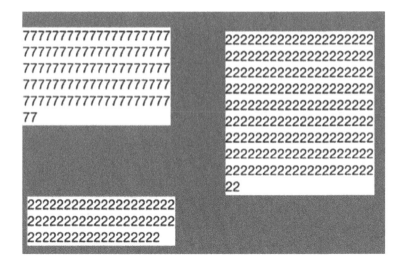

Fig. 5. Objects labeled with numbers

although there is no statistically significant difference in either scroll time or distance between the two systems.

In some cases such as those for Users A and G, the time and distance values for the tabletop environment are much higher. We consider this to be due to the difficulty of recognizing the edges of the virtual workspace. We observed that users spent a lot of time searching for those objects which were placed at the edges of the workspace.

Table 2 shows the results of an evaluation using the AHP. The result shows that the swipe-based system is more effective than the tabletop environment for performing the required task. Considering the first table, the ease of scrolling is seen to be the most important factor while completing the task. Additionally, the second table shows that participants considered scrolling to be easier using the swipe-based system. We consider these aspects, related to ease of scrolling, to be the reason why participants completed the tasks in shorter time using the swipe-based system. Conversely, the ease of remembering the location of numbers within the workspace area was greater in the tabletop interaction environment. This demonstrates a more intuitive grasp of spatial relationships between objects within the virtual space. These effects, however, were not reflected in the overall expressed preference because the factors evaluated were relatively unimportant for the task being performed.

Discussion. In this experiment, participants considered ease of scrolling to be the most important factor, since it accounts for most of work performed during the task. To scroll the tabletop environment participants had to move around the table, because the workspace extended beyond the area physically reachable from a static location. These factors likely contributed to the difference in reported ease of scrolling between the two systems.

In a more realistic task, the frequency of scrolling would be much lower because editing and rearrangement operations also occur on objects within the workspace. Also, the importance of remembering object locations and understanding their spatial relationships within the workspace would increase with the duration of the task being performed. The importance of these factors can be considered to increase the effectiveness of the tabletop environment.

4.3 Collaborative Object Manipulation Experiment

The purpose of this experiment is to investigate the effectiveness of the tabletop environment in terms of communication and behavior for users collaboratively arranging a number of shared objects.

Experiment Design. The task to be evaluated is arranging numbered objects into groups sharing the same number. Objects were labeled with digits from 1 to 9 and participants asked to move them around to form same-numbered groups.

The participants were eight Computer Science students, divided into two groups of four people. Each group performed two tasks, using the two systems one after the other. Eighty objects were arranged in the workspace, labeled with a subset of the possible digits (1–9), as shown in Fig. 5. Each task used a different set of labels, and participants did not know which numbers were present and which were missing. At normal zoom the numbers labeling the objects are visible, but when zoomed out the numbers are too small to read, as shown in Fig. 6. The first group performed the task using the swipe-scroll system with 7 different numbers labeling the objects, then used the tabletop system with 9 different labels. The second group performed the task using the tabletop system with 7 different labels, then used the swipe-scroll system with 9 different labels.

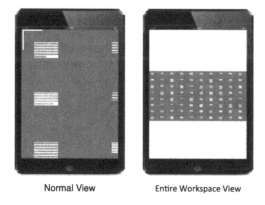

Normal View   Entire Workspace View

Fig. 6. Normal and zoomed workspace views

Fig. 7. An experiment in progress

Before performing these tasks, participants could practice using the systems for 3 min. Figure 7 shows one of the experiments in progress, with participants using the tabletop interaction environment to perform the task.

During the experiment we recorded how participants communicated and cooperated among themselves. After the experiment participants were asked to complete the questionnaire shown in Table 3, and the answers were analyzed to understand the relative advantages and disadvantages of each environment.

Results. Figure 8 shows the results of the questionnaire. Participants felt manipulation operations were easier in the swipe-based system, whereas the tabletop environment was better for communicating with others and for providing a sense of collaboration. For Q13 and Q14 the answers indicated that tasks were shared with other participants, and that each participant took charge of forming some of the groups of same-numbered objects. One of the teams performed the task by having each participant move objects to the center of the workspace if they were labeled with a number for which they were not responsible. In response to Q12 they answered that the zooming function was used in both systems to understand the overall state of the workspace.

Several differences in communication and behavior were observed during the tasks. Using the swipe-based system, although users communicated about where in theworkspace to place objects with a given number and who was responsible for each number, they performed the subsequent manipulation task almost personally and communicated far less than when using the tabletop environment. With the tabletop system, participants communicated throughout the tasks using pointing gestures to indicate specific locations on the table combined with spoken interaction using words such as "here". Some difficulty in passing objects between participants was observed, with users awkwardly stretching their arms or exchanging their physical positions when moving objects into an area near another user.

Table 3. Content of questionnaire

Q	Questions	Answer format	Answer options
1	Which system do you feel easy in scrolling?		'swipe-scroll'
2	Which system do you feel easy in dragging the labels?		
3	Which system do you feel easy in grasping which part of the workspace you are looking at?		
4	Which system do you feel easy in grasping the rough position of the labels in the workspace?		
5	Which system do you feel easy in grasping the precise position of the labels in the workspace?		'no difference'
6	Which system do you feel easy in recognizing which part of the workspace the other users are looking at?	multiple choice	
7	Which system do you feel easy in communicating with others?		
8	Which system do you feel easy in cooperating for manipulation with others?		'tabletop interaction'
9	Which system do you feel more stressful in performing the tasks?		
10	Which system do you feel fun in performing the tasks?		
11	Which system do you feel more sense of collaboration in performing tasks?		
12	How did you use the zooming function on each of the systems (in terms of purpose and method)?		
13	Did you split the task with other users? If so, how was the task split?	free text	
14	Did you have a task flow? If so, how did the task proceed?		

Discussion

Basic Operations. Based on the results of Q1 and Q2, the tabletop interaction environment was found to have disadvantages compared with the swipe-based system for basic operations such as scrolling and dragging. The effort needed to physically move the terminal appears to have affected the ease with which these operations could be performed.

Grasping Viewing Area. We expected that migrating objects between areas and collaborating with others would be easier in the tabletop environment, because users can situate themselves within the workspace by looking at their terminal's position on the table. We see from the result of Q6 that participants found it very easy to situate the working areas of other participants. On the other hand, Q3 reveals that participants found it harder to precisely situate their own working area within the overall workspace using the tabletop system than with the swipe-based. The reason for this is that in the tabletop environment users cannot perform a task while the display is zoomed out to show the entire

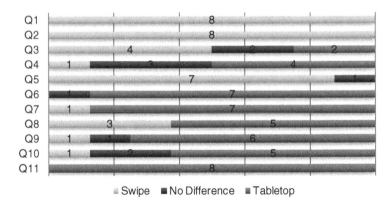

Fig. 8. Results from the questionnaire

workspace (physical and virtual distances must be in 1-to-1 correspondence while the terminal is moving), but they can do so in the swipe-based system. Also, because of the inconsistency in the relationship between terminal position and the viewing area within the workspace, users could not be certain that exactly the same workspace area was being revealed when the terminal was placed at the same position atop the table. Improving the tracking accuracy of terminal movement is a topic of future work.

Situating Objects within the Workspace. According to the results of Q4 and Q5, the tabletop environment was better for roughly situating an object within the overall space, whereas the swipe-based system was better for situating an object precisely. This also is due to the gradually-accumulating inconsistency between the physical and virtual positions of each terminal.

Communication among Users. Responses to Q7 indicate that the tabletop environment made communication easier between users. We understand this to be due to users being able to indicate easily and directly any location within the virtual space by physically pointing to the corresponding tabletop location and using explanatory phrases such as "here" and "over there". In contrast, with the swipe-based system we observed users using spoken phrases such as "upper left" or "lower right" to describe locations within the entire workspace, which seems to be a more limited method for conveying the positions of objects within the workspace.

Cooperation among Users. Participants offered divergent opinions in their responses to Q8. Cooperation was required in the tabletop environment to pass an object from one user to another. We expected that one user would use their terminal to move an object to an agreed-upon location in the workspace, and then a second user would retrieve it by moving their terminal to the same location on the tabletop. However, as described in Sect. 4.3, this operation was not performed as we expected. In the swipe-based system, conflicts occurred between users manipulating the same object at the same time. Both systems therefore presented their own particular disadvantages, which would affect the results of the questionnaire in very subjective ways.

4.4 Summary

Our findings can be summarized as follows:

- Searching for objects was found to be less easy in the tabletop environment compared to the swipe-based system, because of the effort required to physically move the terminal. Advantages of the tabletop environment were found to be better situational awareness and understanding of the working area's location within the overall workspace.
- The tabletop environment, with its tangible physical cues about object location, encouraged the efficient use of physical pointing and spoken explanations concerning objects within the workspace.
- A significant disadvantage of the tabletop environment was the uncertainty that a given object will be at the same location when a terminal is placed in the same position on the tabletop. Precise tracking of terminal movements is therefore required in the tabletop environment and similar systems to eliminate any uncertainty about the correlation between object position and terminal position.

5 Conclusion

We described an interactive tabletop environment using tablet terminals and presented our findings about the effectiveness of the environment to support groupwork compared to a more traditional swipe-scrolling system. We found that the tabletop environment enabled users to communicate more effectively during groupwork, but also reduced efficiency because of difficulties related to 'scrolling' the workspace using physical movement of terminals. Several disadvantages were related to imprecise tracking of terminal movement using a wireless mouse, such as spatial inconsistency and latency. Reducing these to unnoticeable levels should increase the efficiency of our environment, and should be considered of primary importance in environments similar to ours.

The tasks performed in our evaluations were limited to searching for and then spatially organising objects. Building and evaluating more realistic applications within our environment is essential to improve our understanding of its effectiveness.

Acknowledgements. This work was supported by JSPS KAKENHI Grant Number 25330249.

References

1. Dearman, D., Guy, R., Truong, K.: Determining the orientation of proximate mobile devices using their back facing camera. In: Proceedings of the SIGCHI Conference on Human Factors in Computing Systems, pp. 2231–2234 (2012)
2. Fitzmaurice, G.W.: Situated information spaces and spatially aware palmtop computers. Commun. ACM **36**(7), 39–49 (1993)
3. Kokogawa, T., Maeda, Y., Go, H., Itou, J., Munemori, J.: Improvement of web-based idea generation support system GUNGEN-SPIRAL II with multiple tablet devices. IPSJ J. **54**(2), 639–646 (2013)
4. Lin, C.P., Wang, C.Y., Chen, H.R., Chu, W.C., Chen, M.Y.: RealSense: directional interaction for proximate mobile sharing using built-in orientation sensors. In: Proceedings of the 21st ACM International Conference on Multimedia, pp. 777–780 (2013)
5. Luyten, K., Verpoorten, K., Coninx, K.: Ad-hoc co-located collaborative work with mobile devices. In: Proceedings of the 9th International Conference on Human Computer Interaction with Mobile Devices and Services, pp. 507–514 (2007)
6. Marquardt, N., Hinckley, K., Greenberg, S.: Cross-device interaction via micro-mobility and F-formations. In: Proceedings of the 25th Annual ACM Symposium on User Interface Software and Technology, pp. 13–22 (2012)
7. Rädle, R., Jetter, H.C., Marquardt, N., Reiterer, H., Rogers, Y.: HuddleLamp: spatially-aware mobile displays for ad-hoc around-the-table collaboration. In: Proceedings of the Ninth ACM International Conference on Interactive Tabletops and Surfaces, pp. 45–54 (2014)
8. Satty, T.L., et al.: The Analytic Hierarchy Process. McGraw-Hill, New York (1980)
9. Seifert, J., Simeone, A., Schmidt, D., Holleis, P., Reinartz, C., Wagner, M., Gellersen, H., Rukzio, E.: MobiSurf: improving co-located collaboration through integrating mobile devices and interactive surfaces. In: Proceedings of the 2012 ACM International Conference on Interactive Tabletops and Surfaces, pp. 51–60 (2012)
10. Tandler, P., Prante, T., Müller-Tomfelde, C., Streitz, N., Steinmetz, R.: Connectables: dynamic coupling of displays for the flexible creation of shared workspaces. In: Proceedings of the 14th Annual ACM Symposium on User Interface Software and Technology, pp. 11–20 (2001)
11. Yee, K.P.: Peephole displays: pen interaction on spatially aware handheld computers. In: Proceedings of the SIGCHI Conference on Human Factors in Computing Systems, pp. 1–8 (2003)

What Makes a Good Recommendation?
Characterization of Scientific Paper Recommendations

Laura Steinert[(✉)] and H. Ulrich Hoppe

University of Duisburg-Essen, Lotharstr. 63, Duisburg, Germany
steinert@collide.info

Abstract. In this paper we propose several new measures to character-ize sets of scientific papers that provide an overview of a scientific topic. We present a study in which experts were asked to name such papers for one of their areas of expertise and apply the measures to characterize the paper selections. The results are compared to the measured values for random paper selections. We find that the expert selected sets of papers can be characterized to have a moderately high diversity, mod-erately high coverage and each paper in the set has on average a high prototypicality.

1 Introduction

Every year the number of new scientific articles increases. By now researchers can no longer look at all newly published papers even in their respective fields. To this end, paper recommender systems have been developed to help researchers find papers to read or cite. Beel et al. have found over 200 research articles published since 1999 that deal with paper recommender systems [1].

However, the task of recommending papers differs depending on the target group: An experienced researcher might want to get recommendations with a high serendipity. Yet another one might be interested in finding related literature for a new paper. To the best of our knowledge, no recommender system exists that provides a scientist with an overview of a scientific field. The target group of such a system includes students that just started working on their PhDs as well as grant program managers and review panel members looking into unfamiliar research fields. Therefore, such a recommender system can support scientific communities.

But before such a recommender system can be developed the requirements must be analyzed: What characterizes papers that provide an overview of a scientific field? And how can we measure these criteria? In this paper we describe new and existing measures that can characterize sets of papers. Furthermore, we use these measures in a study to determine how papers that give an overview of a scientific field can be characterized.

This work was supported by the Deutsche Forschungsgemeinschaft (DFG) under grant No. GRK 2167, Research Training Group "User-Centred Social Media".

T. Yuizono et al. (Eds.): CRIWG 2016, LNCS 9848, pp. 115–130, 2016.
DOI: 10.1007/978-3-319-44799-5_9

In the next section of the paper we describe related work. Afterward, the characterization measures are given. In Sect. 4 the aforementioned study is described. The following section analyzes the characteristics of papers giving an overview of a field using the results of the study. The paper concludes with a conclusion and remarks on future work.

2   Related Work

Scientific communities are constantly evolving and changing. As such, keeping track of a community can be a challenging task. Computer tools can support scientific communities by aiding the understanding of a field and its community. This can be achieved by identifying key papers and authors as well as emerging research fronts. These tasks are addressed by the *Action Science Explorer* tool [2]. It visualizes scientific papers and their citations and displays information on the papers on demand. Among the displayable information are citation contexts and automatically generated summaries of papers. Furthermore, it helps a user in understanding a field by providing various network analysis measures and plotting options.

Another option to support scientific communities is to provide researchers with paper recommendations. Although a vast number of paper recommender systems exist, it is unknown which recommender system is the best. One problem is that no gold standard exists against which new systems can be compared. Therefore, the comparability of systems is hindered. Additionally, many reported results cannot be reproduced due to insufficiently described algorithms or flaws in the evaluations. One such reported flaw lies in the limited use of evaluation metrics: Most paper recommender systems are only evaluated with respect to the accuracy of the recommendations [1]. However, it has been show that other factors also play an important role, e.g. the diversity of recommendations [9].

In the next section we describe various existing and new measures to characterize papers. Our aim is to understand the characteristics of paper sets that provide an overview of a scientific field. In the future we want to use the results and measures to develop a system that recommends such papers. However, the measures can also be used to evaluate and characterize paper recommender systems for other target groups, e.g. recommending serendipitous papers to experienced researchers. As such, by providing a set of measures we hope to help with the problem of evaluation flaws in paper recommender systems.

3   Measures

For measuring the characteristics of papers, measures can be applied to sets of papers or individual papers. Among the possible measurements for sets of papers are topic diversity, the breadth and depth of the covered topics as well as the extent to which all important subtopics are covered by the papers, i.e. coverage. Other measures might consider the coherence of the scientific papers. While the ranking of recommendations usually plays an important role in recommender systems, all measures presented here treat the papers in a set as unordered.

Each individual paper can also be characterized with regard to various features: These can consider the breadth and depth of the covered subtopics within a single paper, the diversity within the paper or in how far the paper is a representative of a scientific research line, i.e. in how far it is *prototypical.* Moreover, they might take the length or the type of the publication – technical report, conference paper, journal paper – or the comprehensibility of the paper into account.

Measures for set diversity and set coverage have been defined before. These will be described in the following subsections. Moreover, we define additional measures for set diversity, set coverage and paper prototypicality that are also described in this section. Some measures described in this paper use the citation network. This is a directed, acyclic graph $G(V, E)$ in which papers are nodes (V) and citations are edges (E). An edge starts at the paper making a citation and ends at the referenced paper.

It should be noted that the measures used in this paper are specific for the case of scientific paper recommendations. The used data structures are geared to scientific papers, e.g. venues, abstracts, authors and citations. Apart from that, in other domains traits not considered here might be desirable, e.g. recommending products from different price ranges.

3.1 Set Diversity

According to Beel et al. [1] only two paper recommender systems take the diversity of a set of papers into account: Vellino [8] and Küçüktunç et al. [4].

Venue-Based Diversity. Vellino [8] considers diversity for the comparison of existing paper recommender systems. In these systems a user has to specify one scientific article of interest based on which recommendations are generated. For each recommended paper the journal distance between the journal the paper was published in and that of the input paper is computed. The journal distance is computed by using a large database with papers from several journals. Based on these distances the diversity of the set is calculated. The approach does not consider the distance of papers published at conferences. However, in many disciplines most papers are published at conferences – e.g. in computer science. Therefore, we will not use this measure.

Density-Based Diversity. Küçüktunç et al. [4] incorporate a diversification process into their system to make citation recommendations for scientific papers. The used diversity measure was developed by Tong et al. [7] to analyze the diversity of a set of nodes of a graph in general.

The diversity of a set of papers R is measured by using the l-density of the set in the underlying citation network, as given in (1). For this Küçüktunç et al. used $l = 2$.

$$dens_l(R) = \frac{\sum_{p_i,p_j \in R, p_i \neq p_j} d_l(p_i, p_j)}{|R| \cdot (|R| - 1)} \tag{1}$$

The l-density is similar to the normal density. The difference is that two nodes are considered to be connected if they are connected via a path of maximally length l. This is expressed in (2) where $dist(p_i, p_j)$ is the length of the shortest path between two nodes in the citation network. With regard to this shortest path it is unclear whether Küçüktunç et al. use the directed or undirected citation network. However, Tong et al. [7] use the diversity measure for undirected networks. Thus, in this paper the distance $dist(p_i, p_j)$ is also calculated based on the undirected citation network.

$$d_l(p_i, p_j) = \begin{cases} 1 & \text{if } dist(p_i, p_j) \leq l \\ 0 & \text{otherwise} \end{cases} \tag{2}$$

Unfortunately, this diversity score is unintuitive: The lower the diversity score, the better the diversity. To overcome this problem Tong et al. [7] invert the diversity measure which then lies in $[0.5; 1]$. We further normalize the measure to lie within $[0; 1]$ as given in (3).

$$diversity_{density}(R) = (\frac{1}{1 + dens_l(R)} - 0.5) \cdot 2 \in [0; 1] \subset \mathbb{R} \tag{3}$$

Author-Based Diversity. A new approach to calculate diversity looks at the authors of the recommended papers. If all papers have been written by the same set of authors, the diversity can be expected to be low. On the other hand if all papers have been written by completely different authors, a high diversity can be expected. This notion is used in the diversity measure based on authors given in (4) for a set of papers R. Hereby, $author(p_i)$ returns the set of authors of a paper p_i and $uniqueAuthors(p_i, R')$ (5) returns the percentage of authors of paper p_i that do not participate in any paper in the set of papers R'.

$$diversity_{author}(R) = \frac{\sum_{p_i \in R} uniqueAuthors(p_i, R \setminus \{p_i\}))}{|R|} \in [0; 1] \subset \mathbb{R} \tag{4}$$

$$uniqueAuthors(p_i, R') = \frac{|\{a \mid a \in author(p_i) \wedge a \notin \bigcup_{p_j \in R'} author(p_j)\}|}{|author(p_i)|} \tag{5}$$

Similarity-Based Diversity. A different approach considers the topical similarity of the papers in a set. Ziegler et al. [9] and Jones [3] use the similarity of items to measure the diversity. Hereby, a higher similarity of items means a lower diversity. Ziegler et al. use the measure to analyze the topic diversity in commercial book recommendations. Jones uses it to analyze the user acceptance of commercial recommender systems.

Our calculation of diversity based on similarity differs slightly from that used by [9] and [3] in that a higher score indicates a higher diversity. This is shown in (6). For the topical similarity measure the *topic structure similarity* (tss) [5] is used. The tss similarity is a hybrid similarity measure that is a linear combination of a network-based and a content-based similarity. The diversity measure is divided by the maximum tss value – $maxTSS = 2$ – in (6) to normalize it.

$$diversity_{similarity}(R) = 1 - \frac{\sum_{p_i,p_j \in R, p_i \neq p_j} tss(p_i, p_j)}{|R| \cdot (|R| - 1) \cdot maxTSS} \in [0; 1] \subset \mathbb{R} \quad (6)$$

The three diversity measures (3), (4) and (6) will be used in the remainder of this paper.

3.2 Set Coverage

Coverage is defined in various ways in different publications. In our understanding coverage is the extent to which all relevant subtopics are covered by the papers in the set R. A substitute we propose is to use the **average distance** of all recommended papers. Papers on the same topic should be close together while papers on different topics should be farther apart. A very large average distance indicates that most probably several topics are covered by the set of papers. A very small average distance on the other hand can indicate that only some subtopics are covered. Therefore, a moderate distance should be targeted. The coverage of a set of papers $R \subseteq V$ can be measured as given in Eq. (7) where $d(p_i, p_j)$ is the distance of two papers. In this context the standard deviation of these distances is of interest, too.

$$coverage(R) = \frac{\sum_{p_i,p_j \in R, p_i \neq p_j} d(p_i, p_j)}{|R| \cdot (|R| - 1)} \quad (7)$$

Depending on the distance measure, this measure can produce values larger than 1. With regard to the distance measure, three different calculations are considered: A structure-based, a similarity-based and a hybrid distance.

Structure-Based Distance. The structure-based distance is calculated as the length of the shortest path connecting the two papers in the undirected citation network. Let $shortestPaths(p_i, p_j)$ return a set of shortest paths that connect the nodes p_i and p_j in the undirected network and let $length(p)$ be a function that returns the number of edges that make up this path. Then the calculation of this distance measure is given in (8).

$$d_{structure}(p_i, p_j) = length(p), \text{ where } p \in shortestPaths(p_i, p_j) \quad (8)$$

Note that due to the construction of the used citation networks – as explained later – the whole citation network is one weak component. Thus, $\forall p_i, p_j \in V : d(p_i, p_j) < \infty$ holds. Further note that the paths connecting two nodes p_i and $p_j \in R$ are <u>not</u> limited to the subgraph induced by the set of nodes R. The coverage measure using this distance can be normalized by dividing by the diameter of the undirected citation network.

Similarity-Based Distance. The similarity-based distance is calculated using the *topic structure similarity* (tss) [5]. As a higher similarity should infer a lower distance, the distance is calculated as given in (9). Hereby, the maximum value the *tss* similarity can reach is again denoted as $maxTSS$.

$$d_{similarity}(p_i, p_j) = 1 - \frac{tss(p_i, p_j)}{maxTSS} \tag{9}$$

Note that $coverage(R)$ using $d_{similarity}(p_i, p_j)$ is equal to $diversity_{similarity}(R)$ (6). At a first glance it may seem contradictory that a measure for diversity could also be used as an indicator for coverage. However, both concepts are related. If various papers cover different aspects of a topic, they have a high coverage. Likewise, they also have a high diversity. Similarly, if all papers in a set cover the same aspect of a topic, they have a low coverage. At the same time, they also have a high similarity and therefore low diversity.

Hybrid Distance. The third distance is a hybrid of the previously mentioned distances. Let each of the shortest paths be encoded as the list of nodes along it in their natural order and let $p[i]$ denote the *ith* node on a path p. Furthermore, let $length(path)$ return the number of edges that make up this path. The hybrid distance measure is given in (10). The shortest path is again determined based on the undirected citation network. If multiple shortest paths exist between two papers, the one with the shortest hybrid distance is to be taken.

$$d_{hybrid}(p_i, p_j) = min\{d_{hybrid}(path) \mid path \in shortestPaths(p_i, p_j)\}$$
$$\text{with}$$
$$d_{hybrid}(path) = \sum_{l=1}^{length(path)} (1 + maxTSS - tss(path[l], path[l+1])) \tag{10}$$

The coverage measure using this distance can be normalized by dividing by the maximally possible value. This maximum is given as $3d$ where d is the diameter of the undirected citation network.

3.3   Paper Prototypicality

Linked to the diversity of a set of papers is the *prototypicality* of each paper. Prototypicality measures in how far a paper is a prominent representative of a specific line of research. If the same group of authors has published several papers, the youngest should be prototypical for all of them. This notion is used in (11) where the prototypicality of the paper depends on the number of papers in the whole network that are published by the same authors – regardless of the order of the authors on the paper – and were published before this paper.

$$prototypicality_{age}(p_i) = |\{p_j | p_j \in V \wedge authors(p_i) = authors(p_j)$$
$$\wedge \, year(p_i) > year(p_j)\}| \tag{11}$$

Hereby, $authors(p_i)$ is a function that returns the set of authors of a paper p_i. The function $year(p_i)$ on the other hand returns the publication year of a paper p_i. The idea behind the measure is that two papers by the same set of authors most probably fall within the same line of research and the younger paper builds on the older ones. The more previous papers exist, the higher this paper's prototypicality.

On the other hand, a paper that represents a specific line of research should also have influenced many other papers. Therefore, it should have been cited often. Moreover, the citing papers should be similar in topic. This is encoded in (12). Hereby, tss is again the *topic structure similarity* and $N_{in}(p_i)$ is the set of papers that cite paper p_i.

$$prototypicality_{indegree}(p_i) = \sum_{p_j \in N_{in}(p_i)} tss(p_j, p_i) \qquad (12)$$

The venue of a publication also influences its prototypicality. For instance a journal paper should be more prototypical than a conference paper. This is encoded in (13).

$$prototypicality_{venue}(p_i) = \begin{cases} 0.5 & \text{if } venue(p_i) = \text{Technical Report} \\ 1 & \text{if } venue(p_i) = \text{Conference Proc.} \\ 1.5 & \text{if } venue(p_i) = \text{Journal} \\ 0 & \text{otherwise} \end{cases}$$

$$(13)$$

All of these three measures are combined in (14).

$$prototypicality(p_i) = prototypicality_{venue}(p_i) \cdot$$
$$(prototypicality_{age}(p_i) + prototypicality_{indegree}(p_i))$$
$$(14)$$

The measure for prototypicality can be normalized by dividing by the maximally possible prototypicality of a citation network. This maximum is equal to $1.5 \cdot ((|V| - 1) + (maxIn \cdot maxTSS))$ where $maxIn$ is the maximum in-degree in the network.

The prototypicality of papers and the diversity of a set of papers are connected. If each paper in a set has a high prototypicality, most probably each paper represents a different line of research – otherwise the prototypicality values would be low for some papers in the set. This set of papers should therefore also have a high diversity. The opposite is not true in general. Imagine ten papers from completely different research groups on different topics. Moreover, let each of these papers be the first in their respective lines of research. Then the set of these papers is very diverse, while the individual papers are not prototypical.

4   Study

To determine the characteristics of papers that give an overview of a scientific topic, we conducted a study. In this study experts manually picked such papers from one of their areas of expertise. These selected papers were then characterized using the measures defined in Sect. 3.

In a pre-study the expert's area of expertise was inquired. Additionally, three papers from their area of expertise were named by the experts. Based on this information, a list of papers for the chosen topic was created for each expert which was used in the study.

4.1 Hypotheses

The set of papers that provide an overview of a scientific topic should highlight the different subtopics and aspects of the topic. Thus, we expect a high set diversity. The selections are expected to be a trade-off between the number of represented aspects of a topic on the one hand and the depth to which they are explored on the other hand. This first aspect is represented by the coverage. Given this trade-off, we expect moderately high coverage values. We also expect that all papers are more or less similar to one another. Therefore, the average distance as calculated by the coverage is expected to have a low standard deviation. Having a set of papers from the same line of research most probably will not give a comprehensive overview of a scientific topic. Therefore, in a set of papers that give an introduction to a scientific topic we expect each paper to have a high prototypicality on average.

4.2 Pre-study

13 scientific experts from computer science – eleven PhD students, one PhD and one professor – participated in the pre-study. In the actual study experts were asked to select papers from a list that give an overview of a specific scientific field for a starting PhD student. To compile this list for each expert, the experts were asked in a pre-study to state an area of their expertise and name three English papers from that area that had been published in the years 2010 to 2013. The lower bound on the publication year was to ensure that only fairly new papers were named. The upper bound was given by the used dataset. Furthermore, the three papers together should fulfill three further criteria, whereby each paper should meet at least one criterion:

- The expert is an author of the paper, therefore ensuring their expertise
- The paper is known in the scientific community
- The paper is a survey paper

These papers were then used to generate a list of papers for each expert, as described in the following.

4.3 Dataset

These lists of papers were generated by extracting citation networks from the ArnetMiner dataset[1][6]. This dataset contains papers and citations obtained

---

[1] Obtainable from https://aminer.org/citation, dataset V7, last seen on March 31 2016.

from DBLP and is thus mostly limited to computer science papers. For each expert one of the three named papers was chosen – called the *seed* – for which the 2.5 neighborhood network was extracted. The 2.5 neighborhood network of the seed is the graph that consists of all papers connected to the seed via an undirected path of maximally length two and the corresponding edges (2 neighborhood). Moreover, any connections among these papers are included as well (0.5 neighborhood). This is a citation network.

Unfortunately, most papers named by the experts were not present in the dataset or had no or only one edge. These papers had to be discarded. Overall six participants – four PhD students, one postdoc and one professor – named one or more papers that could be used for the study. In the case that more than one appropriate paper had been named, the one that produced the largest and densest citation network was chosen. The papers chosen for the study met various of the three criteria given in the pre-study. Two of the experts – later referred to as experts two and three – had the same dataset.

The extracted citation networks were very large – in one case the network contained more than 3500 papers. As the experts were expected to manually select ten papers out of the citation network, this was not feasible. Hence, it was decided to reduce the citation networks by applying the *k-core algorithm*. The *k-core* of a graph is a subgraph in which each node has at least a degree of k. For this degree count the undirected citation network was considered. For each expert's citation network the minimal k was selected such that the resulting *k-core* consisted of maximally 100 nodes. 100 was chosen since we deem it a small enough number of papers to be given to the experts. The *k-core* of expert six is an exception and contains more than 100 nodes since a higher k resulted in an empty graph.

Table 1 shows the statistics of the citation networks and the selected *k-cores* for each expert. For experts 2 and 3 the same dataset was used, as described above. The undirected diameter – i.e. the longest shortest path in the undirected network – is always equal to four for the complete citation network. This is due to the construction using the 2.5 neighborhood of the seed paper. It can be seen that the diameters of both the directed and undirected networks are in most

Table 1. The statistics of the complete citation networks (CN) and the selected *k-cores* (KC) used in the study; $|V|$: number of nodes, $|E|$: number of edges

Expert	k	$|V|$		$|E|$		Diameter (dir.)		Diameter (undir.)	
		CN	KC	CN	KC	CN	KC	CN	KC
1	9	655	65	2948	517	8	4	4	3
2,3	5	326	90	930	410	6	5	4	4
4	8	706	32	2682	196	8	3	4	3
5	8	3517	95	10525	686	12	4	4	2
6	14	6873	131	36871	1579	13	4	4	3

cases smaller in the *k-cores* compared to the complete citation networks. Thus, the k-cores are far more densely connected than the complete citation networks. Therefore, the datasets used in the study are biased with regard to their density.

For most papers the abstract is missing in the ArnetMiner dataset. Therefore, the abstracts were added manually for the papers in the *k-cores*. Duplicates were removed from the k-cores. Examples for duplicates are pre-published and published versions of the same paper. That way five papers were deleted from the *k-core* of expert one's dataset, four from the dataset of experts two and three, two papers from the dataset of expert four, five papers of that of expert five and one paper from the dataset of expert six. In all cases except that of expert six the seed papers were – coincidentally – not included in the selected *k-cores*.

4.4   Study and Questionnaire

Each expert was given a list with the papers contained in the respective *k-core*. For each paper the list contained information on the title, authors, publication year, venue and abstract. From these lists the experts were asked to select ten papers that provide a PhD student that just started working on their thesis an overview of the scientific topic named by the expert in the pre-study. These papers should together cover all or most main aspects of the scientific topic. Moreover, each paper should cover at least one aspect of the topic of interest and it should be seen as an important paper by the community. In case the topic named in the pre-study was too broad to be sufficiently covered by ten papers or in case the papers covered a slightly different topic than the intended one, the experts were given the option to choose a new topic for which they selected the ten papers.

Additionally, the experts were asked to fill out a questionnaire after selecting the papers. In this they were asked how important various criteria were for their selection on a 3-point Likert scale (Not Important, Moderately Important, Very Important). These criteria were diversity of the set of papers, coverage of the set of papers, depth of the topics covered by the papers, coherence of the set of papers and average prototypicality of each paper.

4.5   Remarks

During the study expert three deviated from the original topic given in the pre-study by selecting a subtopic. Thus, although experts two and three were given the same dataset, both selected papers for different topics and their results cannot be compared to one another.

Furthermore, it should be noted that in the case of expert five the list of papers given did mostly cover a different topic than the one chosen by the expert. The original chosen topic was *Automata Theory* from theoretical computer science. However, the list of papers given in the study mostly dealt with *Binary Decision Diagrams* (BDDs). The seed paper used to generate the list of papers[2]

---

[2] Bonchi, F., Pous, D.: Checking NFA equivalence with bisimulations up to congruence. In: ACM SIGPLAN Notices. vol. 48, pp. 457–468. ACM (2013).

quotes the paper that introduced BDDs in passing. Because of that, a large portion of the citation network deals with BDDs, which happens to be the selected k-core. The expert therefore selected papers that serve as an introduction to the topic of BDDs. However, this topic does not fall within the researcher's area of expertise. Thus, the selections made by expert five have to be interpreted with caution.

5   Results

The datasets used in the the survey along with the anonymized expert selections are available online[3]. Unfortunately, the dataset does not include the information of which type the venue of a paper is. Therefore, in the following it is always assumed that $prototypicality_{venue}(p_i) = 1$ (cf. (13)) holds. To eliminate duplicate papers from the dataset – as described in Sect. 4.3 – the type of the venues for specific papers were looked up manually.

With regard to the author-based diversity measure entity resolution can be problematic. The same author can occur under different names in different papers, e.g. "John Smith", "J. Smith" or "John D. Smith". To solve this problem we converted each author's name to the first letter of the first given name and the last name. Moreover, we converted the names to lower case. For example both "J. Smith" and "John D. Smith" were converted to "j. smith". As our datasets are very small and focus on a single research area the likelihood that two different authors map to the same standardized name is very small.

As will be seen, expert four's selection behaves different from those of the other expert's selections compared to the random samples with regard to nearly all of the calculated measures. Thus, expert four might be an outlier. This might be explained by the relatively small dataset of only 30 papers given to this expert in the study.

To test the suitability of the measures, for each dataset ten random paper sets were selected. Each of these random sets consisted of ten papers – the same size as the expert selections. For these random selections the different measures were also calculated and compared to the values of the expert selections. The results of the study partly confirm our expectations (cf. Section 4.1). In the following the results of the different measures are presented and discussed.

5.1   Questionnaire

Table 2 shows the results of the questionnaire. Hereby the Likert scales have been translated to 1 (Very important), 0 (Moderately Important) and -1 (Not Important).

Regarding the importance of the different criteria the experts' answers vary. The criterion regarded to be most important is set diversity. The second most important criteria are prototypicality of each paper and set coverage. The remaining two criteria are regarded as unimportant or moderately important. Therefore, the measures presented in this paper concern the most important criteria.

---

[3] http://steinert.collide.info/expertstudy2016.html.

Table 2. The results of the questionnaire for the set diversity (Div), set coverage (Cov), topic depth of the set (Dep), set coherence (Coh) and average prototypicality of each paper (Prot)

Expert	Div	Cov	Dep	Coh	Prot
1	1	1	0	0	1
2	1	1	-1	0	1
3	1	0	0	0	-1
4	0	0	0	0	0
5	0	0	0	0	1
6	1	1	0	0	1
Sum	4	3	-1	0	3

5.2 Diversity

Figure 1 depicts the values of the diversity measures for both the expert recommendations and the average of the random paper selections – along with the corresponding standard deviations. The cases for which the expert selections differ significantly from the random selections are again with † ($p < 0.05$) and †† ($p < 0.01$). This significance was measured using a one sample two-tailed t-test. The selection by expert four behaves as an outlier for most of the measures.

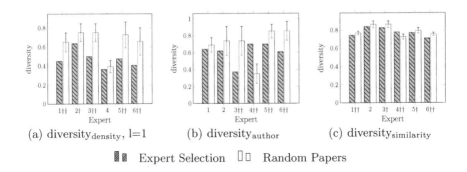

(a) diversity$_{density}$, l=1   (b) diversity$_{author}$ (c) diversity$_{similarity}$

▨▨ Expert Selection   ☐☐ Random Papers

Fig. 1. The values of the diversity measures

The density-based diversity measure was calculated for $l = 1$. Larger values of l were not tested as the underlying networks are k-cores of a 2.5 neighborhood citation network. Thus, any two nodes have a maximum distance of 4 in the complete, undirected citation network. Table 1 shows that the diameter in the undirected k-cores lies between two and four. Therefore, larger values of l are of little interest as the diversity for larger values of l would be 0.

All three diversity measures depict a clear trend: nearly all expert selections have a lower diversity than the random selections. Moreover, the expert selections receive moderately high diversity scores. For the author-based diversity the selection by expert three receives a low author-based diversity value of ca. 0.37. The ten papers selected by this expert have in total a set of 18 authors, out of which seven appear in more than one paper. Out of the ten papers, only one paper has authors that exclusively contributed to this paper within the selected ten papers. All other papers have overlaps in authorship with at least one of the other selected papers. Thus, a small group of authors seems to have contributed a lot of value for the specific scientific topic.

The findings stand partially in contrast to our hypothesis. We would have expected that the expert selected paper sets have a high diversity score and in particular a higher diversity than the random paper selections. However, on second thought, a moderately high diversity makes sense. A too high diversity could easily be achieved by papers that cover completely different topics. However, this is not the target.

For instance in the case of the author-based diversity it is not surprising that a few scientists have shaped a scientific field in such a way that they are authors of more than one paper among the ten papers giving an overview to that field, while the majority of authors occurs in only one of the selected papers. With regard to the density-based diversity measure a moderately high density and therefore a moderately low diversity seems reasonable for papers that introduce a scientific field and various of its subtopics. The fact that the expert selections have a lower similarity-based diversity than the random selections means that the papers chosen by the experts are on average more similar to one another than the randomly selected papers.

5.3   Coverage

Figure 2 depicts the values of the normalized coverage measures (2(a) - 2(c)) for both the expert recommendations and the average of the random paper selections. As the coverage is calculated as the average distance, the standard deviations are shown, too (2(d) - 2(f)). The cases for which the expert selections differ significantly from the random selections are again marked with † ($p <$ 0.05) and †† ($p < 0.01$).

For all three variations of the coverage measure in most cases the expert selected papers have a lower coverage than the randomly selected papers. The exception is expert four's value for the similarity-based coverage measure. However, this selection is not statistically significantly different from the random selections with regard to this measure. For all three measures all expert selections receive moderately high values. This is in accordance with the expectations. The standard deviations are in most cases not significantly different from those of the random selections. Both the expert and random selections have a small standard deviation. This is in accordance with the expectations.

5.4   Prototypicality

Figure 3 depicts the values of the normalized prototypicality measure for both the expert recommendations and the average of the random paper

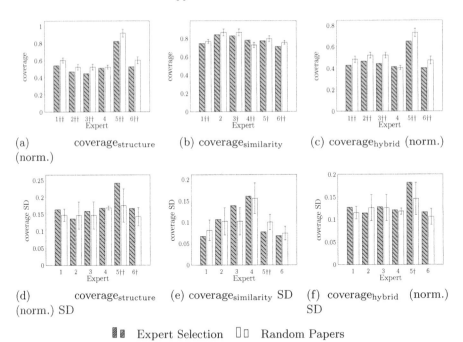

(a) coverage_structure (norm.)

(b) coverage_similarity

(c) coverage_hybrid (norm.)

(d) coverage_structure (norm.) SD

(e) coverage_similarity SD

(f) coverage_hybrid (norm.) SD

▨▨ Expert Selection   ▢▢ Random Papers

Fig. 2. The values of the normalized coverage measures ((a)- (c)) and the corresponding standard deviations ((d) - (f))

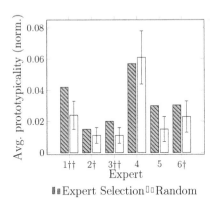

▨▨ Expert Selection ▢▢ Random

Fig. 3. The values of the normalized prototypicality measure

selections – along with the corresponding standard deviations. For the normalization the maximum value for the venue-based prototypicality was changed to one.

The cases for which the expert selections differ significantly from the random selections are again marked with † ($p < 0.05$) and †† ($p < 0.01$). For the average prototypicality the standard deviations shown are calculated for the averages of the random set's averages. The average of the random selections is the average of the averages. Since the random selections are of equal size, it is also the average of all randomly chosen papers. However, it should be noted that the different random samples have overlaps.

The average set prototypicality of the papers chosen by the experts have in general a higher prototypicality than the random selections. This fits our expectations. However, this difference is only statistically significant in four of six cases.

6   Conclusion and Future Work

In this paper we have presented some new measures – an author-based diversity measure, three variants to calculate the coverage of papers and a prototypicality measure – to characterize sets of papers or individual scientific papers. Moreover, we have adapted an existing measure to the domain of scientific papers: a similarity-based diversity measure. In a study experts were asked to select papers that provide an introduction to / overview of a scientific field. The measures were then applied to these expert selected papers and used to characterize papers that provide an overview of a scientific field. The values of the different measures of the expert selections were also compared to the values for randomly selected papers.

The diversity measures show that the expert selected papers in general receive lower diversity scores than random paper selections. However, the expert selections receive moderately high diversity measures. This stands partially in contrast to our hypothesis but is actually reasonable. Similar to the diversity measures, all coverage measures found that the sets of papers selected by the experts most of the time had a lower coverage than the random selections. A moderately high coverage was found in all cases for all measure variants. The standard deviation was low. This is in accordance with our expectations. The average prototypicality of the expert chosen recommendations was higher than that of the random selections. This result also confirms our hypothesis.

All of these measures seem adequate to characterize paper sets that provide an overview of a scientific topic. However, the decision to use the k-core of a citation network as data may have influenced the results of the measures. Therefore, all characterization measures need to be further evaluated in future studies with more participants and different data sets. Additionally, we would like to use the characterization measures to develop a paper recommender system. This recommender system should be tailored to present a scientist with a set of scientific papers that give an overview of a scientific field. Such a system would be a valuable support for scientific communities.

References

1. Beel, J., Gipp, B., Langer, S., Breitinger, C.: Research-paper recommender systems: a literature survey. Int. J. Digit. Libr., 1–34 (2015)
2. Dunne, C., Shneiderman, B., Gove, R., Klavans, J., Dorr, B.: Rapid understanding of scientific paper collections: integrating statistics, text analytics, and visualization. J. Am. Soc. Inf. Sci. Technol. **63**(12), 2351–2369 (2012)
3. Jones, N.: User perceived qualities and acceptance of recommender systems. Dissertation, Ecole Polytechnique Federale de Lausanne (2010). http://infoscience.epfl.ch/record/146784
4. Küçüktunç, O., Saule, E., Kaya, K., Çatalyürek, Ü.V.: Result diversification in automatic citation recommendation. In: Proceedings of the iConference Workshop on Computational Scientometrics: Theory and Applications, pp. 1–4 (2013)
5. Steinert, L., Chounta, I.-A., Hoppe, H.U.: Where to begin? using network analytics for the recommendation of scientific papers. In: Baloian, N., Zorian, Y., Taslakian, P., Shoukouryan, S. (eds.) CRIWG 2015. LNCS, vol. 9334, pp. 124–139. Springer, Heidelberg (2015)
6. Tang, J., Zhang, J., Yao, L., Li, J., Zhang, L., Su, Z.: Arnetminer: extraction and mining of academic social networks. In: Proceedings of the 14th ACM SIGKDD International Conference on Knowledge Discovery and Data Mining, pp. 990–998. ACM (2008)
7. Tong, H., He, J., Wen, Z., Konuru, R., Lin, C.Y.: Diversified ranking on large graphs: an optimization viewpoint. In: Proceedings of the 17th ACM SIGKDD International Conference on Knowledge Discovery and Data Mining, pp. 1028–1036. ACM (2011)
8. Vellino, A.: A comparison between usage-based and citation-based methods for recommending scholarly research articles. Proc. Am. Soc. Inf. Sci. Technol. **47**(1), 1–2 (2010)
9. Ziegler, C.N., McNee, S.M., Konstan, J.A., Lausen, G.: Improving recommendation lists through topic diversification. In: Proceedings of the 14th International Conference on World Wide Web, pp. 22–32. ACM (2005)

Cooperation Isn't Just About Doing the Same Thing – Using Personality for a Cooperation-Recommender-System in Online Social Networks

Jens Lamprecht[✉], Dominik Siemon, and Susanne Robra-Bissantz

Institute of Business Information Systems, Technische Universität Braunschweig,
38106 Braunschweig, Germany
{j.lamprecht,d.siemon,
s.robra-bissantz}@tu-braunschweig.de

Abstract. Through Online Social Networks, like Research Gate, Stack Exchange or Facebook, it's easy to find a partner for cooperation, because Social Networks have the potential to connect thousands of people. To assist finding the right person for cooperation many of these networks have Recommender-Systems, but these systems mostly rely on the matching of keywords for each individual. This article shows on a conceptual level, that current Recommender-Systems for cooperation on Online Social Networks can be improved by additionally using personality for recommendations. Methods like Language Inquiry and Word Count (LIWC) can help to achieve this goal by presenting methods for an automated calculation of personality from user-generated content in these networks, without the need of questionnaires. Based on personality different cooperation types can be derived to improve recommendations for cooperation partners, leading to a better cooperation and therefore help to increase cooperation in Online Social Networks.

Keywords: Cooperation · Online social networks · Personality · Big Five · Five factor model · NEO PI-R · LIWC

1 Introduction

Through Online Social Networks, like Research Gate, Stack Exchange or Facebook, it's easy to find a partner for cooperation, because Social Networks have the potential to connect thousands of people. To assist finding the right person for cooperation through these networks many of them have Recommender-Systems, but these systems mostly rely on the matching of keywords for each individual. Unfortunately these systems don't reflect the current state of the art in cooperation research and can therefore be improved.

Studies have shown, that personality has an significant influence on group work and a proper constellation of personality types can improve the output of teams significantly [1, 2], lead to better decision-making processes and outcomes [3, 4] and help to explain a more divergent or convergent thinking style [5, 6]. Hence personality may have the potential to improve these Recommender-Systems with the aim to form better team constellations and increase cooperation. But measuring personality in Online Social

© Springer International Publishing Switzerland 2016
T. Yuizono et al. (Eds.): CRIWG 2016, LNCS 9848, pp. 131–138, 2016.
DOI: 10.1007/978-3-319-44799-5_10

Networks is quite difficult. Because personality is mainly collected through question-naires, with 60 to 240 items and test times between 10 and 45 min, which is not well suited for online use. Therefore new ways to collect personality, beside questionnaires, are needed. Recent studies have shown promising results in retrieving personality through user-generated content in Online Social Networks [7] based on the Language Inquiry and Word Count (LIWC) method developed by Pennebaker.

In the next sections of this article we will give a brief introduction into cooperation, Social Dilemmas and Social Value Orientation in Social Dilemmas. Followed by an overview about personality and personality can be derived from user-generated content with LIWC. Highlighting relevant works for our concept and showing our approach based on the Design Science Research Methodology (DSRM). Finally describing our concept of a Cooperation Recommender-System and giving a brief outlook for an eval-uation in future work.

2   Cooperation and Social Dilemma

In the case of cooperation at least two partners interact together, however, the relation-ship is based only on a mutual agreement on the respective contributions (inputs) and the result (output) to reach a jointly defined goal [8, 9]. Therefore, cooperation does not require a shared strategy in order to efficiently use the available resources and skills [10]. This implies the effective alignment of the actions of each partner, the alignment of the individual interests [11], the joint production in a defined space and the common task fulfillment [12].

The challenge for cooperation is the absence of a shared strategy. Every individual takes his own choice to either cooperate or behave individualistic in a given situation. Though the strategy of one individual influences the strategy and output of other indi-viduals. In short term individualistic behavior yields a greater output, but if everyone chooses an individualistic strategy everyone gets less than if everyone is choosing to cooperate. Those situations are called Social Dilemmas [13, 14]. Olson [15] described in his work "Public Goods Dilemma", a special case of Social Dilemmas, where every participating individual makes the same use of a public good (e.g. fire fighters, police), but have to pay a different price for this good. Individualists try to minimize their input or accordingly try not to pay anything at all. But if no one pays for the good anymore, the good can't be maintained; therefore cooperation is needed to maintain the supply of the good for everyone [16].

Recent research has shown, that Online Social Networks can be seen as Social Dilemmas as well [17, 18]. Success of Online Social Networks strongly depends on interaction and cooperation in generating content and contributing to the network. Therefore these networks need a cooperative community to function and stay alive.

To describe which strategy each individual will prefer in a Social Dilemma social psychologists developed the Social Value Orientation construct. This construct is based on a hypothetical resource allocation a person would take for herself and another person. Depending on the chosen allocation an individual can either be pro-self (individualistic orientation, competitive orientation) or be pro-social (cooperative orientation, altruistic orientation) [19, 20]. Balliet et al. [21] have shown a medium sized effect on the relationship between Social Value Orientation and actual cooperation in Social Dilemmas.

3   Personality Traits and Language Use

To measure personality there is a variety of personality tests available. These tests mostly rely on questionnaires. A frequently used test is the Five Factor Model (also Big Five personality traits) [22], which uses five factors to describe the human personality. These factors are openness to experience, conscientiousness, extra-version, agreeableness and neuroticism. The item inventory of the Five Factor Model includes 60 items and takes about 10 min to complete. Additionally there are shortened versions of the inventory, for example the Big Five-10 [e.g. 23, 24], with only 10 items and a completion time from about 1 min. This reduction in item count has an influence on the reliability of the test, however [23]. The Revised NEO Personality Inventory (NEO PI-R) [e.g. 25, 26] extends the Five Factor Model. It adds six subordinate dimensions to each of the personality factors of the Five Factor Model. These additional dimensions facilitate deeper insight into personality, but with the cost of a dramatically increased amount of items in the inventory. With an item count of 240 and a completion time of about 45 min the NEO PI-R yields great accuracy but it's not eligible for all situations, especially not for online questionnaires where completion time is a crucial factor [27].

To address this issue a new technique has emerged to measure personality through written text. The Five Factor Model and accordingly the NEO PI-R are based on the Lexical Hypothesis [28] assuming that personality can be determined by language use and by analyzing the usage of words. Extending the Lexical Hypothesis Pennebaker developed the Language Inquiry and Word Count (LIWC) method. The method uses a category-based analysis of language use and the relation to psychological variables [29–31]. Using this method many studies have been conducted to analyze the language use of bloggers in Social Media, showing that there is a strong evidence for a correlation between aspects of the Five Factor Model and the language use of bloggers [7, 32–34].

4   Related Works

Personality has great potential to help understand cooperation. A study has shown that personality can be used to predict cooperation in social dilemmas [35]. Furthermore Social Value Orientation can be derived from personality [36]. Where a pro-social behavior is linked to a high agreeableness [37] and especially altruism correlates well with agreeableness and neuroticism [38, 39].

Chamorro-Premuzic an Reichenbacher [5] showed an positive effect of openness and extraversion on a divergent thinking style. In a later study of Batey et al. [6] only the positive effect of extraversion could be repeated. The Authors also predicted an effect of agreeableness on divergent thinking style. However, this effect was not significant and the authors assumed that one possible explanation might be due to a small sample size.

5   Research Methodology

Our research methodology for the Cooperation-Recommender-System described in this article is based on the Design Science Research Methodology (DSRM) Process Model (Fig. 1) developed by Peffers et al. [40]. An *Objective-Centered Solution* has been chosen as a research entry point, because of the potential to improve the value of "classical" Recommender-Systems through the addition of personality traits. In a first step the problem of cooperation in Online Social Networks has been described and it has been shown, that this problem can be described as a Social Dilemma (see section "Coopera-tion and Social Dilemma"). The *Objective of a Solution*, the second step of the process, is to provide an improved Recommender-System, which leads to a better cooperation in Online Social Networks through a better matching of potential cooperation partners through a recommendation based on personality. The third and last step so far describes the design of the artifact, based on the theory summarized in the previous section and guide to the conceptual design of the artifact in the next section. In the last section "Future Work" a possible *Evaluation* of the concept is presented.

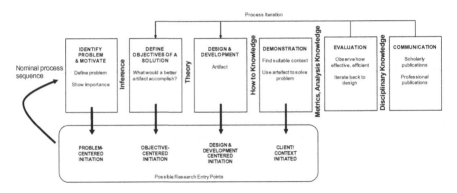

Fig. 1. DSRM process model (Peffers et al. 2007)

6   Predicting Cooperation

Based on this theoretical framework a Social-Recommender-System can be concep-tualized as follows. Beside the recommendation by context, through matching of keywords, a recommendation by personality will be done. Therefore two Information Systems fulfilling different tasks will be used.

One of these systems will perform a text analysis task, where the user-generated content of every single user for a specific Social Network will be collected. After a suitable cleansing of the content (removing links, quotes, pictures etc. from the text) a LIWC analysis will be performed. Through this analysis personality of the user is collected and saved in a database. To reduce the amount of calculations it's not necessary to calculate the personality anew for every new post a user makes in the Online Social Network, but they should be kept up to date to ensure the quality of the recommendation. Therefore these calculations can be done by night, where these platforms are less frequently used and more capacity is available. For this calculations two thresholds have to be considered. The first threshold is the minimum amount of words needed for the LIWC analysis. Yarkoni et al. reported a medium to high reliability for a word count between 2000 and 3000 words [7]. Especially for new users this threshold is critical because recommendation can only be provided after sufficient amount of words can be analyzed. A second threshold is the upper limit of words needed for the analysis. Active users may have generated a lot of posts with a huge amount of words. Using all these words for analysis leads to a longer calculation time but just yields a marginal improvement to the results gained [7]. So an upper limit of words analyzed is needed to keep the calculation time in bound.

The second task highly depends on the first task and is using the personality traits provided by the first task. These are enhanced to cooperation types, which represent the likelihood for cooperative behavior. Derived from this cooperative task an optimal role in a group can be recommended and optimal team composition can be achieved. The enhancing process, to cooperation types, is on the one hand based on current research in this field [e.g. 1, 3], on the other hand enriched with actual usage data from the Online Social Network in relationship to the personality. This helps to determine which users are important for the network and willing to cooperate and which is the perfect role in a group for them depending on specific characteristics, like for example thinking style [5, 6]. Figure 2 shows this conceptual model for a Cooperation-Recommender-System in a brief overview. Bringing together the context based Recommender-System with a personality based Recommender-System.

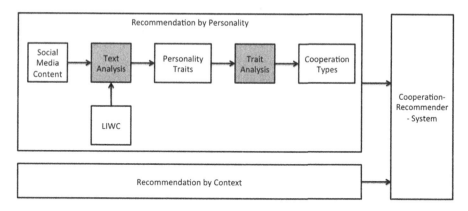

Fig. 2. Conceptual model of a cooperation-recommender-system

7   Conclusion

This article has shown, that a recommendation of potential cooperation partners in consideration of personality can improve cooperation in Online Social Networks. Understanding participation in Online Social Networks as a Social Dilemma helps to understand the underlying strategic choices to cooperate or not on these platforms. Whereas personality can be used to explain strategic behavior. But gathering personality on Online Social Networks is a difficult task, because personality is mostly derived by time-consuming questionnaires. LIWC can help to address this issue by presenting a method for an automated calculation of personality from user-generated content in these networks, without the need of questionnaires. Additionally this automation enables the use of more detailed personality tests, like the NEO PI-R, which isn't suited as a questionnaire for online use, since it's high complexity and long completion time.

Through this automation it's possible to use the gathered personality information to predict cooperative behavior and form cooperative types. Based on these cooperative types roles in a group can be recommended to improve group performance through optimal team composition.

Due to the novelty of the concept, there are limitations. Parameters like the minimum and maximum word count for the LIWC analysis need empirical testing in a proper environment. However the values stated by Yarkoni et al. [7] provide a good approximation.

8 Future Work

In a future work we will develop a prototype to evaluate our concept in a creativity group task. In this task three different group constellations, based on divergent and convergent thinking styles, will be compared. For the first constellation group members will be assigned by random, with no consideration of thinking style (control group). The participants for the second group constellation will be assigned by personality, while the third group constellation will be arranged by the results of "classical" creativity tests. For this purpose we will use tests, which can be done automatically, like the Guilford Test [41], Wallach Test [42] or a Mathematics, Verbal and Spatial Test [43] as well as the more complex Torrence Test [44], which have to be done manually.

The experiment will consist of three phases. In an *initial phase* the participants have to write down an idea for a specific problem. This written idea will be our input for the LIWC analysis to derive the personality for every participant. Additionally every participant has to complete the creativity tests. The second phase will be a *matching phase*, where groups will be formed, like stated above. In the final *group phase* every group has to solve a group creativity task, which consists of divergent and convergent parts. The outputs of the groups will then be rated by a set of experts and be compared to evaluate the use of personality for group constellations in a group creativity tasks.

References

1. Shen, S.-T., Prior, S.D., White, A.S., Karamanoglu, M.: Using personality type differences to form engineering design teams. Eng. Educ. 2(2), 54–66 (2007)
2. Bradley, J.H., Hebert, F.J.: The effect of personality type on team performance. J. Manage. Dev. 16, 337–353 (1997)
3. Volkema, R.J., Gorman, R.H.: The influence of cognitive-based group composition on decision-making process and outcome. J. Manage. Stud. 35, 105–121 (1998)
4. Stumpf, S., Dunbar, R.: The effects of personality type on choices made in strategic decision situations. Decis. Sci. 22, 1047–1072 (1991)

5. Chamorro-Premuzic, T., Reichenbacher, L.: Effects of personality and threat of evaluation on divergent and convergent thinking. J. Res. Pers. **42**, 1095–1101 (2008)
6. Batey, M., Chamorro-Premuzic, T., Furnham, A.: Intelligence and personality as predictors of divergent thinking: the role of general, fluid and crystallised intelligence. Think. Skills Creat. **4**, 60–69 (2009)
7. Yarkoni, T.: Personality in 100,000 words: a large-scale analysis of personality and word use among bloggers. J. Res. Pers. **44**, 363–373 (2010)
8. Gulati, R., Wohlgezogen, F., Zhelyazkov, P.: The two facets of collaboration: cooperation and coordination in strategic alliances. Acad. Manage. Ann. **6**, 531–583 (2012)
9. Hord, S.M.: Working Together: Cooperation or Collaboration? ERIC, Cambridge (1981)
10. Gerosa, M.A., Pimentel, M.G., Fuks, H., de Lucena, C.J.P.: Development of groupware based on the 3C collaboration model and component technology. In: Dimitriadis, Y.A., Zigurs, I., Gómez-Sánchez, E. (eds.) CRIWG 2006. LNCS, vol. 4154, pp. 302–309. Springer, Heidelberg (2006)
11. Ellis, C.A., Gibbs, S.J., Rein, G.: Groupware: some issues and experiences. Commun. ACM **34**, 39–58 (1991)
12. Fuks, H., Raposo, A.B., Gerosa, M.A., de Lucena, C.J.P.: Applying the 3C Model to Groupware Engineering. PUC, Rio de Janeiro (2004)
13. Dawes, R.M.: Social dilemmas. Ann. Rev. Psychol. **31**, 169–193 (1980)
14. Kollock, P.: Social dilemmas: the anatomy of cooperation. Ann. Rev. Sociol. **24**, 183–214 (2013)
15. Olson, M.J.: The Logic of Collective Action. Public Goods and the Theory of Groups. Harvard University Press, Cambridge (1965)
16. Komorita, S., Parks, C.D.: Interpersonal relations: mixed-motive interaction (1995). http://arjournals.annualreviews.org/doi/abs/10.1146/annurev.ps.46.020195.001151
17. Fu, F., Chen, X.J., Liu, L.H., Wang, L.: Social dilemmas in an online social network: the structure and evolution of cooperation. Phys. Lett. A **371**, 58–64 (2007)
18. Fehl, K., van der Post, D.J., Semmann, D.: Co-evolution of behaviour and social network structure promotes human cooperation. Ecol. Lett. **14**, 546–551 (2011)
19. Liebrand, W.B.G.: The effect of social motives, communication and group size on behaviour in an N-person multi-stage mixed-motive game. Eur. J. Soc. Psychol. **14**, 239–264 (1984)
20. Griesinger, D.W., Livingston, J.W.: Toward a model of interpersonal motivation in experimental games. Behav. Sci. **18**, 173–188 (1973)
21. Balliet, D., Parks, C., Joireman, J.: Social value orientation and cooperation in social dilemmas: A meta-analysis. Group Process. Intergr. Relat. **12**, 533–547 (2009)
22. Goldberg, L.R.: An alternative "description of personality": the big-five factor structure. J. Pers. Soc. Psychol. **59**, 1216–1229 (1990)
23. Rammstedt, B.: The 10-Item big five inventory. Eur. J. Psychol. Assess. **23**, 193–201 (2007)
24. Rammstedt, B., John, O.P.: Measuring personality in one minute or less: a 10-item short version of the big five inventory in English and German. J. Res. Pers. **41**, 203–212 (2007)
25. Costa, P.T., McCrae, R.R.: Professional manual: revised NEO personality inventory (NEO-PI-R) and NEO five-factor inventory (NEO-FFI). Odessa FL Psychol. Assess. Resour. **3**, 101 (1992)
26. Terracciano, A.: The Italian version of the NEO PI-R: Conceptual and empirical support for the use of targeted rotation. Pers. Individ. Differ. **35**, 1859–1872 (2003)
27. Galesic, M., Bosnjak, M.: Effects of questionnaire length on participation and indicators of response quality in a web survey. Public Opin. Q. **73**, 349–360 (2009)
28. Ashton, M.C., Lee, K.: A defence of the lexical approach to the study of personality structure. Eur. J. Pers. **19**, 5–24 (2005)

29. Pennebaker, J.W., Booth, R.J., Francis, M.E.: Operator's Manual: Linguistic Inquiry and Word Count - LIWC2007, pp. 1–11 (2007)

30. Pennebaker, J.W., Graybeal, A.: Patterns of natural language use: disclosure, personality, and social integration. Curr. Dir. Psychol. Sci. **10**, 90–93 (2001)

31. Pennebaker, J.W., Mehl, M.R., Niederhoffer, K.G.: Psychological aspects of natural language. use: our words, our selves. Ann. Rev. Psychol. **54**, 547–577 (2003)

32. Fast, L.A., Funder, D.C.: Personality as manifest in word use: correlations with self-report, acquaintance report, and behavior. J. Pers. Soc. Psychol. **94**, 334–346 (2008)

33. Hirsh, J.B., DeYoung, C.G., Peterson, J.B.: Metatraits of the big five differentially predict engagement and restraint of behavior. J. Pers. **77**, 1085–1101 (2009)

34. Pennebaker, J.W., King, L.A: Language use as an individual difference (1999)

35. Koole, S.L., Jager, W., van den Berg, A.E., Vlek, C.A., Hofstee, W.K.: On the social nature of personality: effects of extraversion, agreeableness, and feedback about collective resource use on cooperation in a resource dilemma. Pers. Soc. Psychol. Bull. **27**, 289–301 (2001)

36. Hilbig, B.E., Zettler, I., Moshagen, M., Heydasch, T.: Tracing the path from personality—via cooperativeness—to conservation. Eur. J. Pers. **27**, 319–327 (2013)

37. Graziano, W.G., Habashi, M.M., Sheese, B.E., Tobin, R.M.: Agreeableness, empathy, and helping: a person × situation perspective. J. Pers. Soc. Psychol. **93**, 583–599 (2007)

38. Buss, D.M.: Social adaptation and five major factors of personality. In: Wiggins, J.S. (ed.) The Five-factor Model of Personality: Theoretical Perspectives, pp. 180–207. Guilford, New York (1996).

39. Ashton, M.C., Paunonen, S.V., Helmes, E., Jackson, D.N.: Kin altruism, reciprocal altruism, and the big five personality factors. Evol. Hum. Behav. **19**, 243–255 (1998)

40. Peffers, K., Tuunanen, T., Rothenberger, M.A., Chatterjee, S.: A design science research methodology for information systems research. J. Manag. Inf. Syst. **24**, 45–77 (2007)

41. Guilford, J.P.: The Nature of Human Intelligence. McGraw-Hill, New York (1967)

42. Wallach, M.A., Kogan, N.: Modes of Thinking in Young Children: A Study of the Creativity-intelligence Distinction. Holt, Rinehart and Winston, New York (1965)

43. Mayer, R.E., Dow, G.T., Mayer, S.: Multimedia learning in an interactive self-explaining environment: what works in the design of agent-based microworlds? J. Educ. Psychol. **95**, 806–812 (2003)

44. Runco, M.A., Millar, G., Acar, S., Cramond, B.: Torrance tests of creative thinking as predictors of personal and public achievement: a fifty-year follow-up. Creat. Res. J. **22**, 361–368 (2010)

Applying the 3C Model to FLOSS Communities

Sara Fernandes[(✉)] and Luis Soares Barbosa[(✉)]

HASLab INESC TEC & UNU-EGOV, United Nations University,
Campus de Couros, Guimarães, Portugal
sarasantos.fernandes@gmail.com, lsb@di.uminho.pt

Abstract. How learning occurs within Free/Libre Open Source (FLOSS) communities and what is the dynamics of such projects (e.g. the life cycle of such projects) are very relevant questions when considering the use of FLOSS projects in a formal education setting. This paper introduces an approach based on the 3C collaboration model (communication, coordination and cooperation) to represent the collaborative learning dynamics within FLOSS communities. To explore the collaborative learning potential of FLOSS communities a number of questionnaires and interviews to selected FLOSS contributors were run. From this study a 3C collaborative model applicable to FLOSS communities was designed and discussed.

Keywords: 3C collaboration model · FLOSS · Learning

1 Introduction

In recent years, open software development has become more and more prevalent. With the rise and generalisation of the Internet, communities and individuals worldwide interconnect themselves and cooperate in a variety of ways. Examples range from crowd funding platforms, such as FundedByMe in Sweden or Seedrs in UK, to PulsePoint Respond which is an enterprise-class, software-as-a-service (SaaS) pre-arrival solution designed to support public safety agencies working to improve cardiac survival rates through improved bystander performance and active citizenship. And, of course, Wikipedia, probably the most used collaboration platform in the world.

Open development is essentially a collaborative process, most commonly focused on a product or service whose added value is perceived by heterogeneous communities. Participants may work in different environments, have totally different backgrounds and resources, and act under different conditions [3]. Collaboration in this sense may be seen as the combination of communication, coordination and cooperation. The articulation of these attributes is what remains in the origin of the *3C collaboration model*, originally proposed by Ellis *et al.* [7] and refined in a later work [6]. Communication is related to the exchange of messages and information among people; coordination concerns management of people and communities, their activities and resources; and finally cooperation denotes a shared activity taking place on a shared space. This model appears frequently in the literature as a means to classify collaborative systems [11,19].

© Springer International Publishing Switzerland 2016
T. Yuizono et al. (Eds.): CRIWG 2016, LNCS 9848, pp. 139–150, 2016.
DOI: 10.1007/978-3-319-44799-5_11

The development of Free/Libre Open Source Software (FLOSS) projects across different people and communities, can be regarded as an example of a collaborative and participatory platform, maintained, and to a certain extent owned by a community. Actually, FLOSS communities consist of heterogeneous groups of independent volunteers, who interact even if driven by utterly different motivations [4,17]. Moreover, FLOSS development provides an example of Peer-Production [14], based as it is on collaborative, social modes of interaction and knowledge exchange [2].

In such a setting, the goal of this paper is to explore the application of the 3C collaboration model to FLOSS communities, under the broad objective of boosting their potential as non standard educational agents. This entails the need for a accurate understanding of what are the pillars and the dynamics underpinning FLOSS communities. Therefore, we ran an international questionnaire and performed 4 individual written interviews with active members of such communities in an attempt to understand how learning processes occur within FLOSS communities.

The rest of the paper is structured as follows. After some review of background concepts in Sects. 2, 3 presents the research method. Data gathered through a questionnaire, following up our previous research [8,9], and a qualitative analysis of the interviews, is presented in Sect. 4. Section 5 presents the 3C model applied to FLOSS Communities. Finally, Sect. 6 concludes and presents some directions for future work.

2   Background

Learning can be defined as a persisting change in human performance or performance potential which must come about as a result of the learners experience and interaction with the world [5]. It can be formal, i.e. institutionally framed and hierarchically structured, or informal. Informal learning is a life-long process in which an individual acquires knowledge, attitudes, values and skills while performing daily activity within various contexts. From Jay Cross perspective, people informally acquire much of the knowledge they use in their practice. Through the observation of others, by trial and error, or simply working side by side with more experienced people. In his opinion, *formal education contributes only about 10 % to 20 % of what a person learns in a professional context* [1]. In both settings, the qualifier collaborative refers to sets of activities involving a group of people learning or trying to learn something together.

When several people learn, or attempt to learn, something together, we refer to this activity as collaborative learning. Unlike individual learning, collaborative learning capitalizes on other persons resources and skills, for instance by asking for information, cross-assessment of ideas or mutual monitoring of work progress. It encourages knowledge construction, skill development and deeper understanding by actively engaging people in the learning processes [12].

At the origin of the 3C collaboration model, originally proposed by Ellis *et al.* [7] and later explored in [6], is the combination of *communication, coordination* and *cooperation*. Communication is related to the exchange of messages and information among people; coordination is related to the management of people, their activities and resources; and cooperation refers to any kind of production taking place collaboratively, on a shared space. This model appears frequently in the literature as a mean to classify collaborative systems.

In the paper *Applying the 3C model to groupware development* [11] two instantiations of the 3C model are presented, as well as the classification of AulaNet services based on the 3C model. The first instantiation is for Mackay's Media Space [13], which are multimedia, enhanced communication spaces. The Media Space itself is the shared space. It is aimed at informal communication and its main goal is to create opportunities for informal meetings, which are coordinated by the standing social protocol. Such meeting generate conversation, which may occur using the media provided by the system or any other available mean, such as telephones. The instantiation is depicted in Fig. 1.

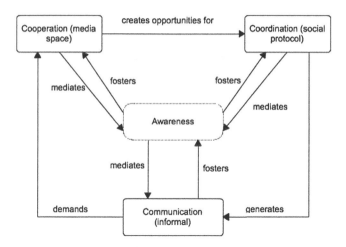

Fig. 1. 3C collaboration model instantiated for the Media Space domain.

A second instantiation is concerned with group work and is depicted in Fig. 2. The 3C collaboration model instantiated to the groupware domain shows that, while communicating, people negotiate and make decisions. While coordinating themselves, they deal with conflicts and organize their activities in a manner that prevents loss of communication and of cooperation efforts. This example shows the iterative nature of collaboration.

Although, as seen above, the 3C model is commonly used for classifying collaborative systems, no attempt was done to use it in the FLOSS development scenario. FLOSS builds on the general idea of open and available source code and goes even further by being both a software development method and a software

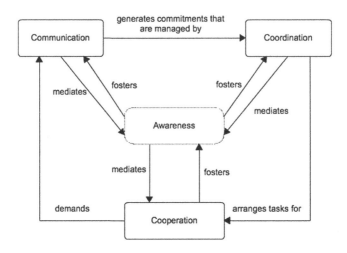

Fig. 2. 3C collaboration model instantiated for group work.

business model [16]. It is further defined by the license used to grant users and developers additional right to the code. FLOSS can freely be used, studied, and modified. Note that it is not necessarily cost free, thus qualifier free does not relate to monetary cost but to freedom or liberty. Copying and redistribution is allowed, but can be restricted by the license as it may require a need to grant the same rights to the modified versions as well. Richard Stallman formulated the first definition of free software in 1983, as any piece of software that grants anyone with a copy the freedom to run, study, redistribute or improve it. Actually, there are four degrees of freedom used to classify FLOSS [10]. A program is free software if it gives users adequately all of these freedoms. Otherwise, it is non free. Those are indexed from zero as geek homage to zero-based numbering often used in computer systems, as follows:

0 The freedom to run the program for any purpose.
1 The freedom to study how the program works, and change it to make it do what you wish.
2 The freedom to redistribute copies so you can help your neighbor.
3 The freedom to improve the program, and release your improvements (and modified versions in general) to the public, so that the whole community benefits.

At the heart of FLOSS is the developer community, a social ecosystem on its own. The structure of the community is often depicted with a layered onion model, where the users of the software form the outmost layer and the most prominent developers and the leader of the project are at the core [15]. As depicted in Fig. 3, the Onion Community Model for FLOSS focuses on the developer community alone.

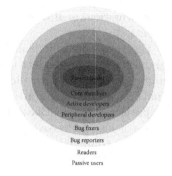

Fig. 3. General structure of a FLOSS community (Onion Model).

3   Research Method

The aim of this study was to understand how collaboration and learning occurs within FLOSS communities; which are the motivations, challenges and difficulties participants in such projects experience, as well as which sort of learning experience they have and how they interact. Research was based on qualitative instruments, as described below. Actually, qualitative research methods produces results that cannot easily be achieved by statistical procedures or similar quantitative methods [18]. The results of this kind of approach are richer and more informative, helping to answer questions involving variables that are difficult to quantify, such as human characteristics like motivations or perceptions.

For this study we used both a survey and structured interviews as data collection method. The survey was made available online using Google Docs and shared among FLOSS communities, as well as sent to a number of individual FLOSS contributors. Its aim was twofold (1) to study the interactions between FLOSS projects participants, and (2) to assess the didactical value of participating in FLOSS projects. A preliminary analysis of this survey was previously made in references [8,9]. The interviews were later conducted to a number of FLOSS contributors selected among those who have previously replied to the online survey.

The questionnaire was structured into three main sections:

– Section A collects respondents demographics, including age, country, language, background and the different FLOSS projects he/she have been enrolled in.
– Section B collects data about the respondents interaction with the project community, and the motivations to start and continue contributing to FLOSS project. It explores the respondents participation in a specific FLOSS project. The respondent is faced with a specific project, to which he/she has (or is) contributing, and is requested to describe how the participation started, the drivers what drove him/her to starting such activity, his/her role in the project, and how many hours he/she devotes to it. The respondent has the

opportunity to describe the type of relationships he has with other community members, how they share information, or if they promote and participate in community meetings or events.

- Section C surveys where the respondents exploit the potential of FLOSS projects as learning environments. The respondent is asked whether the fact of being in a FLOSS community provides him with a learning opportunity, and if his background (professional or academic) facilitates the learning process while participating in a FLOSS project. The identification of the most important agents in this learning process is also addressed, as well as if FLOSS projects can be regarded as (1) learning communities, (2) a possible alternative to formal education, and (3) an interesting complement to formal education.

Each section comprises open-ended and closed-ended questions. In the open-ended questions no possible responses were given, allowing the respondent to write down the answers in his/her own words. In the closed-ended questions, possible answers were provided for the respondent to tick the category that best described his/her choice. In such questions, the clause "Other / please explain" was included to accommodate any response not listed. The use of these two forms of questions revert to the fact that close-ended questions are extremely useful for eliciting factual information and open-ended questions for seeking opinions, attitudes and perceptions. In the closed-ended questions, we not only allowed multi-selection answers but also provided three types of Likert Scale answers: (1) to analyze the respondents perception, including values like *Strongly disagree, Disagree, Not sure/ Not applicable, Agree*, and *Strongly agree*; and (2) to analyze the frequency of certain respondents behavior, including values like *Ever, Once every year, Once a month, At least 3 times per month*, and *More than 3 times per month*; and (3) to assess the relevance that the respondent assigns to a specific issue, including values like *Not at all important, Not too important, Not sure / Not applicable, Somewhat important*, and *Very important*.

The interviews, used in a second phase of this study, aimed at further exploring (1) the motivations to participate in FLOSS projects, and (2) the didactical value of their communities (emphasising namely, the interactions established while contributing to the project or carrying on related activities.

4   Data Analysis

Questionnaire Results. Since the questionnaire was released, data was collected from 28 respondents, 25 men, 3 women, from 16 different countries, including Portugal, United Kingdom, Germany, India, France, Serbia, Finland, Netherlands, Belgium, Slovenia, USA, Macau SAR China, Canada, Argentina, Israel, and Brazil (see [9] for a detailed analysis).

Concerning the first question-objective, we were able to see that, independently of the type of relationships participant maintain with FLOSS communities and the degree of personal acquaintance, such communities act as important personal networks, promoting high-level interactions and creating opportunities to (often virtually) meet and socialize in a variety of events. Although the most commonly given reason for starting contributing to a FLOSS contributors project, was the response to a personal/intellectually rewarding challenge, their interest does not fade out along time and they go on contributing to the project in a quite regular way.

Concerning the second research question, it became evident that FLOSS projects contributors recognize the learning potential of such environments, and that the fact of being active participants in such projects improves a number of different skills. All the respondents identified not only other community members as learning agents, but also include themselves in such a category. This provides evidence of the eminently collaborative natures of the, often non linear but effective teaching and learning processes occurring within FLOSS.

Interviews to FLOSS Contributors. After conducting the questionnaire online, a group of 4 participants from the survey was selected to be interviewed individually. The data collected is summarised and briefly analysed below. As already mentioned, the focus was put on the motivations to participate in FLOSS projects and communities, on the one hand, and the assessment of such an experience as a possible learning one, on the other.

Interview 1. The first FLOSS developer to be interviewed, referred as interviewed **A** in the sequel, was a master student, who acts as a freelance software consultant and developer. For a long time, he has been engaged in several FLOSS projects, such as cwac-caera, UniversalImageLoader, ProgreeWheel and Django. For the purpose of the interview A chose to refer to the cwac-camera project.

A decided to participate in the cwac-camera project after using this software at a professional level. In his case, the interactions with the community were easy and the communication was exclusively done online, via Github, resorting to issues/forums or pull-requests. He communicates weekly with other community members and is willing to help whoever seeks support. The interviewed never had any serious disagreement with community members nor he motived others to join the community. For him, the time of participation on such projects depends only on the personal interest and time available, as the projects can only achieve the most if contributors are motivated and driven to move it forward.

With respect to the possible learning experience developed along the process, **A** believes he has learned a lot, particularly on how others contribute to the same project and how they interact among each other and with code being produced. Moreover, as he is willing to help others, he also likes to share his knowledge.

When asked if participating in FLOSS project in the the context of formal education, **A** believes that everyone studying software development and engineering should at least once experience what it means to participate and contribute to a FLOSS project. This is understood as a privileged way to learn and get proficient in a number of methods, techniques and professional practices, as well as in purely social skills. As a limitation to use FLOSS projects in formal education, **A** points out the control students may or not have of the project and its size. Those are factors that may limit how broad or how deep the learning experience may result. He also mentions that the success or failure of the particular project used in such a context cannot be used as an reliable instrument for assessing one's contribution.

Interview 2. The second interview was made to FLOSS contributor **B**. He holds a PhD and is professionally an university lecturer. **B** has been involved with several FLOSS projects, such as NetBSD, EDOS/MANCOOSI, Coq, or FreeBSD. For the purpose of the interview, **B** selected the NetBSD project.

B decided to participate in NetBSD project because he felt he could contribute with some patches and, moreover, there were some bugs that he knew how to fix. He communicates with other community members once a week through the project mailing lists. Despite his wish, his participation is somehow limited due to lack of time. Since **B** joined the community, a very opinionated one, he became aware of several on-going disagreements and quarrels inside it, but tries to stay away from them, depending on the points being discussed. For **B**, both a long term or a short term period of participation in a project can make sense, both of them bringing a number of advantages. Actually, in his perspective, FLOSS projects should allow both short-term participations for submitting occasional patches (e.g. to fix a bug) and long-term development to mature ideas and practices and bring a sense of continuity to the project. As far as difficulties are concerned, **B** claims they are inevitable, but underlines the support always offered by other community members.

As for the learning experience, **B** recognises he indeed learned some new technical skills and new ways of interacting with other developers. Facing people with strong personalities and commitment, lead to the development of new and improves socially-related skills.

When asked about the possible use of participation in FLOSS projects as an element in formal education, **B** believes it represents a great opportunity to interact with the FLOSS world and with a remarkable formative value. He is promoting a Software Engineering course at his university that uses FLOSS projects as part of the syllabus.

Interview 3. The third interview, referred as **C** in the sequel, also has a PhD. **C** has been involved with several FLOSS projects, such as Parrot VM, Rakudo, Perl, and Dancer.

For the purpose of this interview, **C** selected the project Dancer, a lightweight web framework written in Perl for building websites and similar applications. **C** started participating in the project as, by that time, he was already involved in building application, and decided to help on a new version. **C** communicates in a daily basis with the community, using IRC, mailing lists or the issue tracker available.

The Dance community is very active, and without having much time, **C** have difficulties and keeping up with everything happening, there. However, he tries to remain open to challenges and new problems to solve.

The community does not have disagreements but does have "healthy" discussions. The motivation and the time spent in the project, for **C**, depends on personal interest and the fact that when a difficulty arises, community members are always willing to help.

As for the learning experience, **C** believes participating in FLOSS projects constitutes a source of learning, of new skills and technologies, as many people with different backgrounds and different education paths share their knowledge. What one learns and the knowledge created is, for **C**, the best benefit one can have for participating in a FLOSS project. Also, **C** believes that FLOSS projects should be used as learning experiences and that the active involvement in such communities should be formally included in some courses of at university level.

Interview 4. The fourth interview was with interviewed **D**, a university lecturer, that has been contributing to the Perl community. **D** does not contribute to a single project but is involved in a set of modules, each of which can be regarded as a project in itself.

D was motivated to participate in such project because he was an enthusiast of the language; but also because he got to know someone of the community. He began the interaction via email, with other community members, asking for help to use some of the modules. Now they use IRC channel on a regular basis.

D is motivated by the project mainly because he enjoys seeing the community growing, with a general and active participation. Actually, there are almost no cases of people joining and dropping out of the project in the first month. As far as the time of participation is concerned, only those with more time in the community can advance for the development of more complex projects (modules). Hence, it depends on what is the task to perform. The community is very helpful and every time **D** had a difficulty he found the solution with a community member. Similarly he is willing to help others, a dynamics that seems to be dominant in this sort of communities.

Concerning the learning experience, **D** acknowledges to have learned many different things and progressing in different aspects. For example, he learned how to deal with other people or even to improve the use of English. He also became aware of how people work differently, how to read, analyse and reuse other peoples code and deal with new technologies from a very practical starting point.

For **D** using FLOSS project as a learning platform at different level of education can be beneficial but also represent a risk. Students may lack the basic knowledge he believes to be required, or, on the other hand, FLOSS communities may not have the patience or time to help them. This may be purely out of their horizon. His recommendation is to proceed in a careful way, as there are no two students or two FLOSS communities equal.

Summary of Findings. The data gathered both through the questionnaires and the four interviews to FLOSS developers provide empirical evidence on

- The relevance as well as the complexity of the human interactions involved; remarkably in all interviews FLOSS communities were mentioned as a sort of school for personal relationships.
- The strongly personal motivation for joining and remaining such communities.
- The mutually supportive environment.
- The intense, even if sometimes unbalanced, learning experience offered. Most, but not all, see in participation in such projects an opportunity that could be somehow integrated in a formal education setting.

These findings were taken into consideration in our proposal of a 3C collaborative model for FLOSS communities, detailed in the next section.

5   A 3C Collaborative Model for FLOSS Communities

As referred in Sect. 1, the origin of the 3C collaboration model is the combination of communication, coordination and cooperation. FLOSS communities are all about collaboration, as witnessed by the interviews summarised above. They grow because people gather in the same goal: to develop software. To do it, collaboration is at the core of its success, despite personal motivations, backgrounds or professional activities. However, the outcome of the FLOSS community dynamics is well known and not only such project are often successful in terms of products made available (with a growing commercial impact, it should be noted), but also in terms of the knowledge produced and the communities

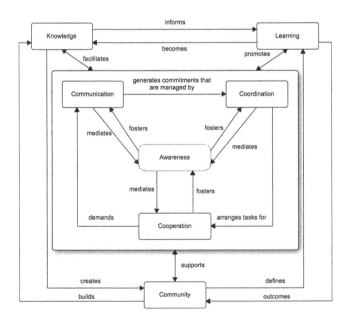

Fig. 4. The 3C collaborative model instantiated for FLOSS communities.

fostered along the process. Indeed all participants, in different ways, have the opportunity to learn both new technical skill, but also new social and cultural skills, new ways of working, etc. Hence FLOSS community can accurately be described in terms of the 3C collaborative model proposed by [7].

Figure 4 depicts our proposal to instantiate a 3C collaborative model applied to FLOSS communities. As previously observed, motivation is the key to start participating in a FLOSS project; it can be a new challenge, the topic, a new idea, etc. The tasks developed are just one of the ways to contribute. FLOSS projects are developed within a communitarian basis. The knowledge each participant brings can help not only the project to succeed, but also others in acquiring new knowledge and skills. As observed in the interviews, new knowledge can be acquired when a FLOSS participant faces difficulties, or sometimes it happens just out of curiosity and personal motivation. Why knowledge happens is of minor importance, in comparison with how knowledge is facilitated and how learning is promoted within a FLOSS community. This instantiation of the 3C collaboration model for FLOSS communities allows for the description of their dynamics which can be regarded as a learning experiences, with relevant didactical potential.

6   Conclusions and Future Work

FLOSS communities consist of heterogeneous groups of independent volunteers who interact among them driven by different motivations, to produce a shared software asset. As we were able to analyze by our sample of respondents to the questionnaire, FLOSS projects participants collaborate and cooperate between them in more systematic and innovative ways than usual in normal, classic professional practice. Al the community dynamics is focused and driven by its shared objective: to develop a new software project. Despite the relevance they give to FLOSS development, it is interesting to see that the FLOSS developers interviewed are skeptical with respect to the possibility that participation in FLOSS projects can be an alternative to formal education, for example, to replace formal courses in Software Engineering in higher education institutions. However, they see that the *learning by doing* concept, typically emerging from FLOSS projects, are an effective and possibly attractive complement to formal education, mainly in Software Engineering degrees. Clearly, the 3C collaboration model can be applied to model FLOSS communities collaborative learning frameworks and help to categorise and assess them.

We are currently working on validating this model in the educational context, through the analysis of data gathered in a pilot project in which MSc students have to join an contribute to a FLOSS project as part of a formal course in Software Engineering.

Acknowledgments. This work was supported by the *Programa Operacional da Região Norte*, NORTE2020, in the context of project NORTE-01-0145-FEDER-000037. The second author is further supported by FCT under grant SFRH/BSAB/113890/2015.

References

1. Arets, J., Heijnen, V.: Interview with jay cross (2015). www.tulser.com/wpcontent/uploads/2015/10/Tulser-interview-Jay-Cross.pdf. Retrieved 9 May 2016
2. Bacon, S., Dillon, T.: The potential of open source approaches for education. Futurelab, 44 (2006)
3. Burnell, L.J., Priest, J.W., Durrett, J.B.: Teaching distributed multidisciplinary software development. IEEE Softw. **19**(5), 86–93 (2002)
4. Cerone, A., Sowe, S.K.: Using free/libre open source software projects as e-learning tools. ECEASST, 33 (2010)
5. Driscoll, M.: Psychology of Learning Instruction, 3rd edn. Pearson Education Inc., Boston (2005)
6. Ellis, C., Wainer, J.: A conceptual model of groupware. In: Proceedings of the 1994 ACM Conference on Computer Supported Cooperative Work, CSCW 1994, pp. 79–88. ACM, New York, NY, USA (1994)
7. Ellis, C.A., Gibbs, S.J., Rein, G.: Groupware: some issues and experiences. Commun. ACM **34**(1), 39–58 (1991)
8. Fernandes, S., Cerone, A., Barbosa, L.S.: A preliminary analysis of learning awareness in FLOSS projects. In: Cerone, A., Persico, D., Fernandes, S., Garcia-Perez, A., Katsaros, P., Ahmed Shaikh, S., Stamelos, I. (eds.) SEFM 2012 Satellite Events. LNCS, vol. 7991, pp. 133–139. Springer, Heidelberg (2014)
9. Fernandes, S., Cerone, A., Barbosa, L.S.: Analysis of FLOSS communities as learning contexts. In: Counsell, S., Núñez, M. (eds.) SEFM 2013. LNCS, vol. 8368, pp. 405–416. Springer, Heidelberg (2014)
10. GNU Foundation. What is free software? (2016). www.gnu.org/philosophy/free-sw.en.html. Retrieved 9 May 2016
11. Fuks, H., Raposo, A.B., Gerosa, M.A., Lucena, C.J.P.: Applying the 3C model to groupware development. Int. J. Coop. Inf. Syst. **14**(02n03), 299–328 (2005)
12. Jara, C.A., Candelas, F.A., Torres, F., Dormido, S., Esquembre, F., Reinoso, O.: Real-time collaboration of virtual laboratories through the internet. Comput. Educ. **52**(1), 126–140 (2009)
13. Mackay, W.E.: Media spaces: environments for informal multimedia interaction. In: Beaudouin-Lafon, M. (ed.) Computer-Supported CooperativeWork. Trends in Software Series, pp. 55–82. Wiley, Hoboken (1999)
14. Magrassi, P.: Free and open-source software is not an emerging property but ratherthe result of studied design (2010). CoRR, abs/1012.5625
15. Nakakoji, K., Yamamoto, Y., Nishinaka, Y., Kishida, K., Ye, Y.: Evolution patterns of open-source software systems and communities. In: Proceedings of the International Workshop on Principles of Software Evolution, IWPSE 2002, pp. 76–85. ACM, New York, NY, USA (2002)
16. Raymond, E.S.: The Cathedral and the Bazaar. O'Reilly Media, Sebastopol (1999)
17. Sowe, S.K., Cerone, A., Settas, D.: An empirical study of FOSS developers patterns of contribution: challenges for data linkage and analysis. Sci. Comput. Program. **91**, 249–265 (2014)
18. Strauss, A., Corbin, J.M.: Basics of Qualitative Research: Techniques and Procedures for Developing Grounded Theory, 2nd edn. Sage Publications Inc., Thousand Oaks (1998)
19. Sung, H.-Y., Hwang, G.-J.: A collaborative game-based learning approach to improving students' learning performance in science courses. Comput. Educ. **63**(1), 43–51 (2013)

Hootle+: A Group Recommender System Supporting Preference Negotiation

Jesús Omar Álvarez Márquez[✉] and Jürgen Ziegler

University of Duisburg-Essen, Duisburg, Germany
{jesus.alvarez-marquez, juergen.ziegler}@uni-due.de

Abstract. This paper presents an approach to group recommender systems that focuses its attention on the group's social interaction during the formulation, discussion and negotiation of the features the item to be jointly selected should possess. The system supports a collaborative preference elicitation and negotiation process where desired item features can be defined individually, but group consensus is needed for them to become active in the item filtering process. Users can provide feedback on other members' preferences and change their significance, bringing up new recommendations each time individual settings are modified. The last stage in the decision process is also supported, when users collectively select the final item from the recommendation set. We developed the prototype hotel recommender Hootle+ and evaluated it in a user study involving groups of different size. The results indicate a good overall satisfaction, which increases with group size. However, the success ratio for bigger groups is lower than for small groups, raising questions for follow-up research.

Keywords: Group recommender system · Group preference elicitation · Negotiation · Decision-making

1 Introduction

Over the recent years, recommender systems (RS) have become an important and widely used technology that can help users in selecting items from large sets of choices, for example, in online shops or media portals [32]. RS are usually aimed at supporting individual users in their search and decision-making, which is appropriate in many cases where an item (such as a news article) is typically only utilized by a single user. Already early on, RS research recognized that there are also situations where groups of people utilize a product or service together, for example, when jointly going to a restaurant or the movies. *Polylens* was the first system that supported group decisions by providing recommendations based on the users' preferences [28]. A number of group recommender systems (GRS) have been developed since [6, 20] but there is still limited research in this area and the question of how to optimally support a group decision process based on recommendations is still open in several aspects. Usually, GRS extract the information they need from existing user profiles, subsequently using one out of two approaches for calculating the recommendations: either they aggregate the user profiles to create a single group profile (model aggregation) before generating group recommendations, or the recommendations are individually calculated for each

© Springer International Publishing Switzerland 2016
T. Yuizono et al. (Eds.): CRIWG 2016, LNCS 9848, pp. 151–166, 2016.
DOI: 10.1007/978-3-319-44799-5_12

user profile and then aggregated, using a variety of different strategies (recommendation aggregation). These approaches fail, however, when user preference data is not available, either for single users or for the whole group, which is the case in cold start situations. This obstacle is especially problematic for ad-hoc groups who gather spontaneously or when user data are distributed over different unconnected systems. A further issue is the situational variability of user preferences, which may amplify the inherent heterogeneity of preferences due to different responses of group members to the situational context. These issues ask for methods that can elicit group preferences on the fly and that can aggregate individual preferences in a manner that best suits the individual users as well as the group as a whole. In addition, other processes occurring in group interaction, such as developing or refining one's own preferences and requirements based on the group discussion, or negotiating with others about the desired features of an item, have so far been under-explored in GRS research.

In this paper, we present an approach to GRS that is based on the intersection of conventional recommender techniques and decision-making support for groups. In a precursor development [1], we obtained promising results but also uncovered some issues that leave space for improvement, which motivated this follow-up research and the development of a revised method and prototype. From the previous development, we kept the underlying basic idea of allowing user to collaboratively create and discuss a preference model (thus addressing collaborative preference elicitation [30]), from which recommendations are generated. Although the old system let participants generate their individual preference model by creating public lists of features ordered by importance that were subsequently aggregated into the group's model, a user study taught us that the information tended to be too complex for unexperienced users, and that it was hard for participants to keep track of the changes, an issue that became more noticeable for larger groups. With these concerns in mind, we reshaped the group interaction process in a way that users do not only change and discuss their individual preference model, but are also able to manipulate the group's preference model directly. In this process, group interaction can happen at two (tightly intertwined) stages: (1) users can online discuss and negotiate preferences proposed and accepted, and (2) they can discuss and rate items taken from the recommendation set to arrive at a final consensus decision.

A major goal in this development was to avoid unfair situations in which some users might not be satisfied with the items proposed by the system. Instead of applying a fixed strategy, as is the case in most GRS, we based our work on the assumption that computer-mediated discussion groups have more equal member participation [35]. Each user can individually specify the features the jointly selected item should possess and propose them to the group. The group decides through public voting which attributes will be accepted and rate their significance, using an explicit preference elicitation approach [29]. Features that are accepted become part of the group preference model, which is used to determine an initial set of recommendations. By group discussion, members may then be able to convince other users to modify their preferences that were included into the group model. Recommendations are continuously calculated and updated after each change, thus allowing users to see the effect of their actions immediately. Different mechanisms are provided for discussing and reaching an agreement, both for the creation of a group preference model and for the final item selection.

In the following, we first survey related research before presenting the conceptual aspects of our approach (Sects. 2 and 3). We then describe the implementation of the prototype Hootle+ and its user interface design in Sect. 4. We report on a user study performed with groups of different sizes in Sect. 5 and conclude by summarizing our work and outlining future work in Sect. 6.

2   Related Work

While the field of recommending items for single users has already received a great deal of attention in recent research, GRS are, in comparison, a still less deeply investigated area. However, various GRS have been developed over the recent years, starting from early systems such as *MusicFX* [21], a group music recommender, that use different approaches for generating recommendations [6, 14]. However, there are still many open research questions concerning, for example, the best approach to aggregating individual preferences, techniques for responding to the situational needs of the group, or supporting the social interaction processes in the group for converging on a joint decision.

To structure the wide range of different aspects involved in group recommending, [16] suggest a design space comprising the dimensions preference input, process characteristics, group characteristics, and output. In the process dimension, an important aspect is how individual, possibly conflicting preferences can be merged to obtain recommendations that best fit the group as a whole. Apart from a few exceptions, group recommenders commonly use one of two schemas for gathering and representing users' preferences [14], already mentioned during the introduction. The first one, prediction aggregation, assumes that for each item, it is possible to predict a user's satisfaction, given the user's profile; then, making use of some specific aggregation strategy, items are sorted by the group's overall satisfaction. In [11] a video recommender that uses this strategy is described; also, Polylens [28], a system that suggests movies to small groups of people with similar interests, based on the personal five-star scale ratings from Movielens [10] uses this method.

The second most used strategy, model aggregation, utilizes single user profiles for generating a group preference model, which is then employed to generate matching recommendations. There exists a high number of methods used for creating the group's model: in *Let's Browse* [17] the group preference model can be seen as an aggregation of individual preference models; in *Intrigue* [2, 3] (which recommends sightseeing destinations for heterogeneous groups of tourists) the group preference model is constructed by aggregating preference models of homogeneous subgroups within the main group; *MusicFX* [21] chooses background music in a fitness center to accommodate members' preferences, also by merging their individual models; *AGReMo* [5] recommends movies to watch in cinemas close to a location for ad-hoc groups of users, creating the group's preference model not only by individual model aggregation but also taking into account specific group variables (e.g. time, weight of each member's vote). Furthermore, the *Travel Decision Forum* [12, 13] creates a group preference model that can be discussed and modified by the members themselves, aiming to non-collocated groups who are not able to meet face to face, allowing asynchronous communication.

Regardless of whether the aggregation is made before or after generating recommendations, an aggregation method that is appropriate for the specific group characteristics needs to be chosen. There are a number of voting strategies, empirically evaluated in [20], that have been used in actual GRS. One of the most typically chosen is the average strategy, where the group's score for an item is the average rating over all individuals (e.g., it is used by *Intrigue* and *Travel Decision Forum*); on the other side, the least misery strategy scores items depending on the minimal rating it has among group members (*Polylens, AGReMo*); placed somewhere in between, the average without misery strategy consists in rating items using an average function, but discarding those where the user score is under a threshold (*MusicFX, CATS* [22–25]); as a final example of most used aggregation methods, the median strategy uses the middle value of the group members' ratings (*Travel Decision Forum*).

On another dimension, the question of preference elicitation has to be solved, which is concerned with how the user-specific preference information needed to generate recommendations is obtained. One approach is to let users rate a number of items in advance and to derive preferences from this set of ratings. *AGReMo*, for instance, requires group members to create their own model of individual preferences before the group meeting takes place by rating movies that they already saw. In *Travel Decision Forum,* each participant starts with an empty preference form that has to be filled with the desired options, so group members define new preferences for each session. A more interactive approach, although for single user systems, is described in [19], which requires users to repeatedly choose between sets of sample items that are selected based on latent factors of a rating matrix. The techniques mentioned also address the cold-start problem when no user profile is available up-front but initially require some effort on the part of the user to develop a sufficiently detailed profile.

However, most preference elicitation techniques do not considerate group interaction. As pointed out in [18], to obtain adequate group recommendations it is not only necessary to model users' individual preferences, but also to understand how a decision among group members is reached. While research on group decision-making [33] is concerned with collaboratively making choices, focusing on the social process and the outcome, these aspects have mostly not been addressed in the development of GRS. Group decision making involves a variety of aspects, such as the discussion and evaluation of others' ideas, conflict resolution and evaluating the different options that have been elaborated. Also interesting for our research is the concept of consensus decision-making [9], which seeks for an acceptable resolution for the whole group. Within this context, Group Decision Support Systems (GDSS) have emerged, that aim at supporting the various aspects of decision-making [26, 27]. Recent examples of GDSS are *Choicla* [34] (domain-independent decision-making tool) or the popular *Doodle* [8] (event scheduling). Only few GRS attempt to include aspects of group decision theory, for instance, by introducing automated negotiation agents that simulate discussions between members to generate group recommendations [4]. However, supporting the entire preference elicitation and negotiation process that may occur when users take recommender-supported decisions is, to our knowledge, not realized by current GRS.

Taking into account the social factor that is involved in group recommendation, one needs to contemplate the question whether a user would be willing to change personal preferences in favor of the group's desires, bringing up the importance of group negotiation. In the Travel Decision Forum again, users are able to explore other members' preferences, with the possibility to copy them or propose modifications. The Collaborative Advisory Travel System (CATS) focuses on collocated groups of persons gathered around a multi-touch table. Recommendations are made by collecting critiques (users' feedbacks respecting recommended destinations) that can be discussed face to face, since the system gives visual support to enhance awareness of each other's preferences. The main difference between CATS and the system we propose is that the former is focused in critiquing items once they have been recommended, whereas the latter allows negotiation already in the preference elicitation stage.

3 Preference Elicitation and Negotiation Method

The approach here described is built on the idea of letting users remotely collaborate to create the set of preferences that will conform the group's preference model. As a result, users do not discuss only about recommendations, but also about which attributes should be examined by the system when exploring the items to recommend. For doing so, preferences are evaluated in a process that involves interaction among group members almost since its very first stage until the last one. The result will be a very well narrowed set of preferences and a collection of recommended items matching the group's overall wishes. The overall process is carried out as follows:

1. Each participant can individually select the features that the recommended items should contain by placing them in a private area.
2. Once a feature is selected, the user may propose it to the rest of the group, together with the importance this user thinks that this feature deserves.
3. By proposing a feature, it becomes visible to the whole group, which will decide whether to accept it as a filter or not using the voting system provided.
4. If the feature is accepted, it becomes an active filter and influences the recommendations depending on its significance. A feature's significance is calculated by aggregating the importance level that each user has given to it. Significance is adjustable at any moment, bringing up new recommendations after any change.
5. Finally, a user is able to highlight specific recommended items and to state an opinion (via voting/discussing) about the ones that have been selected by the rest of users. More features can be proposed, accepted and rated continually, so the recommendations are narrowed until the group finds an item that satisfies their needs.

The proposition pool and the possibility to specify the filters' importance individually, having immediate feedback in the group model and the recommendations increases participants' awareness of others' preferences and the effects their own preferences have on the group results. The approach also entails aspects of critique-based recommenders since users can criticize or accept proposed features or recommended items. In contrast to fully automated recommender system, users have a higher level of control over the process and can easily adapt it to their current situational needs and context.

4   Description of the System

Following the aforementioned guidelines, a new, completely redesigned version of the Hootle GRS described in [1] was implemented. The prototype makes use of content-based techniques and is applicable to many different domains, provided properties of the items to be recommended are available. For demonstration purposes, we chose hotel selection for group travel as application area and used an Expedia dataset consisting of 151.000 hotel entries with descriptive information.

The different areas in which the interface is divided are shown in Fig. 1.

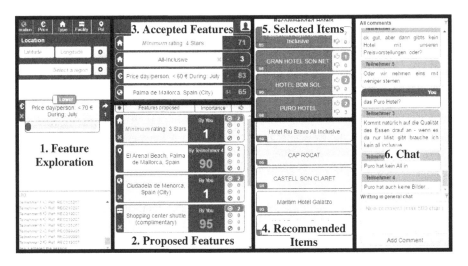

Fig. 1. Areas of the interface.

1. **Feature exploration.** Area for exploring item features by using a set of given filters (e.g. location, facilities or nearby points of interest). It is also possible to provide an importance level and to specify if the attribute is negative or positive.
2. **Proposed features.** Proposed features are shown into this area, which is shared by all participants. Voting is enabled for each proposed attribute, which can be accepted as a group filter, rejected or vetoed, depending on the results.
3. **Accepted features.** This area contains the attributes that have been approved (or vetoed) by the group. Together with their specific significance level (individually set by group members), these attributes conform the group's preference model.
4. **Recommended items.** The system calculates and displays recommendations into this area. The list is constantly updated in real-time when some group filter is added/removed or its significance changes.
5. **Selected items.** Recommended items selected by users are placed here, so other participants can see them as well.
6. **Chat.** Chat to discuss arbitrary questions that come up during the decision process. Specific discussion threads for attributes and items are provided too.

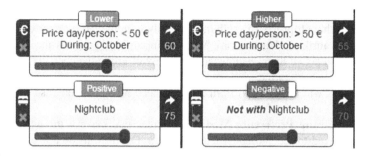

Fig. 2. Definition of two positive attributes and their negative counterparts. Importance level is specified by the slider under the attribute and displayed as a value at the right side.

4.1 Collaborative Preference Elicitation

Selecting New Attributes. This is the first step in a process that might be repeated several times. Users create new attributes by searching them through the filters located into the "feature exploration" area. Creating an attribute to propose it as a group filter (which means being part of the group's preference model) consists in selecting one of the attributes provided by the system and adding the value, type and importance attached to it (Fig. 2). Possible attribute types are *positive* (the attribute should be part of the recommendations features) and *negative* (where the opposite is preferred). For the price related attributes, "negative" and "positive" types are changed for "higher" and "lower" types. The importance level is a number between 1 and 100 that determines how relevant is the attribute in question for its creator.

Proposing an Attribute. Action that means moving a feature into the "proposed features" section of the interface, where attributes become visible for the whole group. When an attribute enters this phase, voting is enabled. Votes are not anonymous, opening the door to discussion and negotiation regarding the acceptance or rejection of the proposed features. Group members have four different choices to vote for (Fig. 3):

- To accept an attribute (blue check mark). The user acknowledges the attribute and agrees in creating a group filter from it.
- To stay neutral (grey dot). The user doesn't care about the attribute, but doesn't have any reason for not including it if others wish to do so either.

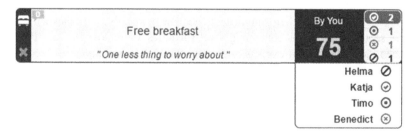

Fig. 3. Proposed attribute showing its importance level and voting results so far.

- To remove an attribute (red cross). A user manifests willingness to remove an attribute, although proposed attributes can only be removed by their creators.
- To veto an attribute (black slash). Vetoing an attribute prevents the system from using it as an active filter, even when a majority of group members has accepted it. An attribute vetoed by the whole groups becomes a veto filter and every single item containing it will be removed from the calculated recommendations.

Creating the Group Preference Model. Attributes that make it through the voting process are moved to the "accepted features" area. Features inside this area, together with their significance, conform the group preference model. Significance of an attribute is calculated using a predefined aggregation function over the importance level that each user has given to the attribute in question. Individually assigned importance levels are public knowledge among the group (Fig. 4).

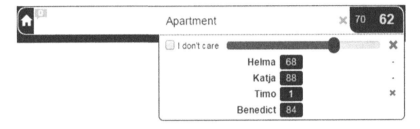

Fig. 4. Accepted feature. Individual importance levels and group significance are displayed.

An attribute that has been already accepted can be removed if the majority of the group want to do so. A removed group filter is returned to the proposed features area.

4.2 Generating Recommendations

The system takes the given preference model and explores the DB using a content-based filtering method (Fig. 5). In content-based filtering, items are described by a set of attributes, which are compared against the preference model of a user (in our case, the collaboratively created group model). Because the preference model is created from scratch in each new session, the system is applicable in cold-start situations where no user profile exists yet. Items in the DB are scored depending on how many positive attributes they contain and their significance (items with negative attributes will receive negative scores, while items containing vetoed features are removed). Once the items have been rated, the system extracts those with the highest scoring.

Every time that the group's preference model changes, new recommendations are obtained, enabling real time feedback. It could happen that none of the collected items completely fulfills the group model. In the case that only the top rated items were selected, it would be possible that for some of the attributes inside the group preference model not a single matching recommendation were provided. Because the system's

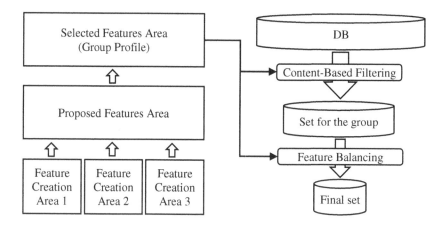

Fig. 5. Scheme of the filtering process.

raison d'etre is to serve as a tool for discussion and consensus finding within the context of GRS, it makes sense to try to return a well-balanced set of recommendations, allowing these who have chosen less popular attributes to be an active part of the negotiation process. Thus, a further step is done before sending the found recommendations to the session's participants, attempting to collect a set of items where there is at least one fitting item per attribute in the preference model.

As firstly said, the system does not require of any previously stored user profiles, something of a great usefulness when dealing with a group situation for the reasons mentioned earlier. Nevertheless, there is still plenty of room for expanding the method with more complex and longer-term user profiles, built upon the user's past choices. The interaction effort needed to specify the desired features could be lightened by starting the session with some auto-generated proposed features or letting the system elaborate a preset group preference model. Increasing the precision of the recommendations could also be a possibility by using attributes that participants have not defined for the current session, but knowing that they were selected in the past.

4.3 Negotiation

Many of the preferences stated by a user depend to a great extent on the situational context of the group and the social interaction that takes place within it. Opinions can be influenced by others through negotiation, making possible the reconciliation of adverse points of views. Thus, group decision making is an important part of the process and group agreement may not be found without an appropriate set of tools supporting discussion, negotiation and consensus finding.

Communication. Being able to talk, explaining the own decisions and questioning the reasons of others are fundamental actions in group decision making; therefore, written communication (for non-collocated groups) is of great importance. It is supported via chat and enhanced by other mechanisms, detailed in the following paragraphs.

- *Chat.* A general chat is provided where users can discuss questions that involve the whole process. Besides it, specific discussion threads for each attribute and recommendation are available too, keeping comments organized.
- *Significance.* A visual mechanism for expressing an opinion in relation with a particular feature. Each attribute has a slider that allows the users to individually define how important a feature is for them (within a scale from 1 to 100). This action, besides helping the system to generate the recommendations, provides to the rest of users a quick view of who likes and who dislikes an attribute.
- *Voting.* Users can express their consent to accept/remove/veto an attribute by voting. Votes are not anonymous, which means that a user knows at any moment what the others think about the feature at issue, giving them the chance to convince the other members and negotiate the outcome of the polling. Much the same happens with the recommended items, where users are able to vote recommendations up and down.

Conflict Resolution. A conflict appears when two or more participants want features that contradict each other. This situation is reflected by the system when the same attribute is proposed twice, once positively and once negatively, or when two incompatible (but different) attributes are added. For the first case, when one of the attributes is accepted by the group as filter, the other one is removed and no further discussion is needed. However, the second circumstance is a little bit trickier, because in many cases the system is not able to notice the contradiction by itself and the task of dealing with them relies on the users. As an attempt to support the participants visually, they have access to information about each recommended item. Those entries in the group preference model that are not fulfilled by an item are highlighted in red color, so a user can easily tell apart the conflictive attributes and try to change the opinion of the members who added them, with the expectation of removing them or lowering their significance.

4.4   Towards the Right Decision

Finding a recommendation that matches the group whishes may require several tries. Usually, it will be necessary to move through the different stages of the process in a cyclic and iterative fashion, modifying the group preference model and exploring the new recommended items once again. When negotiation and discussion are the driving force of this changes, with each new iteration the group should get closer to a solution, optimizing the group filters and narrowing down the recommendations.

Nevertheless, even when the process is carried out properly, the criteria for selecting the "right item" may differ from one scenario to another: in some cases, it could be the one that has been accepted by the majority; in others, it could be unacceptable to choose an item that has been rejected by only one member of the group. While a fixed group recommendation strategy might be used, we believe that the system cannot generally resolve such decision problems. Our approach provides tools for preference specification, discussion and acceptance measuring, but it is not possible to talk about the one right solution when dealing with group decision making in a real life situation. Ultimately, it is up to the users to decide whether a recommendation fits their needs or not and to make the final choice.

5 Evaluation

To evaluate our approach, we performed a user study with several groups comprising either three or six users, which is the range of group sizes we expect to occur in real applications. In a user study with the previous system version, we noticed an interesting correlation effect between group size and satisfaction, but had groups of three, four and five members, which may have limited the reliability of the results due to the limited range. We thus decided to slightly increase the range and focus on the extreme values. We also set up a group who used a limited version of the system with discussion facilities disabled as control, but for practical reasons could only set up one group of each size, leading to inconclusive results that are not further considered here. The main objectives of this study were to determine the usability of the approach and the quality of the resulting recommendations, as well as, more specifically, to analyze the impact of the cooperative preference elicitation and negotiation tools developed.

5.1 Setting and Experimental Tasks

We made use of a hotel database provided by Expedia with 151,000 entries. For each hotel, a full description and a set of attributes, including property and room amenities (within 360 possibilities), locations (258,426) and points of interest nearby (94,512) were available. We prepared two task scenarios with different levels of complexity:

- In an 'introductory' task, the group was instructed to select a hotel knowing beforehand some common, desired attributes, as well as the location of the hotel. This task also served as a training session to allow participants to explore the functions and possibilities the system supplies. The following scenario was presented – *"Your group will be participating at a conference in Berlin. As the conference always provides lunch and dinner, you just need to find a hotel including breakfast. Your conference will take place near the Brandenburg Gate."*
- In the 'open' task, which was always performed after the introductory task, only un-specific instructions were given to the group. The scenario used for this task was – *"It is summertime. You and your friends really need to get out of the daily routine. Discuss where to stay."*

To prevent participants from complying too quickly with the wishes of other users, we artificially induced different backgrounds and objectives for each group member. For this purpose, we created a set of role cards for the second task that were randomly distributed among group's members, with the intent of generating conflicts and discussion. A problem detected in the precursor study was that the roles used were so different one from each other that in many cases they created an artificial situation that is not commonly found in real life, where groups that plan to travel together tend to share similar preferences. Thus, for this occasion the roles were simplified and created with shared characteristics:

1. You love shopping and you are interested in cultural things.
2. You are interested in cultural things and clubbing.
3. You love partying every night. During the day, shopping keeps you awake.
4. You like to spend your time on the beach. When that is not possible, hiking fits well.
5. You prefer to hike the whole day and do sport related activities.
6. You are a sport addict and you love the beach.

5.2   Method

39 people (22 females, 17 males, average age of 22.63, σ 3.65) took part in the study, distributed in 5 groups of 3 participants and 4 groups of 6. Since the system is web-based, all users were provided with a normal desktop computer with a display screen of 21" and running the same browser. They sat in a large lab room but were separated from each other and instructed to communicate only via the means provided by the system.

Each group first received a brief introduction to the system and was asked to work on the two decision tasks, always in the order introductory task – open task. Before beginning the second task, they all received randomly one of the role cards. A task was considered complete when the group found consensus (i.e. agreed on a hotel) or the time ran out (25 min maximum per task).

After completing both tasks, participants were asked to fill in a questionnaire regarding aspects such as the quality of the recommendations or the ease-of-use of the system, using a 1–5 scale. It comprised the SUS items [7] as well as items from two recommender-specific assessment instruments (User experience of RS [15] and ResQue [31]). The recommender-specific items measure the constructs *user-perceived recommendation quality, perceived system effectiveness, interface adequacy, and ease of use*.

5.3   Results and Discussion

Not all groups were able to find a solution, reaching the time limit for the tasks. For the 3 person groups, agreement was always achieved in contrast to the 6 person groups, where only a 25 % of the tasks were completed with consensus regarding the item to select. An average success rate over all sessions of 66 % was reached. Despite the low success ratio for the bigger groups, the percentage of agreement among users (participants who selected the same hotel) was 77 %, as shown in the objective data listed in Table 1. Time needed per task was higher for the 6 people groups, as well as the amount of individual preference changes made per user (importance level, vote selection), but the number of comments written per user in the bigger groups was lower than in 3 people groups. This could mean that participants in bigger groups made a more extensive use of the graphical interface for showing their wishes and opinions to the rest of the group, because relying only in chat communication for transmitting ideas is usually more complicated the more people are writing at the same time. Despite these differences, both group types elaborated preference models with similar sizes.

Table 1. Objective results. Lower (LB) and upper (UB) bounds at 95 % confidence interval.

	3 people groups			6 people groups			Avg.
	m	LB	UB	m	LB	UB	m
Time per task (minutes)	13,60	10.18	17.01	17,63	13.8	21.43	15,61
Preference Model Size	6,10	3.85	8.34	6,38	3.87	8.88	6,23
Changes per user	12,33	6.123	18.54	14,56	11.09	18.03	14,35
Comments per user	7,16	2.42	11.90	6,41	3.77	9.06	6,92
Solution found	100 %	–	–	25 %	–	–	62.5 %
Agreement among users	100 %	–	–	77 %	–	–	88 %

In relation to the usability of the system, it received a SUS score of 65, placing the prototype slightly under the average. An independent-samples t-test was conducted to compare the items of the questionnaire, taking group size as independent variable. While many items did not show big difference between cases (Table 2), some conclusions can be extracted from them. In general, it seems harder for bigger groups to find recommendations that match the participants' individual wishes and to agree with the rest of members, which is a logical consequence of group size increase. Interesting is the fact that the groups of 6 are in general more satisfied with the tool than the smaller groups, despite being easier for the latter to find a solution through consensus.

Discussion. The outcome of the evaluation seems to indicate that some of the issues found during our previous study have been lessened, specifically the one related with how well the system scales up with group size. Even if having bigger groups increases the complexity of the decision-making process, the results point to a greater satisfaction and sense of helpfulness when using the system. This is more noticeable when one looks to the preference model size, which is almost the same through group sizes

Table 2. Some results of the evaluation.

Group size	3		6		Avg.	
	m	σ	m	σ	m	σ
The recommended items fitted my preferences	4.00	0.50	3.83	1.16	3.88	1.02
I liked the items recommended by the system	3.78	0.83	3.79	0.88	3.79	0.86
*It was very easy to find a good solution together	3.78	1.09	2.62	1.31	2.94	1.34
The other team mates agreed my opinion	4.00	0.70	3.29	1.19	3.48	1.12
*Even with different opinions we could find a good compromise	4.44	0.73	3.46	1.06	3.73	1.06
I can make a better choice with the system	3.78	0.97	3.96	1.2	3.91	1.18
I can find a solution in less time using the system	3.56	1.33	4.04	1.08	3.91	1.15
I think the program is easy to use	3.67	0.87	3.46	1.06	3.52	1.00
I think the functions in this program are well integrated	3.56	0.88	4.00	0.72	3.88	0.78
In general, I am satisfied with the system	3.56	1.13	4.33	0.96	3.76	1.00

*Significant ($p < 0.05$)

indicating that users limited the number of preferences expressed in a well-considered manner in order to facilitate consensus finding. The low ratio of solutions found for the 6 people groups could be explained as a consequence of limiting the time to finishing a task to only 25 min, but further research may be needed in order to obtain some final conclusions. In a real world situation, where the time span for finding a solution in a non-collocated group setting could be days or even weeks, and where individual preferences may tend to be more homogenous without artificially inserting roles, a higher success ratio would be expected.

6 Conclusion and Outlook

We have presented an approach to group recommended systems, which enables collaborative preference elicitation on the fly, avoiding a cold-start situation and providing more control during the recommendation process. The system supports negotiation and discussion during the preference elicitation and item selection phases. Participants can freely define and propose features, adding them to a shared pool of attributes where the group will collaboratively select those to conform the group preference model. Once the attributes are extracted, users are able to individually assign an importance level to each one of them and the system calculates their significance to the group. Recommendations are then generated after the given group preference model and will be recalculated each time that it changes. Recommendations are shown to the group members, letting them to select and discuss about those that they like, or to redefine the group preference model to obtain new recommended items.

The technique here described provides higher flexibility and awareness than the fixed strategies typically used in group recommenders. Since preferences and matching recommendations are always visible, participants' awareness of individual and group views and of the effects of their preference settings is increased.

Based on prior work, a novel prototype version of a hotel group recommender Hootle+ was developed, following the ideas described above. The results of the user study we conducted show that the new system appears to handle bigger groups better than the previous system version which did not allow users to influence the group model directly. On the other hand, we obtained a lower success rate per session, which may be due to tighter time constraints.

A work in progress is the idea of having different privileges levels defined within a session, which could be assigned to participants so their opinions would have distinct weights when voting or calculating the significance of an attribute (e.g. expert's opinion). This feature would also allow creating personalized rules for vote counting in relation to the acceptance or rejection of a feature, conferring even more flexibility to the system. It is planned to add moderator specific functions too, enabling a user to control the session's flow and to take the final decision. In future work, we will also further improve the usability of the interface, which raised some negative comments in the study. Furthermore, a detailed empirical comparison to a suitable baseline system is planned. In addition, receiving feedback from real groups of users would be a solution to the problem inherent to the use of artificial roles during the test sessions, so we are considering an online version with a realistic use case for future research.

References

1. Márquez, J.O.A., Ziegler, J.: Preference elicitation and negotiation in a group recommender system. In: Abascal, J., Barbosa, S., Fetter, M., Gross, T., Palanque, P., Winckler, M. (eds.) INTERACT 2015. LNCS, vol. 9297, pp. 20–37. Springer, Heidelberg (2015)
2. Ardissono, L., Goy, A., Petrone, G., Segnan, M.: A multi-agent infrastructure for developing personalized web-based systems. ACM Trans. Internet Technol. (TOIT) 5(1), 47–69 (2005)
3. Ardissono, L., Goy, A., Petrone, G., Segnan, M., Torasso, P.: Intrigue: personalized recommendation of tourist attractions for desktop and hand held devices. Appl. Artif. Intell. 17(8-9), 687–714 (2003)
4. Bekkerman, P., Kraus, S., Ricci, F.: Applying cooperative negotiation methodology to group recommendation problem. In: Proceedings of Workshop on Recommender Systems in 17th European Conference on Artificial Intelligence (ECAI 2006), pp. 72–75. Citeseer (2006)
5. Beckmann, C., Gross, T.: Towards a group recommender process model for ad-hoc groups and on-demand recommendations. In: Proceedings of the 16th ACM International Conference on Supporting Group Work, pp. 329–330. ACM (2010)
6. Boratto, L., Carta, S.: State-of-the-art in group recommendation and new approaches for automatic identification of groups. In: Soro, A., Vargiu, E., Armano, G., Paddeu, G. (eds.) Information Retrieval and Mining in Distributed Environments. SCI, vol. 324, pp. 1–20. Springer, Heidelberg (2010)
7. Brooke, J.: SUS-A quick and dirty usability scale. Usability Eval. Ind. 189(194), 4–7 (1996)
8. Doodle AG. http://www.doodle.com
9. Hartnett, T.: Consensus-Oriented Decision-Making: the CODM Model for Facilitating Groups to Widespread Agreement. New society publishers, Gabriola (2011)
10. Herlocker, J.L., Konstan, J.A., Terveen, L.G., Riedl, J.: Evaluating collaborative filtering recommender systems. ACM Trans. Inf. Syst. (TOIS) 22(1), 5–53 (2004)
11. Hill, W., Stead, L., Rosenstein, M., Furnas, G.: Recommending and evaluating choices in a virtual community of use. In: Proceedings of the SIGCHI Conference on Human Factors in Computing Systems, pp. 194–201 (1995)
12. Jameson, A.: More than the sum of its members: challenges for group recommender systems. In: Proceedings of the Working Conference on Advanced Visual Interfaces, pp. 48–54. ACM (2004)
13. Jameson, A., Baldes, A., Kleinbauer, T.: Two methods for enhancing mutual awareness in a group recommender system. In: Proceedings of the Working Conference on Advanced Visual Interfaces, pp. 447–449. ACM (2004)
14. Jameson, A., Smyth, B.: Recommendation to groups. In: Brusilovsky, P., Kobsa, A., Nejdl, W. (eds.) Adaptive Web 2007. LNCS, vol. 4321, pp. 596–627. Springer, Heidelberg (2007)
15. Knijnenburg, B.P., Willemsen, M.C., Gantner, Z., Soncu, H., Newell, C.: Explaining the user experience of recommender systems. User Model. User-Adap. Inter. 22(4–5), 441–504 (2012)
16. Kompan, M., Bielikova, M.: Group recommendations: survey and perspectives. Comput. Inform. 33(2), 446–476 (2014)
17. Lieberman, H., Van Dyke, N., Vivacqua, A.: Let's browse: a collaborative browsing agent. Knowl. Based Syst. 12(8), 427–431 (1999)
18. Liu, X., Tian, Y., Ye, M., Lee, W.: Exploring personal impact for group recommendation. In: Proceedings of the 21st ACM International Conference on Information and Knowledge Management, pp. 674–683. ACM (2012)

19. Loepp, B., Hussein, T., Ziegler, J.: Choice-based preference elicitation for collaborative filtering recommender systems. In: Proceedings of the SIGCHI Conference on Human Factors in Computing Systems (CHI 2014), pp. 3085–3094. ACM, New York (2014)

20. Masthoff, J.: Group modeling: Selecting a sequence of television items to suit a group of viewers. In: Ardissono, L. (ed.) Personalized Digital Television. HCI, vol. 6, pp. 93–141. Springer, Heidelberg (2004)

21. McCarthy, J.F., Anagnost, T.D.: MusicFX: an arbiter of group preferences for computer supported collaborative workouts. In: Proceedings of the 1998 ACM Conference on Computer Supported Cooperative Work, pp. 363–372. ACM (1998)

22. McCarthy, K., McGinty, L., Smyth, B.: Case-based group recommendation: compromising for success. In: Weber, R.O., Richter, M.M. (eds.) ICCBR 2007. LNCS (LNAI), vol. 4626, pp. 299–313. Springer, Heidelberg (2007)

23. McCarthy, K., McGinty, L., Smyth, B., Salamó, M.: The needs of the many: a case-based group recommender system. In: Roth-Berghofer, T.R., Göker, M.H., Güvenir, H.A. (eds.) ECCBR 2006. LNCS (LNAI), vol. 4106, pp. 196–210. Springer, Heidelberg (2006)

24. McCarthy, K., McGinty, L., Smyth, B., Salamo, M.: Social interaction in the CATS group recommender. In: Workshop on the Social Navigation and Community Based Adaptation Technologies (2006)

25. McCarthy, K., Salamo, M., Coyle, L., McGinty, L., Smyth, B., Nixon, P.: CATS: a synchronous approach to collaborative group recommendation. In: FLAIRS Conference, pp. 86–91 (2006)

26. McGrath, J.E., Berdahl, J.L.: Groups, technology, and time. In: Tindale, R.S., Heath, L., Edwards, J., Posavac, E.J., Bryant, F.B., Suarez-Balcazar, Y., Henderson-King, E., Myers, J. (eds.) Theory and Research on Small Groups. HCI, vol. 6, pp. 205–228. Springer, New York (2002)

27. Nunamaker Jr., J.F., Briggs, R.O., Mittleman, D.D., Vogel, D.R., Balthazard, P.A.: Lessons from a dozen years of group support systems research: a discussion of lab and field findings. J. Manage. Inf. Syst. **13**, 163–207 (1996)

28. O'connor, M., Cosley, D., Konstan, J.A., Riedl, J.: PolyLens: a recommender system for groups of users. In: Prinz, W., Jarke, M., Rogers, Y., Schmidt, K., Wulf, V. (eds.) ECSCW 2001, pp. 199–218. Springer, Heidelberg (2001)

29. Pommeranz, A., Broekens, J., Wiggers, P., Brinkman, W.P., Jonker, C.M.: Designing interfaces for explicit preference elicitation: a user-centered investigation of preference representation and elicitation process. User Model. User-Adap. Inter. **22**(4–5), 357–397 (2012)

30. Pu, P., Chen, L.: User-involved preference elicitation for product search and recommender systems. AI Mag. **29**(4), 93 (2009)

31. Pu, P., Chen, L., Hu, R.: A user-centric evaluation framework for recommender systems. In: Proceedings of the Fifth ACM Conference on Recommender Systems, pp. 157–164. ACM (2011)

32. Ricci, F., Rokach, L., Shapira, B.: Introduction to recommender systems handbook. In: Ricci, F., Rokach, L., Shapira, B., Kantor, P.B. (eds.) Recommender Systems Handbook, pp. 1–35. Springer, New York (2010)

33. Saaty, T.L.: Fundamentals of decision making and priority theory with the analytic hierarchy process, vol. 6. RWS Publications, Pittsburgh (2000)

34. Stettinger, M.: Choicla: towards domain-independent decision support for groups of users In: Proceedings of the 8th ACM Conference on Recommender systems, pp. 425–428 (2014)

35. Walther, J.B.: Computer-mediated communication impersonal, interpersonal, and hyper personal interaction. Commun. Res. **23**(1), 3–43 (1996)

AppWatchSecurity: Improving a Video Surveillance System by Integrating Smartwatch-Based Arousal Detection

Supasit Jansrithep and Thitirat Siriborvornratanakul[✉]

Graduate School of Applied Statistics, National Institute of Development Administration (NIDA), 118 SeriThai Rd., Bangkok 10240, Bangkapi, Thailand
supasit.jan@gmail.com, thitirat@as.nida.ac.th

Abstract. This paper proposes a prototype system that collaborates smartwatches with traditional video surveillance security. By combining concepts of user-centered design, ubiquitous wearable, psychophysiology and Internet of Things (IoTs), we present the upgraded video surveillance system where heart rate-based anomalies can automatically trigger the alarm. As a first prototype, the system was limited to library-like experimental setups and the anomaly was defined by arousal heart rate—unusually high heart beats. Using a smartwatch and a simple three-question questionnaire, we were able to collect referential arousal heart rate data from 25 healthy subjects together with their individual rating scores regarding three habit factors—smoking, drinking alcohol and eating fatty foods. According to our semi-quantitative user testings in a controlled library environment, the prototype was able to wirelessly connect and synchronize all devices, send the alarm, and perform real-time heart rate measurement as well as calculation. Based on confusion matrix evaluation, our anomaly detection gave promising results of 95 % accuracy and 90 % precision. However, major revision was required for the anomaly detection to cover unobserved factors, and there were serious usability problems regarding the smartwatch to be fixed.

Keywords: Smartwatch · Heart rate · Biofeedback · Psychophysiology

1 Introduction

Psychophysiology is the recently growing field in Human-Computer Interaction that studies relationship between physiological activity and psychological manipulation. There are many previous works studying correlation between physiological data and user experiences. For example, [2,4] investigated correlation between physiological data (e.g., skin-conductance, electroencephalography, heart rate, electrodermal activity) and game play experiences (e.g., competence, immersion, flow, tension, challenge). The work of [5] revealed that physiological signals naturally emitted by users significantly improved discovery rates in user researches, particularly in emotional user experiences that were difficult to spot by traditional expert-based observation. Using logged events identified by peaks of the

© Springer International Publishing Switzerland 2016
T. Yuizono et al. (Eds.): CRIWG 2016, LNCS 9848, pp. 167–175, 2016.
DOI: 10.1007/978-3-319-44799-5_13

signals read from simple finger-mounted GSR (Galvanic Skin Response) sensors alone, this work showed that up to 63 % more user experience issues were discovered. Hence, it should be reasonable to include physiological data whenever analyzed targets include user's internal emotions or experiences.

Because of major drives in fitness and health care, heart rate monitoring has become a must feature for recent wearable devices especially smartwatches. It was mentioned in [2,3] that heart rate data were proved to correlate with both positive and negative emotions. Experiments in [2] revealed that, in first-person shooter games, high values of heart beat conveyed tense and frustation whereas low values conveyed positive effects (i.e., competence, immersion and low levels of challenge); the heart rate data here were monitored by a chest-strap accessory of Garmin Forerunner 50 sport watch. In experiments of [3], three physiological signals were measured—GSR (Galvanic Skin Response), ECG (electrocardiography), and EMG (electromyography); heart rate values were indirectly computed and interpolated from the ECG signals read from three electrodes (two on the chest and one on the abdomen). Then, based on fuzzy logic, this work was able to transform a set of physiological signals to arousal and valence (pleasure), and then from arousal and valence to five emotions. Heart rate values were used in the first transformation to modulate the GSR signals for arousal modeling and modulate the low EMG signals for valence modeling.

To monitor real time heart beats, there are three popular alternatives—ECG (electrocardiography) sensing electrodes, chest-strap heart rate monitoring devices and wrist-worn wearable devices. Among the three, the wrist-worn alternative tends to be the most comfortable and fashionable but also the worst in accuracy [6], particularly when the wearer does not wear the device tightly above the wrist bone. Most commercial wrist-worn heart rate monitors use similar optical sensing technologies that shine a light into the blood vessels and detect heart beats by looking at the changes in blood volume. When worn on the wrist, the optical technologies are accurate for casual users that are staying still or at rest. Focusing on wrist-worn smartwatches, the number of previous researches is quite limited and mostly involves the watches' embedded accelerometers rather than heart rate sensors. From our survey, there has been no concrete research presenting the use of smartwatch's heart rate sensors yet.

In this paper, we are interested in monitoring user's real-time heart beats via a commercial smartwatch and using the read data to create an anomaly detector for a traditional video surveillance security system, expanding its anomaly detection to include those triggered by users' anomaly heart beats. To the best of our knowledge, there has been no previous work that couples heart rate anomalies with video surveillance security yet, particularly when heart rate monitoring is done via a commercial smartwatch.

It has been known that the most difficult task in psychophysiology is mapping physiological data read from sensors to correct user's experiences, emotions or activities, and vice versa. As a very first prototype system using only a commercial smartwatch to detect anomalies, here we do not try to resolve a complete linkage between real-time heart beats and user's internal anomalies. Instead we

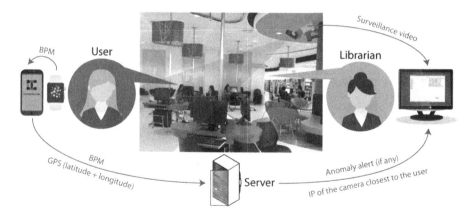

Fig. 1. AppWatchSecurity system's overview in a library setup.

detect anomalies by simply looking for user's arousal heart beats (i.e., user's higher-than-usual heart beats). The main purpose of doing this is to discover whether a commercial smartwatch is ready and reliable enough for this kind of serious detection and IoT applications. In the long run, we expect the complete system to become an optional feature for a household's video surveillance system where the surveillance system works closely in collaboration with authorized smartwatches in order to monitor the watch wearers' safeness. Nevertheless, the experiments presented in this paper focus on quiet library setups in order to limit users' activities and anomalies of the prototype to as few as possible.

2   Proposed Methods

The overview of AppWatchSecurity in a library setup is illustrated in Fig. 1. The current prototype shown in Fig. 2 includes one iPhone 6 plus (iOS 9.0.1), one Apple Watch 42 mm Sport (WatchOS 2.0) operating in the normal mode, one D-Link IP camera, one laptop computer and one Wireless-G Broadband Router with 4-port switch. The iPhone's application includes registering for a new user, logging in for an existing user, receiving an updated BPM (beats per minute) value from Apple Watch every 5 s via Bluetooth, and periodically sending the BPM value and iPhone's location (latitude and longitude) to the server via Internet. The server computer continuously analyzes the BPM data for any anomaly sign; if the anomaly is detected, the server compares the latest iPhone's location to find the closest surveillance camera and sends an alarm to the librarian. The librarian may choose to respond to the alarm immediately or confirm the anomaly first by checking the real-time surveillance video feed provided as an optional click in the librarian-side system.

As mentioned earlier, in this prototype, the anomaly detection is done by looking for any arousal heart rate. To achieve that, referential heart rate data were collected from 25 healthy subjects, including 14 males and 11 females with

Fig. 2. The first prototype of AppWatchSecurity.

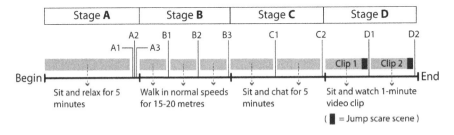

Fig. 3. The overview of how referential heart rate data were measured. (Color figure online)

ages ranging from 24 to 46 (average = 30.84, SD = 5.70). As shown in Fig. 3, we divided the heart rate measurement into 4 continuous stages—A, B, C and D. The A stage is the measurement after the subjects sat and relaxed themselves for 5 min. The B stage is the measurement after the subjects walked for 15–20 m in normal speeds. The C stage is the measurement after the subjects finished chatting and answering simple questions for another 5 min in seated positions. Finally, the D stage is the measurement after the subjects watched a one-minute video clip containing 5–6 s of jump scare scene. To increase reliability of the measured values, the measurements in A and B stages were repeated three times for each subject and the three values were averaged before used. Similarly, the measurements in C and D stages were repeated two times and the two values were averaged before used. Note that we used two different video clips for the two measurements in D stage and the measurements were done immediately at the end of jump scare scenes. Figure 4 shows averaged heart rate information regarding 25 subjects, grouped by genders and measurement stages. One obvious conclusion is that the arousal state (i.e., D stage) is the state with the highest BPM in both genders.

Next, we tried to group 25 arousal heart rate data (i.e., data from the D stage) with two factors influencing heart rates—illness and habit factors. The illness factor was further divided to three subfactors—high blood pressure, low

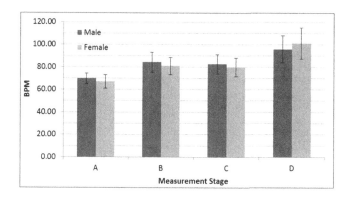

Fig. 4. Relationship between averaged heart rates (vertical axis) and the four measurement states (horizontal axis) regarding 25 healthy subjects.

blood pressure and diabetes, and the habit factor was divided to another three subfactors—smoking, drinking alcohol and eating fatty foods. Using a simple questionnaire, we collected information regarding these six subfactors from 25 subjects. The questionnaire included six short questions—three are yes-no questions for the illness factor and the others are 1 (never), 2 (sometimes) and 3 (very often) rating questions for the habit factor.

Unexpectedly, most subjects could not answer the yes-no questions regarding the illness factor because they were not aware of these detailed health information due to lack of or infrequent medical checkup. Hence, we decided to eliminate the illness factor from this prototype and continued with the habit factor only. The three habit rating scores from each subject were added up, resulting in 7 possible summation scores (i.e., 3–9) for each gender. Mapping between 25 arousal heart rate data and 7 summation scores gave results as shown in Table 1. Note that in Table 1, the representative BPM value for each group was computed by averaging all arousal heart rate data whose habit summation scores matched the group value. For example, because there were two female subjects whose habit summation scores equaled to 6, the representative BPM value for the score of 6 was calculated by averaging the arousal heart rates of both subjects (i.e., $(102 + 119)/2 = 110$).

Using Table 1 as the prototype's reference, a new user registering to AppWatchSecurity via iPhone will be asked to answer the three habit rating questions and their individual threshold value for the arousal state will be stored in a user's profile. For example, if the habit summation score of a new female user is equal to 5, her arousal threshold value will be set to 108 BPM. While real-time monitoring is running, the server computer continuously computes the current representative of heart rate data by averaging 10 latest BPM data receiving from iPhone. Whenever the current representative value exceeds the user's arousal threshold, an anomaly alarm will be sent to the librarian together with an option to click and open the surveillance video feed from the camera closest to the watch's wearer. Note that the server finds the closest camera by compar-

Table 1. Mapping between 7 possible habit summation scores and the averaged arousal heart rate data collected from 25 subjects.

Male								
	Habit summation score	< 5	5	6	7	8	9	
	The number of subjects (person)	2	3	2	5	2	0	
	Representative value (BPM)	85	91	95	101	100	–	
Female	Habit summation score	< 5	5	6	7	8	9	
	The number of subjects (person)	6	3	2	0	0	0	
	Representative value (BPM)	94	108	110	–	–	–	

ing latitude and longitude between iPhone's (dynamic position from GPS) and the surveillance camera's (static position inputted manually). But because there was only one IP camera in the current prototype, issues about efficiency and effectiveness of the closest camera finding algorithm were not investigated.

3   Experimental Results

To test our heart rate based anomaly detection, we conducted two experiments in library or library-like setups. The first experiment included 6 different test subjects (4 males and 2 females). For each subject, a four-minute video was recorded in synchronization with real-time heart rate measurement; while recording, the subject was told to freely sit down or walk around. By averaging all heart rate data during the sitting and walking activities, we got the initial insight as shown in Table 2. According to the table, the number of false positives (FP)—the number of sitting and walking that were incorrectly detected as anomalies—is 3 and the number of true negatives (TN)—the number of sitting and walking that were correctly detected as normalities—is 7. This equals to the false positive rate (FPR) (a.k.a. false alarm rate) of $3/(3 + 7) = 0.3$ or 30 % and the true negative rate (TNR) (a.k.a. specificity) of $7/(3 + 7) = 0.7$ or 70 %.

Table 2. Experimental results regarding the first experiment. * marks the result that exceeds the arousal threshold and will trigger the anomaly alarm.

User information			Arousal threshold	Averaged heart rate	
Code	Age	Sex		Sit	Walk
U1-1	36	Male	85	70	–
U1-2	37	Male	91	87	* 92 *
U1-3	25	Male	95	85	* 96 *
U1-4	31	Female	94	92	* 95 *
U1-5	29	Male	91	65	64
U1-6	34	Female	110	77	–

Table 3. Experimental results regarding the second experiment. * marks the result that exceeds the arousal threshold and will trigger the anomaly alarm.

User information			Arousal threshold	Averaged heart rate				
Code	Age	Sex		Sit	Walk	Talk	Video	Run
U2-1	31	Male	91	63	66	68	68	* 92 *
U2-2	25	Male	95	63	63	70	60	94
U2-3	31	Female	94	71	72	78	78	84
U2-4	27	Male	95	88	92	* 96 *	94	* 97 *
U2-5	46	Male	100	89	91	94	92	* 104 *
U2-6	25	Male	100	60	78	81	71	* 102 *
U2-7	24	Female	110	85	89	95	95	* 114 *
U2-8	24	Female	110	91	97	99	93	* 111 *
U2-9	29	Male	91	58	70	73	65	* 98 *
U2-10	29	Male	100	77	92	89	77	* 101 *
U2-11	36	Male	85	62	72	71	65	* 86 *

Although the FPR and TNR values from the first experiment were not totally unacceptable, we expected better and more coverage results. After closely investigating the three false alarms regarding U1-2, U1-3 and U1-4 subjects, it turned out that the three subjects had a fever when conducting our experiment, making their heart beats quicker than usual. In order not to introduce an illness factor to the current prototype, we conducted the second experiment with 11 different subjects (8 males and 3 females) who showed no explicit signs of illness. In this experiment, each subject was asked to perform a predefined sequence of activities consisting of sitting, walking, talking (seated position), seeing video (comedy, action, tragedy) and running respectively.

Results from the second experiment are shown in Table 3. For our library setups, we considered running as anomaly and the other activities as normality. According to the table, the number of true positives (TP)—the number of anomalies that were correctly detected as anomalies—is 9, the number of false positives (FP)—the number of normalities that were incorrectly detected as anomalies—is 1, the number of true negatives (TN)—the number of normalities that were correctly detected as normalities—is 43, and the number of false negatives (FN)— the number of anomalies that were incorrectly detected as normalities—is 2. In conclusion, our anomaly detection showed impressive performances according to the following indicators: accuracy of $(9 + 43)/(9 + 1 + 43 + 2) = 0.95$ or 95 %, precision of $9/(9+1) = 0.9$ or 90 %, false positive rate of $1/(1+43) = 0.02$ or 2 %, true negative rate of $43/(43+1) = 0.98$ or 98 %, false negative rate of $2/(2+9) = 0.18$ or 18 %, and true positive rate (a.k.a. recall) of $9/(9+2) = 0.82$ or 82 %.

Despite of high performance indicators, we discovered significant problems regarding usability and user experience of Apple Watch's heart rate sensors. In order for heart rate data to be updated all the time, our watch wearer needed to constantly touch the watch's screen every 30 s; this totally contradicts with our concept of no-explicit-workload and automatic anomaly detection. The watch's user experience problem occured during the second experiment when two subjects (i.e., U2-2 and U2-3), both with false positive results, were running without being aware that their wrists were sometimes in the positions that put out the Apple Watch's monitor as well as its real time heart rate monitoring. Also according to Apple Watch's official page [1], there are other factors that may lead to inconsistent or inaccurate heart rate measurement. These factors too have to be included in future studies, unless switching to other smartwatches or sensing devices is proved to be a better alternative.

4   Conclusion

This paper is a prototype system regarding a novel IoT usage scenario that transforms real-time heart rate data read from a commercial smartwatch into an additional anomaly detector in a video surveillance system. As a first prototype, the anomaly is detected by arousal heart beats and all experiments are limited to library setups. Based on referential heart rate data collected from 25 healthy subjects and a simple questionnaire, we assign an individual arousal heart rate threshold to each user. Whenever the real-time measured heart beats exceed the threshold, an anomaly alarm will be wirelessly sent to a librarian. Results from our two experiments with limited user activities show that despite of its simplicity, our anomaly detection algorithm is accurate and precise.

Future works include collecting more referential heart rate data of more activities from more diverse user demographics, adding an illness factor to the algorithm, conducting more user researches to help identify and prioritize related factors, and fixing usability as well as user experience problems regarding the current smartwatch.

References

1. Apple Inc.: Your heart rate. what it means, and where on apple watch you'll find it. Apple official website (2015). https://support.apple.com/en-us/HT204666. Accessed 3 May 2016
2. Drachen, A., Nacke, L., Yannakakis, G., Pedersen, A.: Correlation between heart rate, electrodermal activity and player experience in first-person shooter games. In: Proceedings of the ACM SIGGRAPH Symposium on Video Games (Sandbox 2010), pp. 49–54 (2010)
3. Mandryk, R.L., Atkins, M.S.: A fuzzy physiological approach for continuously modeling emotion during interaction with play technologies. Int. J. Hum. Comput. Stud. **65**(4), 329–347 (2007)
4. Mirza-Babaei, P., Nacke, L., Gregory, J., Collins, N., Fitzpatrick, G.: How does it play better? Exploring user testing and biometric storyboards in games user research. In: Proceedings of the SIGCHI Conference on Human Factors in Computing Systems (CHI 2013), pp. 1499–1508 (2013)

5. Mirza-babaei, P., Long, S., Foley, E., McAllister, G.: Understanding the contribution of biometrics to games user research. In: Proceedings of the International Conference: Think Design Play (DiGRA 2011), vol. 6 (2011)
6. Palladino, V.: Who has the most accurate heart rate monitor? Tom's guide (2015). www.tomsguide.com/us/heart-rate-monitor,review-2885.html. Accessed 3 May 2015

Author Index

Printed in the United States
By Bookmasters